An Object-Oriented
Introduction to Computer Science
Using Eiffel

PRENTICE HALL
OBJECT-ORIENTED
SERIES

An Object-Oriented
Introduction to Computer Science
Using Eiffel

Richard S. Wiener

For book and bookstore information

http://www.prenhall.com

Prentice Hall PTR
Upper Saddle River, New Jersey 07458

Library of Congress Cataloging-in-Publication Data

Wiener, Richard, 1941–
    An object-oriented introduction to computer science using Eiffel / by Richard S. Wiener.
       p. cm. -- (Prentice Hall object-oriented series)
    Includes index.
    ISBN 0-13-183872-5
    1. Object-oriented programming (Computer science) 2. Eiffel (Computer program
    language 3. Computer science.. I. Title. II. Series.
QA76.64.W44   1996
005.13'3--dc20   96-2186
                                      CIP

Editorial/production supervision and Interior Design: *Joanne Anzalone*
Manufacturing manager: *Alexis R. Heydt*
Acquisitions editor: *Paul Becker*
Editorial assistant: *Maureen Diana*
Cover design: *Design Source*
Cover design director: *Jerry Votta*

© 1996 by Prentice Hall PTR
Prentice-Hall, Inc.
A Simon & Schuster Company
Upper Saddle River, New Jersey 07458

The publisher offers discounts on this book when ordered in bulk quantities.
For more information, contact:
Corporate Sales Department
Prentice Hall PTR
1 Lake Street
Upper Saddle River, NJ 07458

Phone: 800-382-3419, Fax: 201-236-7141
E-mail: corpsales@prenhall.com

Printed in the United States of America
10 9 8 7 6 5 4 3 2 1

ISBN 0-13-183872-5

Prentice-Hall International (UK) Limited, *London*
Prentice-Hall of Australia Pty. Limited, *Sydney*
Prentice-Hall Canada Inc., *Toronto*
Prentice-Hall Hispanoamericana, S.A., *Mexico*
Prentice-Hall of India Private Limited, *New Delhi*
Prentice-Hall of Japan, Inc., *Tokyo*
Simon & Schuster Asia Pte. Ltd., *Singapore*
Editora Prentice-Hall do Brasil, Ltda., *Rio de Janeiro*

This book is dedicated with all my love to my sons
Henrik, Marc, and Erik.

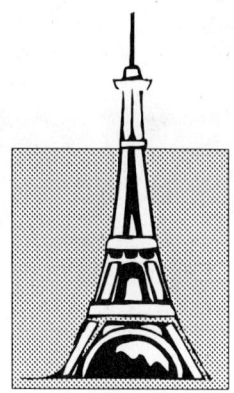

Contents

CONTENTS

Preface

There is a strong need for a CS 1 book that from the very beginning presents the basic principles of computer science from an object-oriented perspective and is supported by a friendly, consistent, and relatively easy to learn object-oriented programming language. An object-oriented perspective represents a further evolution in the trend to emphasize abstractions in computer problem solving and the use of abstract data types in particular in early computer science courses.

This book is aimed at the beginning computer science student enrolled in a rigorous computer science curriculum. It is also aimed at practicing software development professionals new to the object paradigm who wish a gentle introduction to many features of the Eiffel language and the object paradigm.

This book presents the basic ideas of object modeling from the very beginning. Before a student learns to "program," he or she should be introduced to modeling. It is important that the beginning student as well as practicing software development professionals view programming as only part of the intellectual process associated with software development and computer science. Booch class and object scenario diagrams are introduced early as a means of providing notational support and more importantly support for the notion of object modeling.

The object-oriented perspective is quite distinct from the older traditional approach of having students learn the rudiments of programming from the bottom up. That is, first learn about scalar types, variables, assignment operations, branch and loop program control structures, and much later the concept of functional abstraction. Although in recent years functions have been introduced earlier in some CS 1 books, it is often the case that they are first introduced in the middle of the book.

Using an object-oriented perspective, functions and the underlying data model that they are manipulating are introduced from the very beginning. The class is introduced early as a frame from which to introduce and implement simple algorithms and provide a model for objects.

Some computer science departments have been moving towards C or C++ to support CS 1. This author believes that this is a grave mistake. Although both of these languages are commercially important and widely used outside of the university, which probably accounts for their adoption as a CS 1 language, they are poor candidates to support CS 1. Both languages are complex, are relatively hard to read, provide relatively little safety to the beginning programmer, and are relatively inconsistent (particularly C++). They both require the student to take a fairly low-level systems view quite early. It therefore becomes quite challenging for the beginning student to master low-level details and at the same time develop a high-level vision and sensitivity concerning the safe construction of software systems. The Eiffel language is much better suited for this task.

Eiffel is quite readable, friendly, and consistent. The dangerous artifact of pointers is totally missing. Memory management is handled automatically. Eiffel's assertion handling mechanism provides an opportunity to emphasize safe and defensive programming. Its clean and simple syntax and semantics for handling generic components, late-binding, and inheritance allow a student to focus on the fundamental concepts of software construction and algorithm design without having to become distracted with the myriad of complex language details required, for example, if one uses C++.

Chapter 1 provides a short historical perspective related to computation and computers.

Chapter 2 introduces the concept of objects and object modeling. Objects as abstractions of reality are presented. The noun-verb metaphor, the notion of state, object scenarios and messages, classification, inheritance, aggregation and the uses relationship are introduced. An introduction to object-oriented programming is provided through a simple example. Some of the Booch analysis and design notation and the concepts behind the notation are introduced.

Chapter 3 introduces the reader to the world of programming using Eiffel. The basic elements of an Eiffel software system are presented. These include creating and destroying objects, basic types, reference versus value semantics, object assignment, object copying, object cloning, branching, iteration, and the construction of routines. In addition the use of basic Eiffel libraries is introduced.

Chapter 4 focuses on the design of algorithms. A graduated set of problems of increasing complexity are used to illustrate the rudiments of algorithm design and develop sensitivity to algorithm complexity.

Chapter 5 presents the reader with some first examples of complete Eiffel software systems. A preview is provided concerning the use of inheritance, late-binding, and assertions. A pair of ordinary dice are simulated. Then a pair of unusual non-standard dice are constructed using inheritance. A race horse game to be played by a person against the computer is built that uses the non-standard dice. Finally, a counterfeit coin weighing game is created that allows a person to play with the assistance of the computer.

Chapter 6, "The Construction of Eiffel Classes," presents more detail related to the various sections of an Eiffel class and their use. Object creation, routine redefinition and renaming, and export scope are among the topics covered. The important facility of assertion handling is presented in this chapter.

Chapter 7 discusses the issue of building reusable container classes. Several classic container classes are presented including STACK, QUEUE, UNORDERED_LIST, ORDERED_LIST, DEQUE, and SET. The BIT data type is introduced and used as part of the implementation of SET.

Chapter 8 introduces recursion as a design technique. First the mechanics of recursion are presented. The relationship between recursion and iteration is discussed and illustrated. Several smaller examples that illustrate recursive designs are presented including binary search of an array and quicksort. The chapter ends with an intermediate sized example involving a depth-first search of a graph. The reader is introduced to the flavor of more advanced algorithm design, an important foundation subject in computer science.

Chapter 9 presents polymorphism and late-binding as a design principle. After illustrating the principle with a simple and somewhat sterile example, an initial and improved version involving the analysis, design, and implementation of a complete software system are presented. Booch class and object scenario diagrams are used to support the analysis and design.

Acknowledgments

I would first like to thank Paul Becker, publisher at Prentice Hall, for his support and encouragement from this project's inception to its completion.

I am in debt to several outstanding reviewers who have provided extremely useful and constructive criticism of the first-draft manuscript.

Jim McKim of the Hartford Graduate Center, friend, Eiffel mentor, and outstanding critic, has examined every line of code in this manuscript and has made many useful suggestions. As before, Jim, my simple words of thanks are really not enough to thank you for your efforts way above and beyond the call of duty. The entire Eiffel community owes you many thanks for the continuing contributions that you are making.

Brian Henderson Seller, from the University of Technology in Sydney, has provided many helpful comments, particularly regarding the sections of the book dealing with object modeling.

Meilir Page Jones, President of Wayland Systems, has provided tremendous help in his critical but extremely constructive review of the manuscript. His many annotations in the first-draft manuscript have provided significant help in improving the book.

I am particularly appreciative of the timely help provided by Jim, Brian, and Meilir because I know how busy they are. Thank you all for finding the time to fit this manuscript review into your busy schedules.

I thank Margaret Reek for looking at a near final version of the manuscript and providing useful and constructive comments.

I wish to thank Interactive Software Engineering in Santa Barbara for continuing to provide me with their latest Eiffel software. It is my hope that the Professional Version of Eiffel for MSDOS/Windows will make this elegant language much more accessible to students and professionals alike.

I wish to thank Bertrand Meyer, the original designer and implementor of Eiffel, for his encouragement and support.

I also wish to thank Rock Howard and Madison Cloutier and everyone at Tower Technology for their technical support, tremendous encouragement and latest Eiffel products. Their outstanding contributions to the Eiffel community are noteworthy.

With great love and appreciation, I thank my wife Hanne for her help, constructive criticism, and continual encouragement.

Richard Wiener

Chapter 1

Programming and Software

1.1 Computer science

Many readers of this book may be enrolled in their first computer science course. Welcome to computer science! Other readers may be wishing to learn more about object-oriented software development. Welcome to this exciting paradigm! (The word paradigm means "a set of forms all of which contain a particular element" —*Random House Dictionary*.)

Typically a first course in computer science introduces a programming language and focuses on programming. Some students may leave a CS 1 course with the impression that computer science is the study of programming. This is not true.

Software is the end product of an engineering process that involves requirements, specifications, analysis, and design. Software is a tangible and visible entity. It is the instructions that permit a digital computer to perform a variety of tasks. Software is a product often shrink-wrapped with a fancy cover. Software is a multibillion dollar business.

A programming language provides a notation in which to express algorithms and information structures. Reasoning can be done with this notation. But to many computer scientists, programs represent the least creative, most routine, and perhaps most tedious part of the software development process. In fact, some computer scientists do not even program.

To other computer scientists, the creation of programs and software systems is what computer science is all about. The theory of programming languages underscores the importance of programming. But computer science is much more than programming.

Computer science deals with the art, craft, and science of computation using a digital computer. Computer science is a theoretical as well as practical discipline; a theoretical as well as applied science. The theory of automata, artificial and natural languages, learning and cognition, information, data structures, complexity, and algorithms play a central role and serve as a theoretical underpinning for all of computer science. The major application areas of computer science include operating systems, compiler design, data structures and algorithms, graphics, numerical analysis, databases, programming languages, artificial intelligence, machine learning, and software engineering. As a computer science student, you will be required to take courses in many or all of these areas.

Most applied sciences require their practitioners to express their ideas in one or more technical languages. Chemists learn the language of chemical symbols and the operators and connectors that allow chemical equations to be written. Physicists use the language of calculus, differential equations, and other advanced mathematics to express their models and their ideas. Electrical engineers learn the language of circuit diagrams. Computer scientists also use a variety of notations and languages to express their concepts and produce their results.

A physics student must first learn some basic mathematics in order to have a notation that can be used for discussion and reasoning about physics. A computer science student needs to learn a high-level programming language and problem solving techniques in order to be able to reason about computation. Programming no more defines what a computer scientist does than calculus defines what a physicist does.

Computer scientists, like their natural science and engineering colleagues, are concerned with model building, abstractions, analysis, design, and implementation. A program or software system often represents the final step in a reasoning and problem solving process.

This book will introduce techniques for reasoning and problem solving using objects. The fundamental principles of object-oriented programming will be explored and introduced. Through this exploration, many important principles of computation will be revealed.

1.2 Computer programs

A program consists of a sequence of instructions written in a precisely defined language called a programming language. These instructions are translated by a compiler into a low-level language, machine language, that the computer can respond to.

Software applications are generally divided into two broad categories: systems programs and applications programs. System programs are aimed at controlling a computer component such as a storage device, output device, or the computer itself (e.g., operating system). Application programs solve a specific problem external to the computer such as a banking application, air-traffic control system, word processing system, spreadsheet, or some other application area.

Computer programs represent the end product of the software development process. They are tangible entities that can be delivered to a customer, billed for, and shrink-wrapped. Commercial programs usually come packaged with a User's Guide and other supporting written documentation.

1.3 Programming languages

Three broad categories of programming languages have been developed: machine languages, assembly languages, and high-level languages. The earliest computers could be programmed using only a machine language. Such a language uses a sequence of 0's and 1's (bits) that represent precise instructions for computation and data access.

Assembly languages use alphabetic characters (letters) to represent the bit configurations in machine language. The letters usually describe the operations to be performed. Assembly languages represent a higher level of abstraction than a machine language. Some modern assembly languages support control structures that were previously found only in high-level languages.

High-level languages resemble natural languages. Data and operations are represented by descriptive statements.

As an example, suppose we wish to add two numbers and deposit the sum in a third number. In many high-level languages this operation would be symbolized:

```
c := a + b
```

The operands *a* and *b* represent the two numbers to be added and the variable *c* represents the sum. The operator ":=" is the assignment operator. It reads, the sum of the values in *a* and *b* will be assigned to *c*.

In a typical assembly language, the instructions might read:

LOAD A

ADD B

STORE C

In a machine language the instructions might read:

00011000 00000101

00100001 00000011

00101101 11100001

As you can see, only a computer would want to read machine language.

1.4   Structured and object-oriented programming

The word **paradigm** has become popular in recent years. One hears or reads about the object-oriented paradigm.

In the world of software development the 1970s and 1980s were dominated by an approach to problem solving or paradigm called structured programming. The dominant languages of this era included FORTRAN, Cobol, Algol, Pascal, Ada, and C. Considerable investments in building software tools to support the programming and software development process were made during this period. The methods and techniques for structured analysis and design put forth by Larry Constantine, Tom DeMarco, and Edward Yourdon have significantly influenced the way in which large and complex software systems are constructed. Powerful and expensive software tools for computer aided software engineering (CASE) have been developed to support this structured programming paradigm.

The structured approach to problem solving decomposes a problem into functions. This approach is called functional decomposition—a complex operation is factored into several smaller operations. Each of these into still smaller and less complex operations and so forth until each operation is manageable in size and complexity. A software system is viewed as a process of transformation—processing input data through a series of functional transformations to produce output. Data serves as the input to a particular function or to an entire process, gets "processed," and produces useful output. To several generations of programmers, this has been the most natural approach to problem solving. It has become a way of life.

In the mid 1970s a major but quiet research effort dealing with a different paradigm of software construction was performed by the Xerox Corporation at their Palo Alto Research Center (PARC). In 1980 this effort culminated in the commercial release of the object-oriented programming language Smalltalk-80. Inspired by the thinking of Alan Kay and his associates, this language was aimed at returning to the individual programmer a highly individualized and robust software development environment that in many ways resembles the modern workstation environment. An extremely "friendly" graphical user interface mechanism was a by-product of this work and later led to the development of the kind of graphical environment typically found on most workstations as well as personal computers. In 1980 a mouse as an interface device, a series of windows, pull-down menus, push buttons, dialog boxes, etc., which have now become fairly commonplace, were almost unheard of except in a few research labs.

But most significantly, Smalltalk exemplified an entirely new approach to software development and problem solving—the object-oriented approach. In this approach data decomposition rather than functions becomes the center of focus. Functions become attached to a data model and serve this data model. Problem solving becomes concerned with describing and modeling how objects interact with each other.

In the mid 1980s several additional object-oriented languages of considerable importance emerged. These include Objective-C, Eiffel, CLOS, and C++. All of these languages are still being used today although it is clear that C++ has become the most widely used object-oriented language. Of the object-oriented languages mentioned, only Smalltalk and Eiffel are "pure" object-oriented languages. By pure is meant that these two languages are not based on some other non-object-oriented substrate language as are C++ or Objective-C. In these C based languages constructs that support both structured as well as object-oriented programming are able to co-exist. This often leads to a mixed mode of problem solving. Only Smalltalk and Eiffel offer the programmer an ability to do only object-oriented programming. This author considers this to be a great advantage of using these two languages.

The next chapter explains the object-oriented approach in much greater detail.

Other paradigms of programming have been created in addition to structured and object-oriented. Functional programming, exemplified by the LISP programming language and logic programming exemplified by the PROLOG programming language are two examples. Functional programming has been used extensively in artificial intelligence applications and PROLOG in machine learning applications.

1.5   Common software tools

Included among the common software tools generally available to programmers are program editors, word processors, compilers, linkers, debuggers, profilers, and browsers. Each of these will be briefly described.

A program editor is a stripped-down word processing system that enables a programmer to enter the text of a program. Some program editors, namely context-sensitive editors, provide a syntactical structure that enables a programmer to enter a key word in a particular programming language and the editor then generates the remainder of an expression automatically. Most program editors support operations such as *search* (locate a word in the text), *search/replace* (search for and replace a given occurrence or all occurrences of a word with a replacement word), *auto-indent* (indent the text of a program a specified number of spaces or tab units based on the context within the program), and *goto* (move the marker or cursor to a specified line in the text).

A word processor is a program that supports the generation of documents. It often allows the integration of graphical components with textual components. Modern word processing systems are quite powerful and complex.

A compiler is a programming language specific program that translates the text of a program written in a high-level language into machine language. This is an essential process that must be performed before the program can run.

A linker is a program that integrates various pieces of a software application that have each been compiled into the executable code that comprises the application. Often, compiling and linking are performed as one integrated operation in order to translate the text of a software system into executable code.

A debugger is a system program that allows an application program to be executed under the control of the programmer. Program execution can be halted at predetermined spots in the high-level program text or after each step. The programmer can then inspect the values of various entities in the application program to determine whether this program is performing its functions properly. Generally debuggers are used when a fault is detected in an application.

A profiler is a program that is run in conjunction with an application. It computes and reports the amount of time the application spends in various branches and sections, allowing the programmer to determine where more efficiency needs to be designed into the completed application. A profiler essentially is a performance analysis tool.

A browser is a program that allows a visual inspection of a large and complex software application. Such a tool is essential for large software projects in which one programmer needs to be able to inspect other portions of the software system perhaps developed by other programmers or needs to inspect the code of reusable software libraries.

1.6 Programming

A computer **program** is a set of instructions written according to the syntax rules of some computer language. The instructions are translated by another computer program called a **compiler**. The compiler emits low-level machine instructions that permit your digital computer to execute the instructions that you have provided in your program. Such low-level machine instructions are typically quite difficult to read and understand and perhaps even more difficult to write directly. Fortunately, for most programmers this is rarely if ever required.

A well-written program should

(1) Be clear and easy for another programmer to understand.

(2) Solve the specified problem correctly.

(3) Be easy to modify if the specifications of the problem are changed.

1.6.1 Programming languages

There have been hundreds of programming languages invented to assist in the solution of many types of problems. These languages have been grouped into several broad categories based on their characteristics and approach to problem solving. These categories include:

(1) Assembly languages - These languages are each tuned for a specific processor with its unique low-level instruction set. Assembly language programs are typically difficult to write because the ability to formulate abstractions in an assembly language is very limited, quite prone to errors, and not easily adaptable if the specifications of the problem are changed. However programs developed with assembly language typically run quite fast. The earliest programming languages were assembly languages.

(2) Procedural languages - These languages were the first "high-level" languages. The first of these, FORTRAN, was developed during the early 1950s. It was used mainly for mathematical and scientific computations. The basic unit of abstraction in FORTRAN is the subroutine. Subroutines are similar to the services contained in a class description. Data is passed into a subroutine through its parameters. Computation is typically performed on this data and output is returned as a result. Other popular procedural languages are C, Pascal, Algol, and PL/1.

(3) Functional languages - LISP ranks as the grandparent of functional languages. The acronym LISP stands for list processing. LISP and its derivative languages are widely used in the application area of artificial intelligence, machine learning, and cognitive science. Although some commercial applications have been written in LISP, many still consider this language to be a research tool.

(4) Logic languages - PROLOG and its variants provide the opportunity to formulate a set of logical assertions and have the language derive deductions from these assertions. PROLOG, like LISP, has been used as a research tool in the area of artificial intelligence and machine learning.

(5) Object-Based - Modula-2 and Ada are the two most prominent object-based languages. Each supports the notion of abstract data types (to be explained later in this chapter). These are the first procedural languages to provide a clear separation between a data model and its surrounding services (between the external, user's view of data, and its internal representation). Neither of these languages support inheritance.

(6) Object-oriented languages - Simula, developed in Norway in the late 1960s is the first object-oriented programming language. In the 1970s the Xerox Palo Alto Research Center did some seminal research on the object model that led to the development of the Smalltalk programming language. This language was commerically released in 1980. It was soon followed by C++, Objective-C, CLOS (Common Lisp Object System), and Eiffel as well as a spate of other less well known more experimental object-oriented languages. The two most popular object-oriented languages in use today are C++ and Smalltalk. Eiffel is gaining rapidly in popularity but lags behind these other two at the time of this writing.

1.7   Goals of this book

This book is aimed at providing the reader with a solid foundation in the fundamental principles of programming (in this case object-oriented programming) and problem solving.

The object-oriented perspective taken in this book represents a further evolution in a trend to emphasize abstractions in computer problem solving and the use of abstract data types in particular (these are defined and discussed in the next chapter). Object modeling is introduced in this book. It is this author's belief that a beginning student will benefit greatly by learning early that the software development process does not begin with coding. Rather a systematic process of analysis and design occurs first. It is important for the reader to learn that programming is only part of the intellectual process associated with software construction and computer science.

Using an object-oriented approach, you the reader will be introduced to the simple and appealing notion that a software system is composed of harmoniously interacting objects that communicate with each other by way of messages. These messages are precisely defined in a class description.

As many experienced software professionals are discovering, the object-oriented perspective is quite distinct from the older, traditional approach of learning the rudiments of programming from the bottom up (learning first about scalar types, variables, assignment operations, comparison operations, branch and loop constructs, and much later the concept of a function).

Although the approach taken in this book is bold, it is not radical. The notion of function is introduced from the very start (in Chapter 2) and used throughout the book. The principle of encapsulation which unifies a data model with a functional abstraction forms the centerpiece of Chapter 2. Although a focus on implementation details are deferred until Chapter 4, the reader is introduced to the object-oriented problem solving process in Chapters 2 and 3.

Eiffel was chosen to support this effort because of its relatively simple syntax, its consistency, and its clean and rich support for programming with objects. Among the various object-oriented languages developed in the past 10 years, it is the most elegant and perhaps most powerful.

For those readers who are not using this book as a first course in computer science but are using this book as their introduction to the object paradigm, let me say a few words about why C++ is not the language of choice for this book. Although I recognize the enormous popularity of C++ and the likelihood that the reader may need to "get up to speed" in this language, I also strongly believe that the complexity of C++, its somewhat arcane syntax, its lack of safety, and its continued reliance on low-level artifacts such as pointers and references distract from the goal of learning to problem solve with objects. C++ neither encourages or discourages object-oriented problem solving. It is a hybrid language that is culturally embedded in the "C mind set." Although this mind set has proven to be extremely productive, it does not lend itself to learning a new set of problem solving mechanisms.

In my opinion, it is important to first become proficient at the object-oriented problem solving process before embarking on the challenge of mastering a most complex language. The "++" part of C++ is not a small increment from C.

I believe you will find, as I have, that Eiffel is not only an outstanding language from which to learn the basic principles of object-oriented software construction but also a rich and powerful language to use for actual problem solving after you have mastered the principles of Object-Oriented Programming (OOP).

It is my hope that this book will inspire your interest and enthusiasm in object-oriented problem solving and provide you with a solid foundation in some basic principles of computer science.

1.8   Exercises

1. List several ways in which computers have affected your life. (Please restrain yourself from using foul language!)

2. List several jobs that involve a computer.

3. Discuss the major components of a computer.

4. What is the advantage of using a high-level language over a machine language?

5. What are the traditional steps in the life cycle of a software system?

6. Why are you interested in computers or computer science? You may wish to keep your answer to this question in a safe place for several years and re-read your answer in three years.

Chapter 2

An Object-Oriented Approach to Problem Solving

This chapter is about objects and classes and how each are used in the construction of software. When you have finished this chapter, you will have learned: (important technical words are shown in boldface type):

- An **object** is an instance of a **class**.

- An object has **data** and **behavior**.

- An object can receive either a **command** or **query** from another object.

- A command provides the means for modifying the data maintained by an instance of a class.

- A query provides access to the data maintained by an instance of a class.

- The **state** of an object is captured by the values of all its queries.

- Classes can be related to each other in three different ways: **inheritance**, **aggregation**, and **uses** (association).

- Some classes are **abstract** whereas others are **concrete**.

- Objects are created within a **program** and interact with each other as a program runs.

2.1   Object, objects everywhere

2.1.1 Ordinary objects

What is an object? An ordinary object is characterized by its behavior as well as its internal state. For ordinary objects, a boundary separates the inside or body of the object from the region lying outside the object. Features that characterize ordinary objects include texture, color, smell, sound, or cost.

An infant early in life is able to distinguish objects that surround her. These include parents or caretakers and the inanimate decorations hanging near or above her crib. It is fair to say that human beings are all "object-oriented" creatures. As we get older we learn to further categorize objects based on their shape and behavior. Our "object orientation" is strengthened by observations of the world around us and later by the formal process of education. For example, in Chemistry we learn to understand a particular atom based on its classification in a Periodic Table of Elements. In Biology, we learn to classify many living organisms based on an elaborate hierarchical classification of species.

When, as youngsters, we observe objects around us, we often distinguish or classify objects based on their similarities and differences in shape and behavior. But quite amazingly, we are able to quickly learn to classify similar types of objects such as cars independent of their precise shape, size, color, or texture. A toddler can usually recognize a rough sketch of a car in a book, a matchbox-size toy car, and a real car as all being different examples, incarnations, or "instances" of the classification, CAR. Many toddlers can further distinguish a car from a truck not based on some precise shape, size, color, or other precise truck "signature" but instead based on some of the abstract visual properties of cars and trucks. It seems that human beings possess a natural ability to classify objects. These classifications we will call classes.

The word **instance** will be used to mean a particular member of a class. For example, the small matchbox-sized red car that is the favorite play toy of a toddler is an instance of class CAR (upper-case characters will be used for classes) just as the rough sketch of a car in a children's book or the real automobile in the garage are other instances of CAR.

Many children develop a high level of enthusiasm for toy cars, trucks, airplanes, boats, and trains. This fascination appears to be based on the common ability of all of these objects to move from location to location and, most importantly, the ability of the child to control this movement. Before long, children are able to obtain an understanding of a VEHICLE abstraction. This abstraction represents the common features of all vehicles including cars, trucks, airplanes, boats and trains (and other vehicle types encountered later on when one's life experience and purchasing power broadens). A child seems able to perform this generalization before learning the word "vehicle." As human beings we seem to be able to perform such generalizations naturally. This approach to classification serves as the basis for an "object-oriented" approach to problem solving.

The VEHICLE class whether formally defined or informally understood is considered to be an **abstract class** in contrast to a **concrete class** such as a CAR, TRUCK, PLANE, BOAT, and TRAIN. Rarely will a child request of his parent: "Please bring me the red vehicle from my room." An abstract class (such as VEHICLE) is one that has no actual instances but can be used to spawn instances of concrete classes (such as CAR, TRUCK, PLANE, BOAT, or TRAIN). It is a generalization of a concrete class.

The abstraction of a class VEHICLE which contains the common features of CAR, TRUCK, PLANE, BOAT, and TRAIN forms the basis for the notion of **inheritance**. The concrete classes acquire (inherit) characteristics from their parent class (the abstract class). Each inherited characteristic from the abstract class is found in instances of the concrete classes.

In our perception of ordinary objects it is difficult or nearly impossible to precisely define the characteristics of each concrete class. We can quickly develop the ability to accurately identify a car. We may never develop the ability to precisely define the class CAR. Our pattern recognition abilities are based on complex phenomena that cannot easily be modeled. When we "model" a CAR class, we attempt to extract essential features or characteristics while ignoring inessential details. It is at least comforting to know that although we may not be able to precisely model a car, we can at least drive one.

2.1.2 Objects as abstractions

As soon as we think about, write about, or talk about cars, we are developing an abstraction of such an entity. This is not an activity that comes easily or early in life. Both artists and engineers need to perform such an abstraction when attempting to depict a car. Each will do this quite differently. The artist will focus on the shape, texture, and color aspects of a car whereas the engineer will focus on both the shape and behavioral features of a car. In particular, the engineer is concerned with the relationship between shape and behavior. The abstract model of the car developed by the engineer must unify shape and behavior. This unification is called **encapsulation**.

The features of shape, texture, and color might be considered to be the "data" aspects of the car. In addition to these "data" characteristics, the engineer is concerned with issues such as the cornering ability of the car, its braking ability, its acceleration, etc. These phenomena involve the response of the vehicle to various inputs (e.g., pushing down on the accelerator pedal, pushing down on the brake pedal, moving the steering wheel, etc.). A car's behavior is strongly influenced by its "data" characteristics. A big and heavy car generally requires much more power to attain a given level of acceleration performance than a small light car. It is generally less maneuverable than a light car.

For the purposes of understanding the acceleration characteristics of a car, the only "data" features (henceforth called **attributes**) that may be relevant are the car's mass, torque, tire friction, and drag coefficient. These variables form the internal state or attributes for class CAR. Other attributes such as its color, brand name, or cost are irrelevant. Features such as the car's current speed could be computed from a knowledge of its attributes.

If one is developing an abstraction of a car as a business commodity, then the attributes that we might use to represent a car's internal state include the loan amount, the interest rate on the loan, the number of months of the loan, the number of payments already made, and the current "blue book" (wholesale and retail) value of the car. From these attributes the "behavior" of the car as a business commodity can be fully described.

The modeling of objects is similar to the modeling of any entities in science. The level of detail defined in the model is dependent on the goals of the problem. If it is desired to study the thermodynamic properties of the four-stroke cycle associated with an internal combustion engine, then a model that includes a much finer granularity of detail is appropriate. This would include information about the geometry of each cylinder and the geometry of each piston.

Therefore, the description of an object, the object abstraction, is based on the problem domain in which the object exists. Features of the object that play an essential role in finding a solution to the given problem must be represented in the object model (the class) whereas features that are not essential are ignored. An abstraction represents a simplified depiction of reality. The *Oxford Dictionary* (1966) suggests the following about abstractions: "The principle of ignoring those aspects of a subject that are not relevant to the current purpose in order to concentrate more fully on those that are."

2.2   The object model

Coad and Yourdon [1] define an **object** as "an abstraction of something in a problem domain, reflecting the capabilities of a system to keep information about or interact with it; an encapsulation of attribute values and their exclusive services."

Since "problem domain" can refer to almost anything, the key concepts in the definition given above are abstraction, information, interact with, attribute values, and exclusive services.

Abstraction, as indicated above, involves a separation of essential from inessential features. In defining an abstraction, the essential features (and thus inessential features) are relative to the problem that is being solved. This was illustrated in section 2.1.2 with two models of a car, a physical model and a business model.

The concept of **information** and **attributes** in the above definition of object implies data storage. Each attribute represents a separate component of the overall data storage model. This was illustrated in section 2.1.2 with the car attributes mass, torque, tire friction, and drag coefficient. The queries in the external section of the class (the portion of the class that is publicly available) allow the values of some attributes to be obtained.

The concept of **interact with** and **exclusive services** in the definition above suggest action and behavior. The services associated with an object describe the things that you can do to or with the object. This is the **behavior** of the object. The commands in the external section of the class specify precisely what services are available for objects of the class.

The object model involves two principal components: a data model and a behavior model. These models are contained in the class description of the object. The data model provides a precise specification of what information is stored in each object whereas the behavior model provides a precise specification of the services that can be performed on or by the object. Only the services provided in the behavior model can be performed by the object. If additional services are needed they must be added to the behavior model of the class defining that object.

2.2.1   An object model example

Let us consider a simple example to illustrate the object model. Suppose we wish to build an object model of a "counter." No, not a kitchen counter, but a numerical counter. This counter can be used to track the number of times a "counting event" occurs. Examples might include counting the number of vehicles to arrive at an intersection in a traffic simulation or counting the number of airplanes to land on a runway within a specified time period.

We construct a COUNTER class to illustrate the object model.

The state of a COUNTER object, an instance of class COUNTER, is totally described by the value of a query. The value of the query, *count*, holds the instantaneous value of the number of times the COUNTER object has been told to increment its count. This query completely and uniquely specifies the information contained in a particular COUNTER object.

The commands (the services that can be performed by or on a counter object) include:

(1) *create* - construct a new counter object with initial value equal to zero

(2) *increment* - add the value 1 to the current state of the counter

(3) *reset* - set the value of the current state back to 0

Figure 2.1 shows a graphical description of class COUNTER.

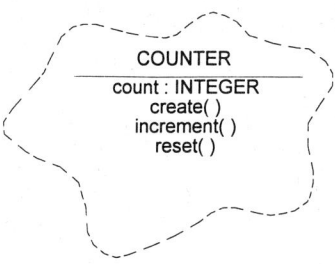

Figure 2.1 Graphical Description of Class COUNTER

This notation in which a class is surrounded by a dotted cloud was created by Grady Booch [2] and is referred to as a "Booch cloud" or just class diagram. The name of the class is given above the horizontal line. Below this line the commands and queries are shown. The empty parenthesis pairs next to each command indicates that these commands require no external information coming in.

2.2.2 The noun-verb and noun-noun metaphors

We introduce a notation to represent the actions that we can perform on an object. We continue with the COUNTER example introduced in the previous section. The four things that we can do to a COUNTER object are create one, increment its value by 1, access its current *count*, and reset its value to 0. These are the **responsibilities** of a COUNTER object.

Suppose we let the entity *car_count* represent a counter object that is used in a traffic simulation program to keep track of the total number of vehicles to arrive at a bridge toll booth. The commands and query that we can perform on such a *car_count* object are

<u>Commands</u>
car_count.create
car_count.increment
car_count.reset
<u>Query</u>
car_count.count

In each of these actions, the object receiving the action is connected to the operation on the object using a dot ("*.*") connector. It would be reasonable to say that the above notation suggests that we are taking actions on a particular object for the commands or obtaining information from the object for the query.

For the commands, the object is a noun and the action is a verb. For the query both the object and query are nouns.

2.2.3 Internal state

Suppose that there are three COUNTER objects in our traffic simulation program: *car_count, truck_count, and bus_count*. As vehicles arrive at the bridge's toll booth, suppose the following sequence of actions are recorded:

car_count.reset
truck_count.reset
bus_count.reset
car_count.increment
car_count.increment
bus_count.increment
car_count.increment
truck_count.increment
car_count.increment
truck_count.increment

The first three actions initialize the three counters to 0. After the remaining seven actions are taken, the objects have the following internal state: *car_count (4), truck_count (2), bus_count (1)*. The object's internal states are different from each other because of the different *increment* actions taken on each.

The point here is that although there are three distinct COUNTER objects, each characterized by the same object model (class description given in Figure 2.1), the internal states of each of these objects dynamically evolve.

2.2.4 Object scenarios and messages

The class diagram of Figure 2.1 represents a static model of class COUNTER. The dynamic behavior is not shown. An **object scenario diagram** may be used to depict the dynamic interactions among objects.

For each command given in the behavior model of a class (e.g., *create*, *increment, reset*), a message corresponding to this service may be sent to an instance of the class. These messages take the form given in section 2.2.3 where ten actions are recorded. Each of these expressions involve sending a message to an object.

The dynamic behavior of class COUNTER is shown in Figure 2.2. This figure includes objects from other classes that use the COUNTER objects.

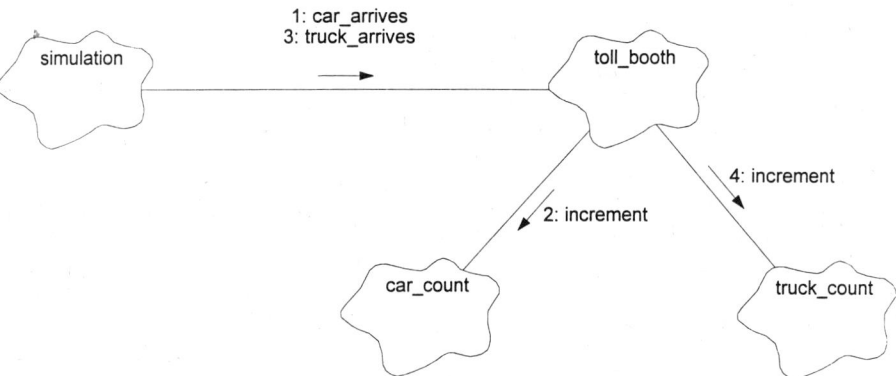

Figure 2.2 Object Scenario Diagram

In Figure 2.2, four objects are shown by the solid "Booch" object clouds. The object *simulation* is an instance of the class SIMULATION (details not shown here). The object *toll_booth* is an instance of class TOLL_BOOTH (details not shown here). The objects *car_count* and *truck_count* are instances of class COUNTER.

The number labels indicate the sequence of actions. The first action is associated with the *simulation* object sending the *toll_booth* object the message *car_arrives*. The second action is associated with the *toll_booth* object sending the *car_count* object the message *increment*. The third action is associated with the *simulation* object sending the *toll_booth* object the message *truck_arrives*. The fourth action is associated with the *toll_booth* object sending the *truck_count* object the message *increment*.

It must be emphasized that only messages that correspond to the available commands are allowed. For example, it would be illegal to send the *car_count* object the command *increase_value_by_three*. Such a message which attempts to increase the *count* by 3 would be allowed only if this command were included in the static description of class COUNTER.

2.2.5 Parameters

Suppose it were desired to be able to increment a COUNTER object's value by more than 1 (e.g., several cars arrive in different lanes at the toll booth at the same time). An additional command must be added to the behavioral model of class COUNTER. We might specify this command as *increment_by (amount : INTEGER)*. The entity *amount : INTEGER* inside the parenthesis pair specifies that *amount* is a parameter and *INTEGER* is its description or type. The parameter *amount* causes the state, *count*, to be increased by the value of the parameter *amount*. We further assume that *amount* must be positive.

A modified class diagram is shown in Figure 2.3 and a modified object scenario diagram that uses the new service *increment_by* is shown in Figure 2.4.

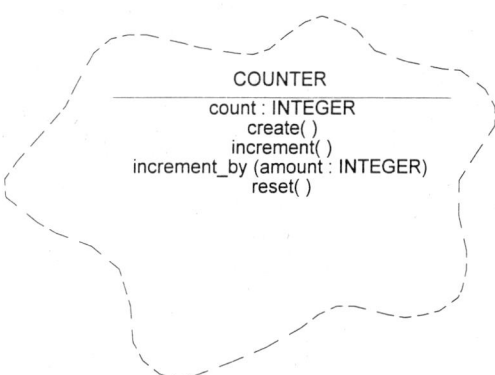

COUNTER
count : INTEGER
create( )
increment( )
increment_by (amount : INTEGER)
reset( )

Figure 2.3 Modified Description of Class COUNTER

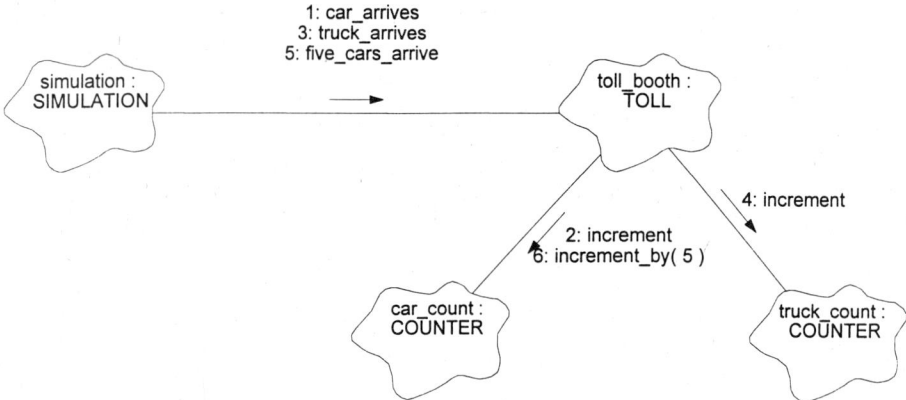

Figure 2.4 Modified Object Scenario Diagram

A command can have one or more parameters, each of a specified type. These provide external input to the command that helps determine the action performed by the command.

As an example of a multiparameter command, consider an application that includes constructing a window on a computer terminal (a geometric region defined by borders in which text and graphics can be displayed). The external information required to construct such a window includes the length and width of the window and its upper-left coordinate. The specification of such a command in a class, WINDOW, might be

create (corner : POINT; width : INTEGER; height : INTEGER)

The first parameter, *corner*, is specified to be of type POINT. Type POINT is another class that includes among its services *make(x : INTEGER; y : INTEGER)* for creating a point object of given *x* and *y* coordinate.

The following actions given by two messages might be taken to create a window object whose corner coordinate is (5, 10) and whose width is 100 and height 200.

a_point.make (5, 10)
a_window.create (a_point, 100, 200)

The first command creates and initializes a point object (*a_point*) with *x* coordinate equal to 5 and *y* coordinate equal to 10. This point object is used to create and initialize a window object (*a_window*) with an upper-left corner given by *a_point* and a width of 100 and height of 200.

Both of the actions given by the two messages above are critically dependent on the external information sent in to the two parameters of class POINT's *make* and the three parameters of class WINDOW's *create*.

As a final example that illustrates the importance of allowing the commands defined in a class to include parameters, consider a class VEHICLE. Suppose we wish to create a vehicle with a specified color, weight, cost, and horsepower. A *create* command for class VEHICLE might be specified as

create (color : STRING; weight : INTEGER; cost : REAL; horsepower : INTEGER)

The parameter *color* is of type STRING. This is a class that represents a sequence of characters as its data model (an ordinary word). The characteristics of such a class are discussed later in the book. Parameters *weight* and *horsepower* are of type INTEGER whereas parameter *cost* is of type REAL.

Although it might not be immediately apparent to the reader and in fact seem unnatural, numerical values of integer type have properties (behavior) different from numerical values of real type. An integer type can have only whole values. A real type can have decimal values. When arithmetic is performed on integer type values, an exact answer is computed. On the other hand, when arithmetic is performed on real type values, an exact answer may not always be possible. This "round-off" error present in the arithmetic processing units of digital computers is caused by the finite storage size of each decimal operand. A quantity such as 1 / 3 (a repeating decimal requiring an infinite number of digits of precision) can only be represented with finite precision. This potentially causes a small error to be introduced in any computation that involves this decimal quantity.

Since integer numbers behave differently than decimal numbers (type REAL), their behavior is specified in two different classes.

2.3 Relationships among objects

Rarely are we concerned with isolated objects. Science in general and computer science in particular are concerned with modeling and understanding systems. Object-oriented systems involve many objects of different types working together to achieve some desired end.

It is important that we examine the kinds of relationships that objects can have with each other. Several important relationships that objects can have to each other are based on the relationships between their classes.

These include **inheritance** (examined in section 2.3.1), **aggregation** (examined in section 2.3.2), and **uses** relationships (examined in section 2.3.3).

2.3.1 Inheritance

The word **inheritance** suggests the acquisition of characteristics from one or more ancestors. This is precisely the sense in which we shall use this term in connection with object-oriented problem solving.

Suppose we wish to construct a new class, a subclass, that represents a specialization of an existing class. We wish the subclass to possibly add some attributes to the data model of the parent as well as some additional commands or queries. We also wish the subclass to share the features of the parent's data model as well as provide the services of the parent class.

There is an important consistency principle that should be satisfied whenever one class is a subclass of another. This principle has three parts:

(1) The subclass should have a logical relationship to the parent that can be expressed as "the subclass is a kind of" the parent class.

(2) The attributes of the parent class must all make sense as part of the state of the subclass.

(3) The services of the parent class must all make sense as part of the behavior of the subclass.

As an example, consider the relationship between a class VEHICLE and class CAR. Clearly, class CAR is a specialization of class VEHICLE. There are many vehicle types that are not cars but no cars that are not vehicles.

Suppose, for the purposes of this simple example, that class VEHICLE has the attributes *color, weight, maximum_speed*, and *price*. Class CAR has the additional attributes *number_cylinders* and *horsepower*.

Now let us consider class AIRPLANE, another subclass of VEHICLE. In addition to the attributes *weight, maximum_speed*, and *price* inherited from class VEHICLE, it has the additional attribute *wing_span*.

Consider now two subclasses of AIRPLANE, JET_PLANE and PISTON_PLANE. Class JET_PLANE introduces the attribute *maximum_thrust* (a characteristic of its jet engine) and class PISTON_PLANE introduces the attribute *displacement* (the volume of each cylinder).

Since this is a simple example, no attempt will be made to model the commands and queries for each of these classes. The Booch class diagram in Figure 2.5 shows the inheritance hierarchy for these basic vehicle classes. The arrows are drawn from subclass to parent.

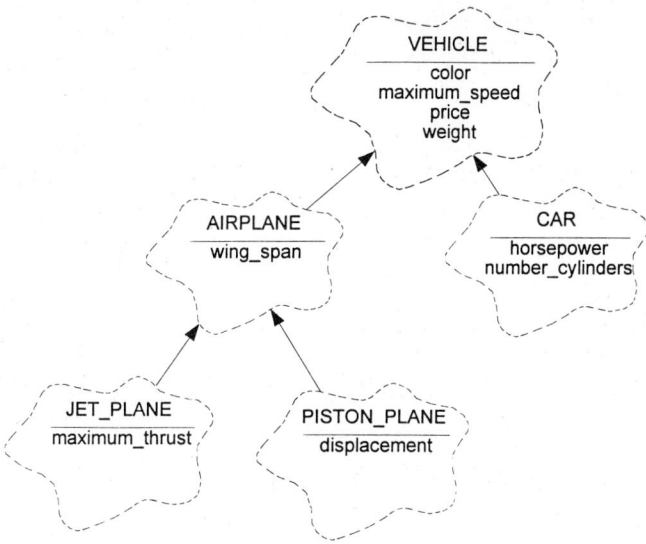

Figure 2.5 Inheritance Relationship for VEHICLE Classes

2.3.1.1 Classification

It was mentioned earlier that the process of classification can be used to manage complexity. Whenever a group of related but somewhat dissimilar objects needs to be modeled, a careful consideration of their similarities and differences may lead to a hierarchy of classes. Attributes that are shared by many subclasses should be placed into classes "high" in the hierarchy. Services that are to be shared by many subclasses should also be placed "high" in the hierarchy. The primary basis for classification is usually based on the distribution and reuse of attributes (i.e. the data model).

As an example, let us consider the world of purebred dogs. The American Kennel Club recognizes several subgroups of dogs, based on their physical as well as behavioral characteristics. Figure 2.6 shows a partial hierarchy of purebred dog classes.

Several of the classes are marked with a triangular adornment with the letter "A" inside of the triangle. This symbol indicates that the class is an **abstract** class. An abstract class will never have instances. Its purpose is to factor common attributes as well as services that are needed in descendant classes. These attributes and services are not shown in Figure 2.6.

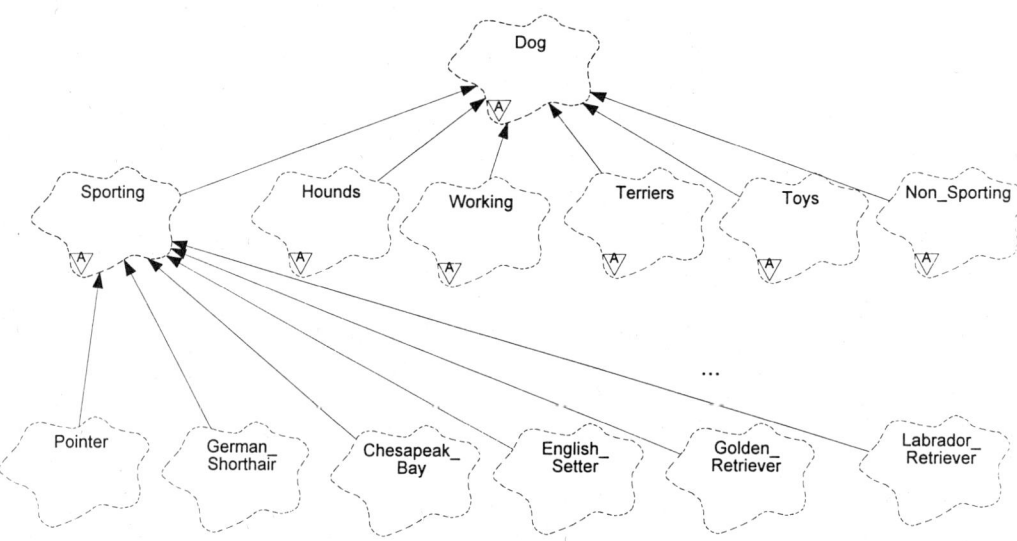

Figure 2.6 Classification of Dogs

A dog fancier is able to know a great deal about a particular breed by knowing where its class sits in the dog hierarchy. Likewise, a software engineer is able to know a great deal about the expected behavior of an object by knowing where its class sits in the hierarchy of classes surrounding it.

2.3.2 Aggregation

The objects around us are generally made from the fabric of other objects or composites. Your computer is composed of a central processing unit, random access memory, high-speed cache memory, and secondary storage. Each of these objects may in turn be partitioned into smaller objects. Ultimately, of course, if one continues to decrease the granularity of components, you will find yourself at the molecular or atomic level. As usual, the problem being solved determines the appropriate level of granularity in modeling one object as an "aggregation" of other objects.

Let us again revisit an object model of a car. A car is composed of an engine, a transmission, a chassis, a set of wheels and tires, an electrical system, a suspension system, an exhaust system, and interior components. Each of these are essential parts of the car and may themselves be modeled as classes.

The object must be able to satisfy the "has-a" relationship with respect to each of its composite parts.

Figure 2.7 shows the aggregation relationship for a car.

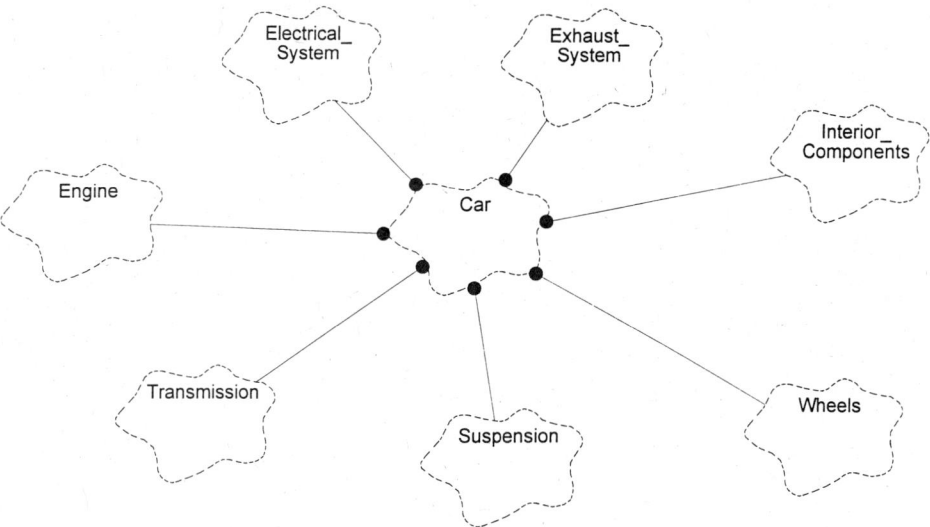

Figure 2.7 Aggregation Relationship between Classes

The dark circle connecting class Car with the aggregates Engine, Transmission, Suspension, Wheels, Interior_Components, Exhaust_System, and Electrical_System indicate the "has-a" relationship and aggregation.

2.3.3 Uses relationship

Often a class needs to use the resources of another class that may not be closely related to it. For example a simulation class may need to perform mathematical operations including sine, cosine, and square root. Suppose these services are found in class MATH. In addition, the simulation class needs to draw geometric figures on the screen. Suppose the services for doing this are found in class GRAPHICS.

Figure 2.8 shows a "uses" relationship between class SIMULATION and classes MATH and GRAPHICS. The light circles attached to class SIMULATION indicate a "uses" relationship to classes MATH and GRAPHICS.

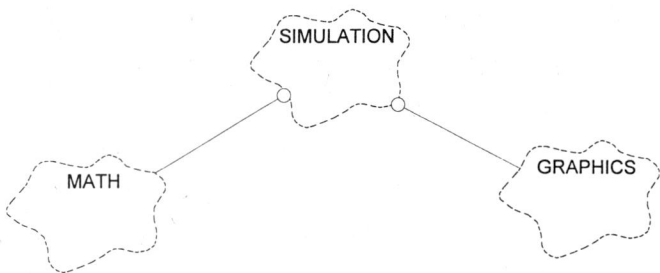

Figure 2.8 A Uses Relationship between Classes

2.4 Abstract data types

An abstract data type (ADT) is a data model and an associated set of operations that can be performed by or on the data model. The COUNTER class defined earlier is a perfect example of an abstract data type. The data model consists of a simple integer, *count*. The operations that define the behavior of this data model are *make*, *increment*, and *increment_by*. The abstract data type COUNTER can be thought of as a single unified element whose purpose is to count events or things. The things that one can do to a COUNTER object are reset its value to 0, increment its count by 1, or increment its count by an arbitrary non-negative integer value. That is all. One cannot add, subtract, multiply, or divide a COUNTER object by another COUNTER object or by an ordinary integer. That is because the abstract data type has defined unique properties that do not include such arithmetic.

Abstract data types provide powerful abstractions that can be used as the basis for problem solving. The low-level details of the data model (the internals of the ADT) become unimportant when deciding how ADTs interact with each other. Only the external properties of the ADT (defined by the set of operations) are important in determining its use.

Abstract data types are represented by classes in an object-oriented language. In procedural languages such as C and Pascal, there is no direct language syntax or support for abstract data types. Careful and disciplined programming allows the programmer to simulate ADTs.

The term **data-hiding** is used to mean that the data model (internal state) of an ADT cannot be directly modified by the user. The internal state can be modified only through the set of operations that have been defined for the ADT. There is no implied secrecy associated with the term data-hiding, only protection. The internal state of an object (an ADT) is protected from inadvertent corruption.

How might one define an abstract data type for a traffic light?

The data model of the light must allow for the internal states green, amber, and red. These values might be defined as having a type LIGHT_COLOR (such a data model would allow only three values for an instance of LIGHT_COLOR).

The commands that could be performed on the light might include

(1) *set (color : LIGHT_COLOR)*

(2) *advance*

The *set* operation allows the user to fix the internal state of the light. The *advance* operation moves the light through the sequence green, amber, red when applied repeatedly. The behavior of the traffic light is completely specified by the operations *set* and *advance*.

2.5 Producers and consumers

A software system generally is composed of many individual components. In an object-oriented setting these components are given by classes. A class library contains a collection of classes unified by their support for some application area. Class libraries have been built to support graphical user interfaces for windows style programming, databases for storing complex information, mathematical computation for engineering and scientific applications, data structures for representing abstract data types, input and output operations, and other application areas.

A **producer** is a programmer whose main focus is building a class library for other programmers to use or other parts of an application to use. A **consumer** is a programmer who is using a class library for a specific application. Often a programmer plays the dual role of both producer and consumer—producing some classes for later reuse by others or in the same application and using existing classes in a specific application.

It is generally desirable to use the available resources of existing libraries to build a new application unless you wish to develop new applications from first principles (i.e. reinvent the wheel). A knowledgeable programmer may be able to assemble a software application by using existing software components that are connected together with minimal new code. This would be a consumer activity.

As an example, suppose we consider a typical first programming application. We wish to write a program that displays your name on the output terminal of your computer system.

Most programming languages are supported by a library or libraries for performing input and output. Input is the process of interaction between a user and computer in which the user transfers information to the computer program. Output is the process of interaction between a user and computer in which a program transfers information to the user.

The first program that we wish to construct involves only simple output. The program is to display the user's name on his or her video terminal. Listing 2.1 presents such a typical first program.

The formatting follows the recommended style guidelines for Eiffel.

Listing 2.1 A first program—Displaying your name

```
class FIRST_PROGRAM

creation
    start

feature

    start is
        do
            io.putstring ("My name is xxx")
        end;

end -- class FIRST_PROGRAM
```

In Listing 2.1, class FIRST_PROGRAM contains one routine, **start**, that triggers the application. A configuration file called an Ace file informs the Eiffel system that FIRST_PROGRAM is the application class and specifically that *start* is the entry point into the application. The reader should consult his or her Eiffel system User's Guide for details relating to the construction of an Ace file.

Routine *start* contains only a single executable line of code, *io.putstring("My name is xxx")* where the user should replace the "xxx" with his or her name. The object *io* is defined in a standard input/output Eiffel library and is available in all Eiffel systems. This library is an important reusable software component. The routine *putstring* is one of many routines defined in this library. It allows the user to display a "string" of characters on the display terminal. A "string" of characters is a sequence of character symbols.

The formal details for writing Eiffel programs and using existing Eiffel libraries are introduced in Chapter 3. Nevertheless, the reader may wish to type in the code from Listing 2.1, compile it, and run it. It is always quite thrilling when one's first program is successfully completed.

The author of Listing 2.1 acted as a consumer. The resource that was consumed or used was the standard IO library. In later chapters you will be shown how to inspect the interface to libraries and use their resources. Throughout this book important routines from important Eiffel libraries will be used in constructing specific applications. You will also be introduced to the business of creating reusable routines for others to use.

One must first become a competent consumer before embarking on becoming a competent producer. Several later chapters focus on the responsibilities of the producer.

2.6 Object modeling

Object modeling is concerned with analysis and design. Because of the introductory nature of this book, only the fundamental concepts of object analysis and design will be explored in this section.

2.6.1 Analysis

Software analysis, both object-oriented and otherwise, is concerned with understanding and modeling the domain of the problem. The major elements of the problem domain are mapped into software components. The initial architecture of these software components is constructed in a manner that precisely describes the relationships that exist among various entities in the problem domain. In an object-oriented context these entities are objects, each an instance of a particular class.

Object-oriented analysis is concerned with the discovery of key classes and their relationship to other key classes. As discussed earlier, each class encapsulates a data model and a set of associated services. These services represent the behavioral model of the class. Much of the work of object-oriented analysis is concerned with determining the data and behavior model of each class.

The static architecture, developed at the analysis level, is given by associations between classes. These associations include aggregation (whole/ essential part) relationships, uses relationships, and generalization/specialization relationships (inheritance). These relationships are discussed and illustrated next.

2.6.1.1 Aggregation relationship

An aggregation relationship is a "whole/essential part" or "intrinsic" relationship. The "whole" object "is composed of" the "part." This part must be essential for the integrity of the whole.

Aggregation is a natural type of association. Many of the objects surrounding you are composed of constituent parts. For example, your video monitor is composed of a plastic case, a video tube, and control buttons or dials. Each of these constituent parts are essential for the functioning of the monitor.

The engine in a car might reasonably be considered to be an essential part of a car. Although it could certainly be argued that engines have an identity of their own (even their own serial number), may be manufactured at a separate site, and can be swapped in and out of cars, for most applications the car is associated with a particular engine that will not be changed. Furthermore, the functioning of the car is totally dependent on the presence of the engine. From this viewpoint, the identity of the car (the whole object) is not separate from the engine (the constituent and essential part). The car's transmission system could also be reasonably considered to be an essential part of a car. One could therefore say that the car (the whole) has an aggregation relationship to its engine and transmission (the parts). There are of course many other essential car components not mentioned.

In a diamond ring, it is fair to argue that the ring (the whole object) has an aggregation relationship to its essential parts, a gold band and a diamond stone. Although each may be manufactured separately, from a modeling viewpoint the identity of the gold band and diamond stone is not critical. What is critical is the identity of the whole object, the ring.

The Booch notation for an aggregation relationship is shown in Figure 2.9. The class with the dark rectangle is the "part" and the class with the dark circle is the "whole."

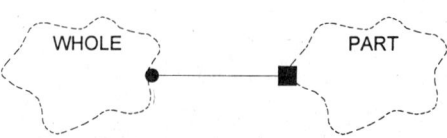

Figure 2.9 Aggregation Relationship

2.6.1.2 Uses relationship

An example of a "uses" relationship is a room, some desks, and some chairs. The room has an identity separate from its desks and chairs. The room still exists even when it is empty. The desks and chairs can be changed, rearranged, swapped, or easily removed.

The Booch notation for a uses relationship is shown in Figure 2.10. Here a room is shown to have a uses relationship to zero or more chairs and zero or more desks.

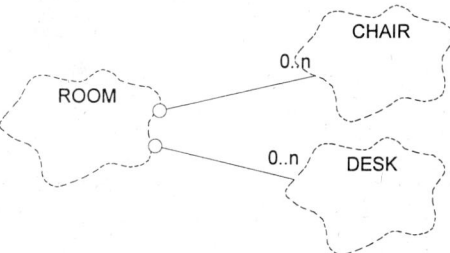

Figure 2.10 Uses Relationship

2.6.1.3 Inheritance relationship

Inheritance in an object-oriented software context implies specialization. A parent class defines general attributes and behavior that are shared by its children. Each child class contains more specialized attributes or behavior (services) that are not present in the parent.

For example, a car can be considered to be a special type of vehicle. A plane can be considered to be another special type of vehicle. A car and plane may share certain attributes (color, weight, price) but have separate attributes (e.g., number of pistons for a car, wing span for a plane).

The Booch notation for inheritance is shown in Figure 2.11 using classes VEHICLE, CAR, and PLANE. The arrows point from the child to the parent (in the direction of generalization).

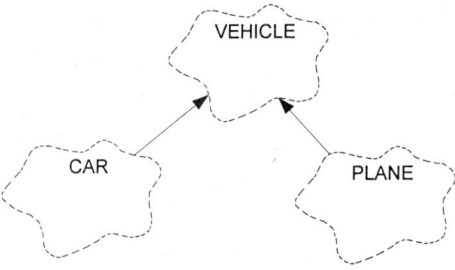

Figure 2.11 Inheritance Relationship

2.6.2 Analysis of an elevator

We discuss some simple elements of the object-oriented analysis of an elevator in an office building.

What are the features that are relevant to the problem domain? There is of course an elevator. There is a set of buttons, each with a numeral indicating a particular floor in the office building. The elevator is painted with a certain color. But certainly this is not relevant to the functioning of an elevator and will not be included in the analysis model. Finally, there is a user, a human being who enters the elevator and wishes to be transported from a given level to some higher or lower elevation in the office building.

Based on the description of the problem domain, a whole/part relationship exists between the elevator and its buttons. Each elevator has a set of buttons that contain all of the legal locations that the elevator is allowed to travel to. These are an essential part of the elevator.

In Figure 2.12, a simple class diagram showing class ELEVATOR and class BUTTON is shown.

Figure 2.12 Class Diagram for Elevator

Each dotted cloud represents a class. The class name is given inside of the cloud. As indicated earlier, the solid line with a solid dot that connects class ELEVATOR to class BUTTON indicates a whole/part relationship or an aggregation relationship. The class with the solid dot "has" or "is composed of" the class without the dot.

The notation, *1..n*, at the end of the connection line indicates that there are 1 or more buttons that are part of the elevator. The solid rectangle at the end of this connection indicates that class ELEVATOR owns its set of buttons (they are not shared by any other objects).

When a person enters the elevator, he or she pushes one of the buttons. This action is shown in the object-scenario diagram given in Figure 2.13.

Each solid cloud represents a specific object with a name given inside the cloud. The numbers followed by a colon represent the sequence of actions. The three events that are shown in Figure 2.13 are (1) a person enters the elevator, (2) the person selects one of the many buttons, and (3) a person pushes this selected button.

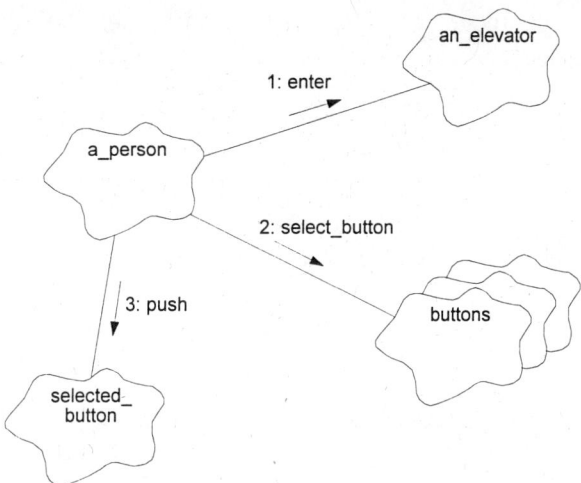

Figure 2.13 Object Scenario Diagram for Person Entering Elevator

The first event, a person entering the elevator, is depicted in Figure 2.13 by the object, *a_person*, sending the message, *enter*, to the *object an_elevator*.

The second event in Figure 2.13 is shown by the object *a_person* sending the message *select_button* to a collection of button objects, *buttons*, shown by the three clouds. The button that is selected is shown with the name *selected_button*.

The third event shown is the object *a_person* sending the message *push* to the *object selected_button*.

2.6.3 Design

If one looks toward the problem domain when doing analysis, one must look toward the solution domain when doing design. The solution domain is a software system containing various objects that interact with each other. Each object is typically defined by a class. During design, one precisely identifies additional classes that interact with the domain classes identified at the analysis level to complete a solution to the problem.

The introductory nature of this book makes it inappropriate to pursue the subject of design.

2.7   Summary

- Ordinary objects are characterized by their behavior as well as their attributes.

- It seems that human beings possess a natural ability to classify objects. We will call these classifications classes.

- The word "instance" will be used to mean an object whose properties are specified in a class.

- The description of an object, the object abstraction, is based on the problem domain in which the object exists.

- An abstraction represents a simplified depiction of reality.

- Features of the object that play an essential role in finding a solution to the given problem must be represented in the object model (the class) whereas features that are not essential are ignored.

- An abstraction represents a simplified depiction of reality.

- Coad and Yourdon define an **object** as "an abstraction of something in a problem domain, reflecting the capabilities of a system to keep information about or interact with it; an encapsulation of attribute values and their exclusive services."

- The data model provides a precise specification of what information is maintained in each object.

- The behavior model provides a precise specification of the commands that can be performed on the object.

- An object receiving an action is connected to the operation on the object using a dot (".") connector.

- A class diagram is used to depict the static architecture of the software system.

- An object scenario diagram is used to depict the dynamic interactions among objects.

- A specific service can have one or more parameters, each of a specified type. These provide external input to the service that helps determine the action performed by the service.

- Science in general and computer science in particular is concerned with modeling and understanding systems.

- Object-oriented systems involve many objects of different types working together to achieve some desired end.

- The process of classification can be used to manage complexity.

- Whenever a group of related but somewhat dissimilar objects need to be modeled, a careful consideration of their similarities and differences may lead to a hierarchy of classes.

- Attributes that are shared by many subclasses should be placed into classes "high" in the hierarchy.

- The primary basis for classification is usually based on the distribution and reuse of attributes (i.e., the data model).

- A subclass should have a logical relationship to its parent that can be expressed as "the subclass is a kind of" the parent class.

- The attributes of a parent class must all make sense as part of the state of the subclass.

- The services of a parent class must all make sense as part of the behavior of the subclass.

- The objects around us are generally made from the fabric of other objects or composites.

- An abstract data type (ADT) is a data model and an associated set of operations that can be performed by or on the data model.

- Abstract data types provide powerful abstractions that can be used as the basis for problem solving.

- The internals of an ADT become unimportant when deciding how ADTs interact with each other. Only the external properties of the ADT (defined by the set of operations) are important in determining its use.

- Abstract data types are represented by classes in an object-oriented language.

- The term data-hiding is used to mean that the data model (internal state) of an ADT cannot be directly accessed by the user. The internal state can be modified only through the set of operations that have been defined for the ADT.

- A producer is a programmer whose main focus is building a class library for other programmers to use or other parts of an application to use.

- A consumer is a programmer who is using a class library for a specific application.

- Often a programmer plays the dual role of both producer and consumer—producing some classes for later reuse by others or in the same application and using existing classes in a specific application.

- One must first become a competent consumer before embarking on becoming a competent producer.

- Software analysis, both object-oriented and otherwise, is concerned with understanding and modeling a problem.

- The major elements of the problem domain are mapped into software components.

- The initial architecture of these software components is constructed in a manner that precisely describes the relationships that exist among various entities in the problem domain. In an object-oriented context these entities are objects, each an instance of a particular class.

- The static architecture, developed at the analysis level, is given by associations between classes.

- Associations between classes include aggregation (whole/ essential part) relationships, uses relationships, and generalization/specialization relationships (inheritance).

- If one looks toward the problem domain when doing analysis, one must look toward the solution domain when doing design.

- During design, one precisely identifies additional classes that interact with the domain classes identified at the analysis level to complete a solution to the problem.

2.8   Exercises

1. Write a list of the distinct objects that you see around you. What connections, if any, do these objects have to each other?

2. Draw a Booch diagram that shows the relationships, if any, between or among the classes that you have included on your list in problem 1.

3. Draw a Booch class diagram for a vehicle hierarchy. The top class in this hierarchy should be class VEHICLE. Indicate the attributes associated with each class in your vehicle hierarchy. Are the first two elements of the consistency principle satisfied for your hierarchy? Explain in detail.

4. Add some methods (behavior) to each class in your vehicle hierarchy of problem 2. Is the third element of the consistency principle satisfied for your hierarchy?

5. Draw a Booch class diagram that describes the classes that model a university classroom setting. Include the students, professor, teaching assistant, and any other things that you can think of. Show the relationships that these objects have to each other in your class diagram.

6. Illustrate the principle of composition by constructing a class that is made up of composite objects. Draw a Booch class diagram of your class.

7. Depict the key steps involved in writing a personal check by using a Booch object scenario diagram. Show all of the objects involved in your scenario and the sequence of messages sent to each object. Describe in words (English) the meaning of your diagram.

8. Show the appropriate associations among the classes that describe the following entities: tulip, rose, flower, petal, honeybee, flower pot.

9. Show the appropriate associations among the classes that describe the following entities: motorcycle, bicycle, car, boat, seaplane, plane, jet-plane, glider, and moped.

10. Show the appropriate associations among the classes that describe the following entities: library, books, card catalog, shelves, sections of shelves, and users.

11. Show the appropriate associations among the classes that describe the following entities: university, classrooms, students, professors, black-board, desks, computer terminals, chairs, notebooks, and courses. If you wish to add some additional entities to enrich your object modeling, feel free to do this. Indicate for every additional class its purpose and show its association to the classes specified above.

2.9   References

1. Coad, Peter, Edward Yourdon, *Object-Oriented Analysis*, second edition, Yourdon Press Computing Series, 1991.

2. Booch, Grady, *Object-Oriented Analysis and Design With Applications*, second edition, Benjamin-Cummings, Menlo Park, CA, 1994.

Chapter

3

The Basic Elements of Eiffel Programs

3.1 Programming

We begin programming in this chapter.

A software system is an interconnected collection of units sometimes called modules. Each module contains a logically coherent set of operations and an underlying data model. In an object-oriented context, a module is the same as a class: a unification of a data model and behavioral model consisting of a set of functions called **queries** and **commands** that can access and manipulate the information contained in the data model. In principle each module represents a potentially reusable body of code.

A "systems" viewpoint is quite different from the more traditional monolithic "program" viewpoint. Using the "program" approach, all of the desired behavior of the software must be embedded in and accounted for by the single entity called your program. Using the "systems" approach, each module is responsible for only a small but well-focused portion of the desired behavior of the software.

Most modern programming languages, including Eiffel, favor a "systems" approach to software construction. This is the approach that we shall take from the very beginning. Using this approach, our first Eiffel program that outputs "My first program" is given in Listing 3.1.

To conform with the latest Eiffel formatting standard, all characters are written in italic and in addition, reserved words in the language are written in boldface. The indentation also follows the Eiffel formatting standard.

Listing 3.1 First Eiffel program

```
class APPLICATION

creation
    start

feature

    start is
        do
            io.putstring ("My first program.")
            io.new_line
        end

end -- class APPLICATION
```

The two output commands, *putstring* and *new_line*, sent to the standard input/output object *io*, cause the string "My first program" to be displayed on the standard output device (your video console) with the screen position cursor then moved to the next line. Because input/output is so necessary and standard, the object *io* does not need to be explicitly declared. Its existence in all Eiffel applications occurs by default.

Even to be able to write this first simple Eiffel software system, the programmer must have some knowledge of the output services available in class STANDARD_FILES. A summary of these services may be obtained by using a tool called **short**. This tool strips out all of the implementation details and reveals only the interface information that would be relevant for a user of this class. Listing 3.2 displays portions of these interface details using the result of applying *short* to the class. Only the output routines contained in this class are shown. These enable a programmer to output characters, integers, decimal fractions (floating point numbers), character strings, and booleans.

Listing 3.2 Portions of interface to class STANDARD_FILES from short

```
class interface STANDARD_FILES

    feature specification
        -- Output routines
```

putchar (c : CHARACTER)
-- Write 'c' at end of default output.

putstring (s : STRING)
-- Write 's' at end of default output.

putreal (r : REAL)
-- Write 'r' at end of default output.

putdouble (d : DOUBLE)
-- Write 'd' at end of default output.

putint (i : INTEGER)
-- Write 'i' at end of default output.

putbool (b : BOOLEAN)
-- Write 'b' at end of default output.

new_line
-- Write line feed at end of default output.
-- Many routines not shown

end interface *-- class STANDARD_FILES*

The APPLICATION class in Listing 3.1 serves to initiate the execution of the software system. It is the root class of the application. All Eiffel software systems must have an accompanying **Ace** file that specifies the file locations of the standard libraries, the programmer generated files that constitute the given application, the name of the root class, and the name of the startup routine within the root class. The Ace file that controls the application given in Listing 3.1 is shown in Listing 3.3.

Listing 3.3 Ace file for Listing 3.1 (Using ISE Eiffel 3 system)

```
system test

root application (ROOT_CLUSTER): "start"

default

        assertion (all);
        precompiled ("$EIFFEL3/precomp/spec/$PLATFORM/base")

cluster

        ROOT_CLUSTER: "/disk2/EIFFELWORK3/WORK";

end
```

The reader may wish to consult the instruction manual that comes with his or her Eiffel system for more details concerning Ace files.

3.2   The Eiffel Language

The Eiffel language was "born" in the late 1980s. It is a pure object-oriented language. This implies that functions can be invoked only through objects and not as stand-alone logical entities. This is in sharp contrast to the popular but complex object-oriented language C++ which allows a mixture of object-oriented and procedural programming in the same application. C++ is called a hybrid language.

As a pure object-oriented language, the class in Eiffel is the basic logical unit of encapsulation as well as the basic physical unit, a module. Eiffel software is organized as a set of interrelated and cooperating classes.

In the next several sections the basic elements of Eiffel programming are introduced. Many of these elements are similar to those of other languages. The designer of Eiffel, Bertrand Meyer, has been a great student of programming language technology and designed a syntax that utilizes some of the best features found in other languages. I believe you will find the syntax of Eiffel consistent, logical, and readable.

3.3   Creating and destroying objects

Programs consist of classes which create objects. These objects are created during program execution, perform their tasks, and then are typically destroyed. When an object is created, storage space is allocated to hold the object. When an object is destroyed, its storage space is deallocated and may be reused by other objects that will be created later.

An object in Eiffel and in other object-oriented languages is an instance of a class. Its attributes are given by the data model of its class. The commands that it can respond to (i.e., the routines that one can invoke through the object) are specified by the set of routines given in the class description.

Before an object can be created in Eiffel, it must be declared to be a variable of a given type. Its type is the name of the class that the object will be an instance of (after it is created). When an Eiffel type declaration such as *my_car : CAR* is given, the compiler verifies that a class called CAR has been defined. Usually the file that defines this class must reside in the same working subdirectory as the class in which the declaration exists.

The declaration, *my_car : CAR*, does not create an instance of class CAR. No memory storage for an object, *my_car*, is allocated by virtue of this declaration. In fact, the object *my_car*, like any object that has only been declared, assumes a default "value" Void. In such a state an object cannot receive any commands or perform any useful tasks.

In order for *my_car* to become an instance of class CAR and have storage properly allocated, a creation routine or creation operator must be used.

Consider the case where class CAR does not have any creation routines specified. One could bring the object *my_car* to life (i.e., allocate storage for it) by using a creation operator as follows: *!!my_car*. The result of this expression is to allocate storage for *my_car* but provide no initialization for any of the attributes that may be defined in class CAR. Some attributes such as those declared to be of type INTEGER, REAL, BOOLEAN, or CHARACTER assume default values.

Consider the other case where class CAR provides three creation routines: *make, build,* and *construct*. A portion of class CAR is the following:

class CAR

    creation
        make, build, construct

    feature
        make (color : STRING; price : REAL; weight : INTEGER) **is**
        -- Details not shown
        end *-- make*

        build (color : STRING; price : REAL; weight : INTEGER;
                horsepower : INTEGER) **is**
        -- Details not shown
        end *-- build*

        construct (color : STRING) **is**
        -- Details not shown
        end *-- construct*

Several expressions that would bring the object *my_car* to life include:

!!my_car.make ("White", 25600, 3100)

!!my_car.build ("Red", 12000, 3500, 125)

!!my_car.construct ("Blue")

In all three of the expressions above, the object *my_car* is created and initialized with the values given as parameters in the various creation routines. In the first case given above (i.e., *!!my_car*), *my_car* is created but its attribute values assume their default values.

It should be clear from this discussion that objects must be explicitly created either using the creation operator (!!) in front of the object you wish to create or using a specified creation routine in conjunction with the creation operator, as shown in the three examples above.

How are Eiffel objects destroyed? Eiffel systems provide for "automatic garbage collection." As an Eiffel application runs, a garbage collection process is running in the background and detecting when storage is no longer connected to a variable name. At an opportune moment the garbage collection process recycles (effectively destroys) the unneeded storage. The following code segment shows an example of storage that is no longer needed:

```
my_car : CAR

!!my_car.construct( "Blue" )

!!my_car.construct( "Red" )
```

The statement, *!!my_car.construct("Blue")*, causes memory storage to be allocated and the object name *my_car* attached to this storage. The third statement, *!!my_car.construct("Red")*, causes new memory storage to be allocated and the object name *my_car* to be attached to this new storage leaving the old storage detached from any object name.

The sequence of actions is shown in Figure 3.1.

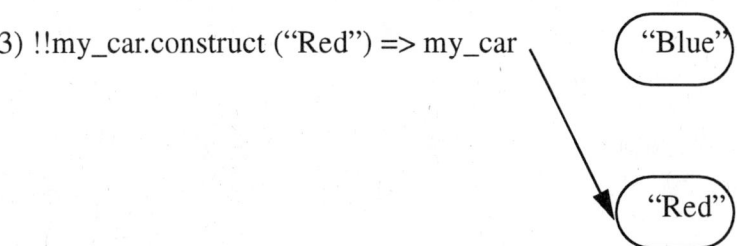

1) my_car : CAR => my_car --> Void

2) !!my_car.construct ("Blue") => my_car ⟶ "Blue"

3) !!my_car.construct ("Red") => my_car   "Blue"

                                             "Red"

Figure 3.1 Garbage Production

The detached storage containing "Blue" should be reclaimed by the automatic garbage collector while the program is running. It is not the Eiffel programmer's responsibility to do this.

3.4 Basic types, default values, and assignment

There are several basic object types that do not require explicit creation in order to be used. The important ones are INTEGER, CHARACTER, REAL, and BOOLEAN. Consider the following declarations:

an_integer   : INTEGER

a_character   : CHARACTER

a_real   : REAL

a_boolean   : BOOLEAN

Each of these objects of basic types receives a default value that is not *Void*.

Objects of type INTEGER have a default value of *0*. Objects of type CHARACTER have a default value of the NULL character (ASCII value 0). Objects of type REAL have a default value of *0.0*. Finally, objects of type BOOLEAN have a default value of *false*.

The basic types introduced in the previous section have "value" semantics. This implies that the declaration of objects causes memory storage to be automatically allocated and default values assigned to the objects.

When a basic type object, the source object, is assigned to another basic type object, the destination object, this destination object resides in storage separate from the source object. The assignment operator in Eiffel is ":=".

The statement, $a := b$, reads: "a is assigned the value b."

Figure 3.2 shows an integer object assigned to an integer object.

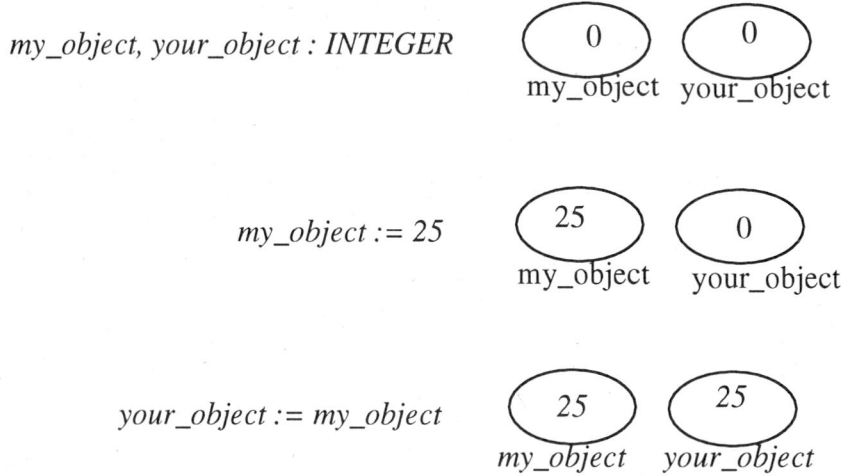

Figure 3.2 Assigning Basic Type Objects

3.5   Ordinary or reference type objects

Ordinary objects (non-basic type objects) have "reference" semantics. This implies that the programmer is responsible for explictly allocating storage using a creation operator possibly in conjunction with a creation routine as discussed in section 3.3. The default value of an ordinary object is *Void*. After the programmer creates storage for such an object the object name is attached to the storage (see Figure 3.1).

What does it mean to assign an ordinary object to another?

Consider the following segment of code:

```
my_car          : CAR

your_car        : CAR

!!my_car.make ("Green", 10000, 2000)

your_car := my_car
```

Figure 3.3 depicts the semantics of the code segment given above.

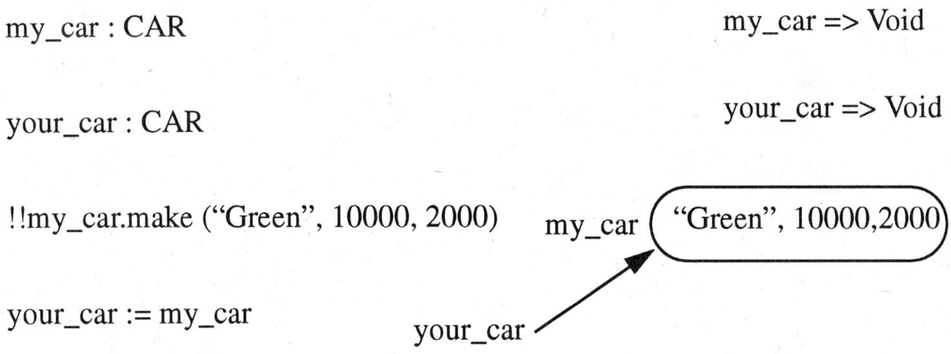

my_car : CAR   my_car => Void

your_car : CAR   your_car => Void

!!my_car.make ("Green", 10000, 2000)   my_car ("Green", 10000,2000)

your_car := my_car   your_car

Figure 3.3 Assigning Reference Type Objects

After the assignment of *your_car* to *my_car*, both object names are attached to the same storage. This implies that if one of the attributes of *my_car* were modified by sending a command such as *my_car.set_weight (2500)*, the weight attribute of *your_car* would also be modified to 2500. There are not two independent objects, but only two different names for the same object storage (only one object exists in computer memory).

3.6 Copying objects

Suppose that we desire the object *your_car* from the previous section to have the same values for its attributes as *my_car* but be an autonomous object that is not attached to the same storage as *my_car*. Assume that *my_car* has been created and initialized. This can be accomplished as follows: (1) Create the object *your_car* and (2) use the *copy* routine that is available to all Eiffel objects.

your_car.copy(my_car) -- Assume that *your_car* has been created

It is essential that the object *your_car* already have storage associated with it in order for the *copy* routine to work. A run-time exception will be raised and an error reported if you invoke the *copy* routine on a *Void* object.

The semantics of the copy routine is depicted in Figure 3.4.

Before copying:

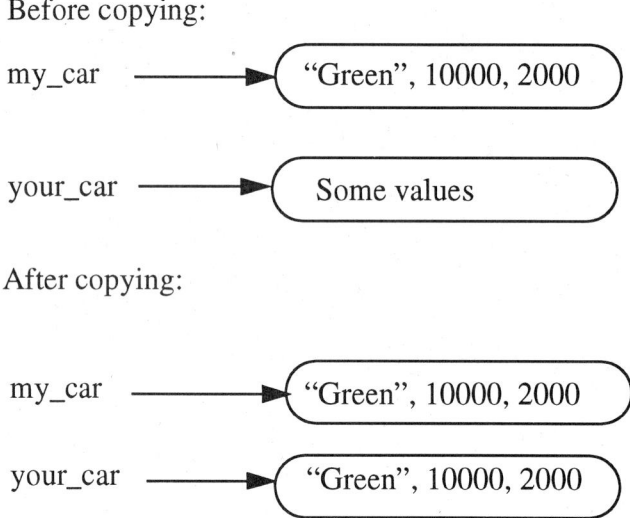

After copying:

Figure 3.4 Semantics of Copying

3.7 Cloning

Suppose that you wish to create storage for *your_car* at that same moment that you wish to copy the attribute values from *my_car* to *your_car*. This can be accomplished using the *clone* routine available to all Eiffel objects. This can be done as follows:

your_car := clone(my_car)

The semantics of the clone routine are depicted in Figure 3.5.

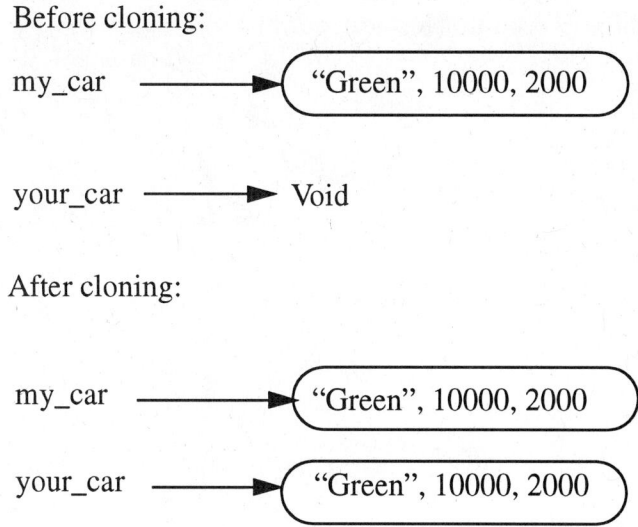

Before cloning:

my_car ⟶ "Green", 10000, 2000

your_car ⟶ Void

After cloning:

my_car ⟶ "Green", 10000, 2000

your_car ⟶ "Green", 10000, 2000

Figure 3.5 Semantics of Cloning

3.8 Basic operators with examples

Equality operator (=): Two objects are equal if they are attached (bound) to the same storage. If one wishes to test whether the objects x and y are equal, an expression of the form $x = y$ would be used.

Example:

```
my_value, your_value : REAL
if your_value = my_value then -- If the values are the same take some action
        -- some action
end
```

Inequality operator (/=): To test whether the objects x and y are not equal, an expression of the form $if\ x\ /= y$ would be used.

Example:

```
my_value, your_value : INTEGER
if my_value /= your_value then -- if the values are unequal take some action
        -- some action
end
```

INTEGER operators:
+ (Binary operator for addition)

Example:

a, b, c : INTEGER
b := 3
c := 4
a := b + c -- value is 7

- (Binary operator for subtraction)

Example:

a, b, c : INTEGER
b := 3
c := 4
a := b - c -- value is -1

* (Binary operator for multiplication)

Example:

a, b, c : INTEGER
b := 3
c := 4
a := b* c -- value is 12

^ (Binary operator for raised to power)

Example:

a, b, c : INTEGER
b := 3
c := 4
a := b ^ c -- value is 81

// (Binary operator for integer division)

Example:

a, b, c : INTEGER
b := 11
c := 4
a := b // c -- value is 2

\\ (Binary operator for remainder)

Example:

a, b, c : INTEGER
b := 11
c := 4
a := b \\ c -- value is 3

< (Binary operator for less than)

Example:

b, c : INTEGER
b := 10
c := 4
if b < c then -- take action only if b is smaller than c
    -- some action
end

<= (Binary operator for less than or equal)
> (Binary operator for greater than)
>= (Binary operator for greater than or equal)
REAL operators:
+ (Binary operator for addition)
- (Binary operator for subtraction)
* (Binary operator for multiplication)
/ (Binary operator for division)
^ (Binary operator for raised to power)
< (Binary operator for less than)
<= (Binary operator for less than or equal)
> (Binary operator for greater than)
>= (Binary operator for greater than or equal)
BOOLEAN operators:
not (unary operator for logical negation)

Example:

b, c : INTEGER
b := 10
c := 4
if not (b < c) then -- take action only if c is equal or less than b
    -- some action
end

or (binary operator for logical "or")

Example:

```
b, c : INTEGER
b := 10
c := 4
if b > 0 or c > 2 then -- take action only if b is positive or c is greater than 2
      -- some action
end
```

and (binary operator for logical "and")

Example:

```
b, c : INTEGER
b := 10
c := 4
if b > 0 and c > 2 then -- take action only if b is positive and c is greater
than 2
      -- some action
end
```

implies (used in assertions)
or else (binary operator for "short-circuited" logical "or")

Example:

```
b, c : INTEGER
a := 12
b := 10
c := 40
if b = 0 or else c // b > 2 then
-- take action only if b is zero or c // b is greater than 2
-- evaluate the expression c // b only if b is not equal to 0
      -- some action
end
```

and then (binary operator for "short-circuited" logical "and")

Example:

```
b, c : INTEGER
a := 12
b := 10
c := 40
```

```
if b > 0 and then c // b > 2 then
-- take action only if b is positive and c// b is greater than 2
-- evaluate the expression c // b only if b is positive
        -- some action
end
```

The last two operators, "or else" and "and then," are sometimes called "short circuit" operators. For the "or else" operator, if the first expression is true, the second expression is never evaluated. For the "and then" operator, if the first expression is false, the second expression is never evaluated.

3.9   Branching

The simplest type of branch is the *if* clause. This control structure is used when the execution of one or more lines of code, a code block, is based on the outcome of a logical test that is performed before entering the block of code. The logical test requires the evaluation of a boolean expression. Such an expression evaluates to either TRUE or FALSE. The form of this structure is

```
if a_boolean_expression then
      statement(s)
end
```

Example:
```
if ground_speed > 160 then
          -- plane takes off
end
```

Another simple control structure is the *if-then-else* structure. It is used when a choice must be made between two blocks of code. The choice is based on the evaluation of a boolean expression. This control structure is built as follows:

```
if boolean_expression then
      block_1
else
      block_2
end
```

Here, *block_1* and *block_2* represent one or more lines of code.

Example:
if ground_speed > 160 **then**
       -- plane takes off
else
       -- plane puts on brakes and takeoff is aborted
end

The *if-then-else* construct can be nested. Consider the following segment of code:

```
if expr1 then
      statement1
else
      if expr2 then
          statement2
      else
          statement3
      end
end
```

If *expr1* evaluates to *true,* then *statement1* will be executed. Otherwise if *expr2* evaluates to *true,* then *statement2* will be executed; otherwise *statement3* will be executed.

Suppose that one of several alternative branches is to be executed based on the evaluation of some control expression which evaluates to *true* or *false.* The *if-elseif-else* construct might be appropriate.

This construct is formed as follows:

```
if expr1 then
      statement1
elseif expr2 then
      statement2
elseif expr3 then
      statement3
else
      statement4
end
```

The *else* clause in the above construct is optional. There is no limit on the number of *elseif* clauses.

Example:
if ground_speed > 220 **then**
    -- slow down

```
elseif ground_speed > 200 then
      -- make power down landing
elseif ground_speed < 170 then
      -- speed up
else
      -- make normal landing
end
```

If the number of *elseif* clauses becomes too large, the resulting expression is awkward to look at and may be inefficient to evaluate. The *inspect* construct might be more appropriate. A control expression that returns either an INTEGER or CHARACTER value is used to determine which block of code is executed.

The syntax for the *inspect* construct is

```
inspect control_expression
when range then
      block_1
when range then
      block_2
      ...
else
      block_n
end
```

Example:
```
inspect input_value
when 1 ..9 then
      io.putstring ("Value is a one digit number")
when 10 .. 99 then
       io.putstring ( "Value is a two digit number")
when 100 .. 999 then
      io.putstring ("Value is a three digit number")
when 1000 then
      io.putstring ("Value equals 1000")
else
      io.putstring ("Value has more than three digits")
end
```

3.10 Iteration (loop)

Iteration or looping is a fundamental logical operation in computing. Either a single statement or more typically a block of statements are executed repeatedly until some stopping condition is satisfied. If the stopping condition is never satisfied, the execution of the statements within the loop will continue indefinitely and the program will typically appear to "hang" (a non-technical term that means the program appears to be doing nothing useful and is producing no output).

In a properly constructed loop, the stopping condition will eventually be met.

The general form of this iteration construct is

from
      initialization_instructions
until
      loop_exit_conditions
loop
      body_of_loop
end

The statement or statements that comprise the *initialization_instructions* are executed exactly once. The *loop_exit_conditions* are tested before each execution of the loop. If the expression evaluates to *false,* the loop is executed; otherwise the loop is terminated and control is transferred to the line below the *end* statement. Clearly some action must occur in the body of the loop (the statement or statements between the reserved words *loop* and *end*) that eventually makes the *loop_exit_conditions true.*

For example, suppose we wish to display all of the integers that are powers of 2 up to the value 65536. The segment of code that accomplishes this using the loop construct is

```
from index := 1
until index = 65536
loop
      index := index * 2
      io.putint (index)
      io.new_line
end
```

The statement *index := 1* represents the *initialization_instructions*. It causes *index* to assume a first value of 1. The statement *index = 65536* represents the *loop_exit_conditions* and the three lines of code below *loop* represent the *body_of_loop*. The statement *index := index * 2* replaces the old value of *index* with a value twice as large. The statement reads "index is assigned index multiplied by 2."

We examine other examples that illustrate the use of iteration.

In the next example, suppose we wish to compute the sum of the finite series

$1 + 2 + 3 + 4 + 5 + 6 + ... + 1,000,000.$

An Eiffel code segment for computing this sum is given below. The various parts of the loop construct are shown as comments.

```
index, sum : INTEGER
from
        -- loop initialization statements
        sum := 0
        index := 0
until index = 1000000 -- loop termination condition
loop
        -- body of loop
        index := index + 1
        sum := sum + index
end
io.putstring ("sum = ")
io.putint (sum)
io.new_line
```

The statement *index := index + 1* reads "the new value of index is assigned a value equal to the old value plus 1."

The initialization statements, *sum := 0* and *index := 0*, are correct but unnecessary. Both objects assume default values of 0 by virtue of their declaration. Incidently, for those who are interested, the output of this segment is *sum = 1784293664*.

As another application, let us approximate the well known geometric series: $1 + 1 / 2 + 1 / 4 + 1 / 8 + ... + (1 / 2)^n + ...$, whose theoretical value equals 2. We wish to continue adding numbers until the next number in the series is equal or less than 10^{-9}. The following code segment uses an iteration construct to approximate this sum.

```
next_term, sum : REAL
from
        sum := 1.0
```

```
        next_term := 0.5
until next_term < 0.000000001
loop
        sum := sum + next_term
        next_term := next_term / 2.0
end
```

The initialization portion of the *loop* construct sets the value of *sum* to 1.0 and *next_term* to 0.5. In the body of the loop, *sum* is incremented by the current value of *next_term*. Next, the value of *next_term* is set equal to one-half of its previous value.

The sum produced by the code above equals 2.

Many additional examples of loop constructs will appear in later program listings.

3.11 Routines

Routines come in two flavors: commands and queries. Routines are invoked when an object is sent a command or query. For example, the command *my_point.set_x_coordinate (50)* changes the *x* attribute of *my_point* to a value equal to 50. The query *my_point.angle* computes the polar coordinate *angle* of *my_point*.

Commands typically change the internal state of the object that they are invoked on. Queries never change the internal state of the object that they are invoked on. A properly constructed query returns information about an object without changing its state. Although the Eiffel language allows one to define a routine that both changes the internal state as well as returns information about an object, this practice is seriously discouraged.

Commands and queries are specified in a feature section of a class. Both the interface information as well as implementation details are given. The user of a class (consumer) needs access to only the interface portion of a routine. The producer of the class needs access to the implementation details when performing maintenance on the routine. (Maintenance is an activity that occurs when (1) errors are reported and corrected, (2) enhancements in capability are desired, (3) improvements in efficiency are sought.)

We will consider only the simplest structure for a routine in this chapter. In later chapters additional components of a routine such as pre-

and postconditions will be discussed. The syntax structure of a simple routine is the following:

routine_name [(optional parameter_list)] [: optional return_type] **is**
local
      object_declarations
do
      -- body of routine
end -- routine_name

The name of the routine (*routine_name* above) should be carefully chosen. It should describe the purpose of the routine. For a command routine, a verb should be used. For a query routine, a noun that is descriptive of what is returned should be used. For example, a command routine for setting the weight of a car might have the name *set_weight*. If another function routine computes the volume of the car, its name might be *volume*.

The parameter list, if present, contains the input information that is used by the routine.

The return type, if present, indicates the type of information that the query computes and returns to the caller (the routine that invokes the function).

The object declarations are a list of object names followed by their respective class types. Recall that no object creation or initialization is implied by any of the object declarations (except for the basic types INTEGER, CHARACTER, REAL, and BOOLEAN). Each object assumes a default "value" of Void until the object is explicitly created by the programmer or unless the object is a basic type.

The statements contained between the delimiters *do* and *end* represent the body or implementation details of the routine.

To illustrate the concept of command and query, we construct a highly simplified class TAXES whose details are shown in Listing 3.4.

The attribute *taxable_income* can be accessed but not assigned to. It has "read-only" semantics. If one wishes to change the value of this attribute, only the command *make* can be used for this purpose.

Listing 3.4 Class TAXES to illustrate command and query

class TAXES

creation
      make

feature

```
-- Attribute query
taxable_income: REAL

-- Creation and ordinary command
make (amount: REAL) is
    do
      taxable_income := amount
    end

-- Function query
tax_owed: REAL is
-- Computation of tax based on attribute taxable_income
    do
      if taxable_income < 6000.0 then
        Result := 0.0
      elseif taxable_income < 22000.0 then
        Result := 0.15 * taxable_income
      else
        Result := 3300.0 + 0.28 * (taxable_income - 22000.0)
      end
    end

end -- class TAXES
```

In the function query *tax_owed*, the tax that is due is $0 if the taxable income is less than $6000, is 15 percent of the taxable income if the income is between $6000 and $22,000 and is $3,300 plus 28 percent of the taxable income in excess of $22,000 if the income is greater than $22,000. This roughly corresponds to the current income tax code.

The command *make* can be used as a creation routine or as an ordinary command. The value passed as a parameter sets the current value of the *taxable_income* attribute.

Listing 3.5 shows a simple application class that exercises TAXES.

Listing 3.5 Simple test program for class TAXES

```
class APPLICATION

creation
    start

feature
```

```
start is
    local
        my_taxes: TAXES
    do
        -- Use creation command make to create and initialize object my_taxes
        !! my_taxes.make (40000.0)
        io.putstring ("The tax owed on $")
        -- Use query attribute taxable_income to return information
        io.putreal (my_taxes.taxable_income)
        io.putstring (" = $")
        -- Use query routine tax_owed to return information
        io.putreal (my_taxes.tax_owed)
        io.new_line
        my_taxes.make (200000.0)
        io.putstring ("The tax owed on $")
        io.putreal (my_taxes.taxable_income)
        io.putstring (" = $")
        io.putreal (my_taxes.tax_owed)
        io.new_line
    end

end -- class APPLICATION
```

The two classes TAXES and APPLICATION constitute a complete application. The object *my_taxes* is brought to life and initialized to 40000 using the creation command *make* with parameter 40000. The current taxable income is accessed directly using the attribute query *taxable_income*. This value can be read but not directly assigned to. The function query *tax_owed* is used to access the tax owed on the current taxable income.

The value of taxable income is reset to 200000 using command *make* with a parameter of 200000. Then the attribute query and function query are used to display new tax data.

3.12 Arrays

Arrays are used to hold a collection of "similar" elements. The meaning of "similar" is given shortly. Each array element has a unique address called its **index**, an integer value. Through the index one can either insert an element into a unique location or access an element from a unique location in the array.

Some languages provide the array as a basic type whereas other languages, such as Eiffel, provide external library support for arrays. Eiffel arrays are supplied through a standard class ARRAY.

Figure 3.6 depicts an array of elements with an index range from 1 to 5.

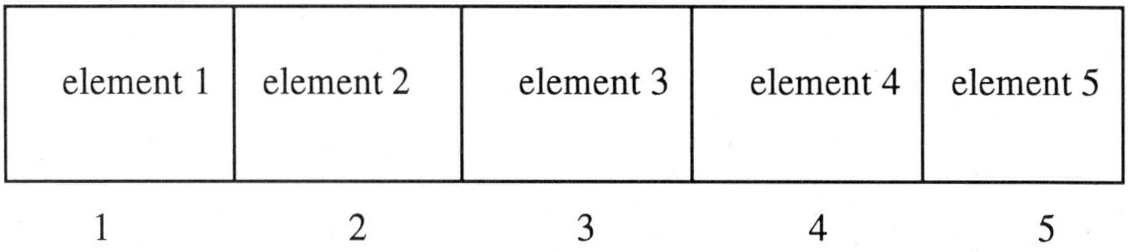

element 1	element 2	element 3	element 4	element 5
1	2	3	4	5

Figure 3.6 An Array of Elements

What are the nature of the elements in an array such as the one depicted in Figure 3.6?

In the context of object-oriented programming (our context), the elements are objects. Each object is an instance of some specified "base" class or one of its descendant classes. In this sense the objects are "similar" in type. Often the elements in an array are of the same type.

A typical declaration of an array is

my_array : ARRAY [SOME_TYPE]

where SOME_TYPE is the "base" type that all the actual instances must conform to.

The ARRAY class command, *put*, for inserting an object, *my_object*, at a specified *index* is

my_array.put (my_object, index)

In the expression above, *my_array* is the name of the array that *my_object* is inserted into. Of course *index* is a specified integer.

Figure 3.7 depicts the insertion of *my_object* as the fourth element of the five-element array given in Figure 3.6.

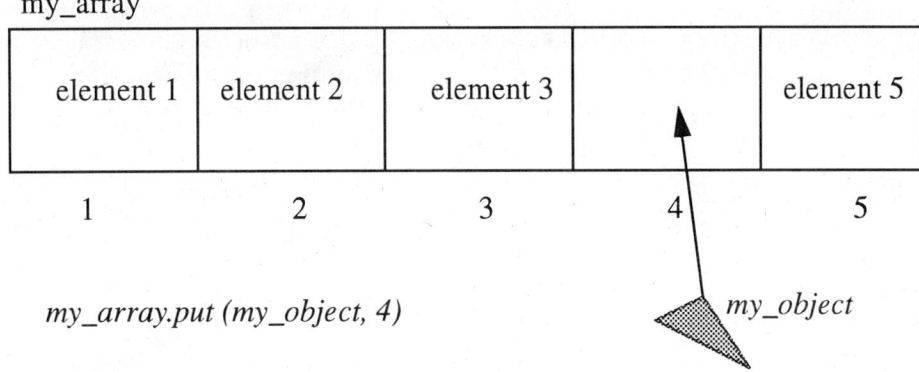

Figure 3.7 The *put* Command

The ARRAY class query, *item*, for accessing an object at specified index is

my_array.item (index)

Of course *index* must be an integer value within the legal range for the given array. The array in Figure 3.7 has a legal range from 1 to 5.

Figure 3.8 shows the element in index 4 being accessed with the *item* query.

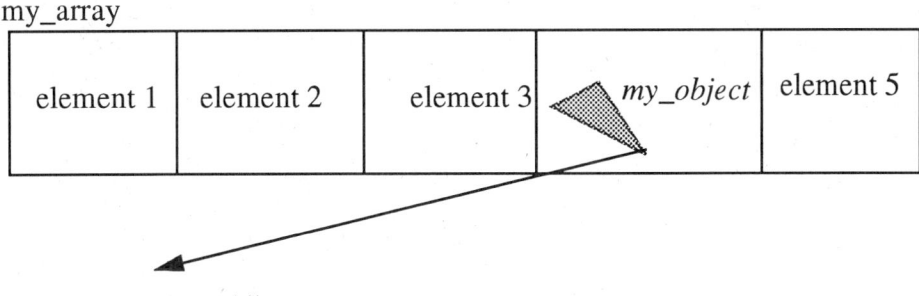

my_array.item (4)

Figure 3.8 The *item* Query

The ARRAY class creation routine, *make*, for constructing an instance of class ARRAY is

!!my_array.make (lower_limit, upper_limit)

The integer values *lower_limit* and *upper_limit* specify the legal index range for the elements in the array. After creating the array, *my_array*, the elements in each index location assume their default values (probably Void).

We illustrate all of the above ideas by constructing an array of vehicles. There will be three types of vehicles in the array: CAR, PLANE, and BOAT. None of the details of the three classes will be shown except for the fact that all three are subclasses of VEHICLE.

```
class VEHICLE
-- Base class. No details shown
end -- class VEHICLE

class CAR
inherit
        VEHICLE
-- No details shown
end -- class CAR

class PLANE
inherit
        VEHICLE
-- No details shown
end -- class PLANE

class BOAT
inherit
        VEHICLE
-- No details shown
end -- class BOAT

class APPLICATION

creation
        start

feature

        start is
            local
                my_array: ARRAY [VEHICLE]   -- Base type is VEHICLE
                my_car:    CAR
                my_boat:   BOAT
                my_plane: PLANE
            do
                !!my_array.make (1, 3)
                !! my_car
```

```
        !! my_boat
        !! my_plane
        my_array.put (my_car, 1)
        my_array.put (my_boat, 2)
        my_array.put (my_plane, 3)
      end

end -- class APPLICATION
```

Figure 3.9 depicts the construction of *my_array* containing three vehicles.

After:

!!my_array.make (1, 3)

my_array

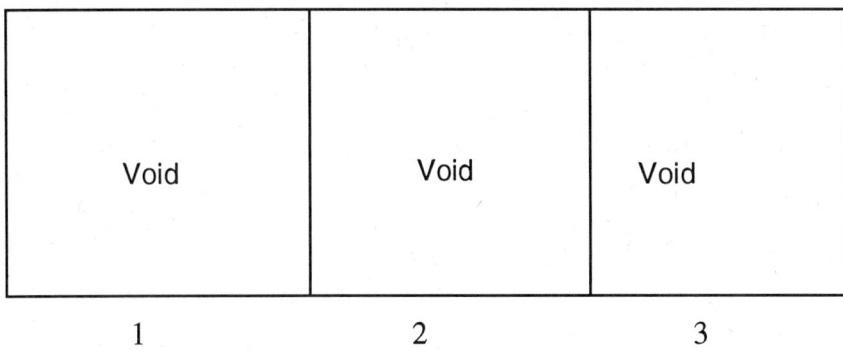

After:
!!my_array.put (my_plane, 3)

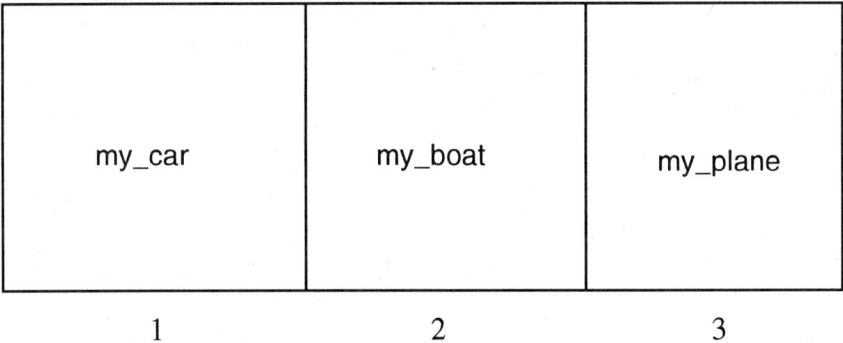

Figure 3.9 Array of Three Vehicles

We next consider the problem of sorting an array of integers of size 3. We return to the subject of sorting in Chapter 4 where we present the subject of sorting in a more serious way and discuss several important sorting methods.

This simple application allows us to review the subject of branching, routines and their parameters as well as arrays.

Suppose we have declared an array as follows:

```
local
    data : ARRAY [INTEGER]

do
    !!data.make (1, 3)
```

Now we wish to insert integer values into index locations 1, 2, and 3. Finally we wish to re-order the numbers in the array so that the smallest is in index 1, the second smallest in index 2, and the largest in index 3. This process is called sorting.

Listing 3.6 presents a sorting routine that accomplishes this mission.

Listing 3.6 Sorting an array of three integers

```
class SORTING_APPLICATION

creation
    start

feature

    start is
        local
            data: ARRAY [INTEGER]
        do
            !! data.make (1, 3)
            data.put (30, 1)
            data.put (5, 2)
            data.put (25, 3)
            sort_3 (data)
            display (data)
        end

    sort_3 (data: ARRAY [INTEGER]) is
        require
            array_correct_size: data.count = 3
```

```
    local
      temp: INTEGER
    do
      if data.item (1) > data.item (2) and data.item (1) > data.item (3) then
        temp := data.item (3)
        data.put (data.item (1), 3)
        data.put (temp, 1)
      elseif data.item (2) > data.item (1) and data.item (2) > data.item (3) then
        temp := data.item (3)
        data.put (data.item (2), 3)
        data.put (temp, 2)
      end
      if data.item (1) > data.item (2) then
        temp := data.item (2)
        data.put (data.item (1), 2)
        data.put (temp, 1)
      end
    end

  display (the_data: ARRAY [INTEGER]) is
    local
      index: INTEGER
    do
      from
        index := 0
      until
        index = the_data.count
      loop
        index := index + 1
        io.putint (the_data.item (index))
        io.putstring (" ")
      end
      io.new_line
    end

end -- class SORTING_APPLICATION
```

The first order of business in routine *start* is the creation of the array *data* with lower index 1 and upper index 3 (index range 1 to 3). Next the values 30, 5, and 25 are inserted into the array. Figure 3.10 depicts the *data* array after this step.

data

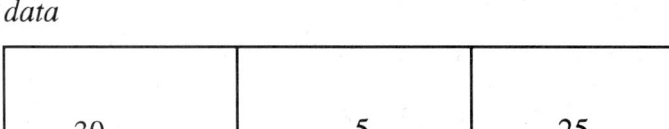

30	5	25

Figure 3.10 Initial Array of Three Integers to Be Sorted

The routine *sort_3* is next invoked with data sent in as a parameter. The *require* clause represents a **precondition** that must be satisfied in order that the routine may perform its task. Preconditions are discussed in detail in Chapter 6.

The first test that is performed is to determine whether the integer in index 1 is greater than the integers in indices 2 and 3 (in other words whether the integer in index 1 is the largest among the 3). If it is, as in this case, the integers in index 1 and index 3 are swapped, thus forcing the largest of the three integers to reside in index 3. Figure 3.11 depicts the *data* array after this swap operation.

data

25	5	30

Figure 3.11 Array of Three Integers after First Swap

Finally, the integers in index 1 and index 2 are compared. If the integer in index 1 is larger than the integer in index 2, they are swapped. This is the case here. Figure 3.12 depicts the data array after this final swap operation.

data

5	25	30

Figure 3.12 Array of Three Integers after Final Swap

The integers are now completely sorted. Can you prove that this "algorithm" (a series of operations that performs some task) always sorts the three integers stored in data?

The *display* routine outputs the values of the integers in index locations 1, 2, and 3. The query *count* is used to get the upper limit of *the_data* array.

3.13 Strings

In the business of programming, a string is *an array of characters*, not something that you tie your shoes with or fasten a box with. These characters can be ordinary upper- and lower-case letters, numerals, or special symbols on the keyboard such as '$', '%', or '&'. Even a blank space is a character.

Because arrays of base type character, namely strings, are so important in programming, we study them as a special type of array. In Eiffel the class STRING encapsulates the properties of this important data type.

In programs we use strings to name people or things. We typically treat a string as a single entity even though its constituent parts consists of characters. So the string with the sequence of characters 'M', 'A', 'R', and 'Y' will generally be thought of as the single entity "MARY" rather than the individual characters shown above. Of course the individual characters of a string can be accessed using the standard array query *item* discussed in the previous section.

A string literal is a sequence of characters delimited by a pair of quotation marks. Several examples of string literals are given below.

Examples of String Literals

(1) "My name is Richard Wiener"

(2) "Testing, testing, 1, 2, 3"

(3) "!@#$%^&*()-+"

(4) "   "

The reader may wish to pause and consider the operations that one might wish to perform on a string. Certainly the most basic operations would include (1) creating a string of given size—an array of characters that can hold a predetermined number of characters, (2) inserting characters into the string at various index locations, (3) filling an entire string at once by using an assignment to a string literal (a set of characters delimited by quotation marks such as "hello" or "goodbye"), (4) accessing characters at specified index locations, (5) copying one string to another (the target string must already be initialized), and (6) returning the length of a string—the number of characters actually in the string, not its potential size.

Are there any additional operations that you might wish to add to this relatively short list? This is the question that a STRING class designer must ask herself when constructing this reusable software component.

Would it surprise you to learn that the STRING class contained in the Eiffel library contains approximately 60 routines that define the behavior (commands and queries) of a STRING object? In order to appreciate the workmanship that goes into the design of such an important reusable software component, let us examine the functionality of the STRING class closely before looking at its formal interface and demonstrating its use through an application.

The STRING class is divided into several *feature* sections, each containing a logically related set of operations. In Table 3.1, the various feature sections are shown with their purpose and a list of some of the routines in the feature sections are listed along with a brief description of their purpose.

Table 3.1   Examination of STRING Class

(1) **Access** - Used to obtain various parts of a STRING object
        has - does STRING include a particular character?
        index_of - position of the first occurence of a character
        item - character at specified index
        item_code - numeric code of character at specified index
        substring_index- position of first occurrence of another string
                      contained within given string
        infix "@" - character at specified index (alternative to item)

(2) **Comparison** - Used to compare two strings
        is_equal - do two strings contain the same sequence of characters?
        infix "<" - is one string lexicographically smaller than another?

(3) **Conversion** - Used to convert string from one form to another
        mirror - reverse the order of characters in the string
        mirrored - test to see whether another string is mirror of first
        to_double - convert to type DOUBLE, if possible
        to_integer - convert to type INTEGER, if possible
        to_lower - convert all upper-case characters to lower-case
        to_real - convert to type REAL, if possible
        to_upper - convert all lower-case characters to upper-case

(4) **Duplication** - Used to copy parts of one string to another
>> **substring** - copy of substring (string contained within a string)
>>> containing characters between one index and another

(5) **Element change** - Used to modify parts of a given string
>> **append** - add a copy of one string to the end of another
>> **copy** - transfer characters from source string to target
>> **extend** - add a character to the end of a given string
>> **fill_blank** - fill a string with blank characters
>> **head** - remove all but the first *n* characters
>> **insert** - add a string to the left of specified index in given string
>> **left_adjust** - remove leading blanks in a string
>> **precede** - add a character in front of a given string
>> **prepend** - add a string in front of a given string
>> **put** - replace character at specified index by given character
>> **replace_substring** - copy characters of another string to
>>> specified positions of given string
>> **replace_substring_all** - replace every occurence of original with new
>> **right_adjust** - remove trailing blank characters from given string
>> **set** - inappropriate to discuss here
>> **share** - make current string share the text of another string;
>>> any change to the text of the other string will affect original
>> **tail** - remove all characters except the last *n* from a given string

(6) **Initialization** - Used to initialize a STRING object
>> **make** - allocate space for at least *n* characters

(7) **Measurement** - Used to obtain numerical features of string
>> **capacity** - allocated space
>> **count** - actual number of characters in string
>> **occurrences** - number of times a specified character appears in string

(8) **Output** - Used to output string
>> **out** - creates printable representation

(9) **Removal** - Used to remove parts of a string
>> **prune** - remove first occurence of a specified character
>> **prune_all** - remove all occurences of a specified character
>> **remove** - remove *i*th character
>> **wipe_out** - remove all characters

(10) **Resizing** - Used to dynamically change the size of a string
>> **adapt_size** - change the size to accommodate current number of characters
>> **grow** - ensure that the capacity is at least the specified integer
>> **resize** - reallocate space to accommodate a specified number of characters

(11) **Status report** - Used to obtain some important characteristics of string
>> **consistent** - can given string be the target of a copy operation?

extendible - may new items be added to given string?
prunable - may items be removed from given string?
valid_index - is specified index within the range of allowable index values?

A small portion of the interface to class STRING is presented in Listing 3.7. The full interface is presented in Appendix 1.

Listing 3.7 Interface to class STRING

class interface STRING

   creation
      make

   feature

      has (c: CHARACTER): BOOLEAN
        -- Does string include 'c'?

      item (i: INTEGER): CHARACTER
        -- Character at position 'i'

      substring_index (other: STRING; start: INTEGER): INTEGER
        -- Position of first occurrence of 'other' at or after 'start';
        -- 0 if none.

      infix "@" (i: INTEGER): CHARACTER
        -- Character at position 'i'

      is_equal (other: like Current): BOOLEAN
        -- Is string made of same character sequence as 'other'
        -- (possibly with a different capacity)?

      infix "<" (other: STRING): BOOLEAN
        -- Is string lexicographically lower than 'other'?
        -- (False if 'other' is void)

      to_double: DOUBLE
        -- "Double" value;
        -- for example, when applied to "123.0", will yield 123.0 (double)

      to_integer: INTEGER
        -- Integer value;
        -- for example, when applied to "123", will yield 123

      to_lower
        -- Convert to lower-case.

to_real: REAL
  -- Real value;
  -- for example, when applied to "123.0", will yield 123.0

to_upper
  -- Convert to upper-case.

substring (n1, n2: INTEGER): like Current
  -- Copy of substring containing all characters at indices
    between 'n1' and 'n2'

append (s: STRING)
  -- Append a copy of 's' at end.

copy (other: like Current)
  -- Reinitialize by copying the characters of 'other'.
  -- (This is also used by 'clone'.)
fill_blank
  -- Fill with blanks.

insert (s: like Current; i: INTEGER)
  -- Add 's' to the left of position 'i' in current string.

put (c: CHARACTER; i: INTEGER)
  -- Replace character at position 'i' by 'c'.

capacity: INTEGER
  -- Allocated space

count: INTEGER
  -- Actual number of characters making up the string

occurrences (c: CHARACTER): INTEGER
  -- Number of times 'c' appears in the string

wipe_out
  -- Remove all characters.

end *-- class STRING*

Appendix 1 provides all of the information that is required to use the STRING class in a given application. As part of the learning process in becoming a competent consumer, the reader should carefully study the interface information in this Appendix.

One highly recommended strategy for becoming comfortable and familiar with the use of a class such as STRING is to create a test program that exercises some of its functions. Although this may take some time and even appear tedious, the payoff is potentially great. Once the programmer gains confidence in the proper use of a reusable class like STRING, then the real benefit of software resuse can come into play.

The string application given in Listing 3.8 is designed to exercise a small sample of the routines of class STRING. Comments throughout the routine indicate the purpose of each code segment. The code segments are separated by two blank lines. The reader is encouraged to carefully review this listing, segment by segment, and to make modifications and additions in order to gain additional insights into the behavior of a STRING object.

Listing 3.8 Application program for class STRING

```
class STRING_APPLICATION

creation
    start

feature

    start is
        local
            message:  STRING
            reverse:  STRING
            str1, str2:  STRING
            r:        REAL
        do
            message := "Testing, testing, 123, 1234"
            io.putstring ("message = ")
            io.putstring (message)
            io.new_line


            -- Create string str1 and copy message to str1 then compare
            !! str1.make (50)
            str1.copy (message)
            if str1.is_equal (message) then
                io.putstring ("str1 = message")
            else
                io.putstring ("str1/= message")
            end
            io.new_line
            str1.put ('t', 1)
            if str1.is_equal (message) then
                io.putstring ("str1 = message")
```

```
else
   io.putstring ("str1/= message")
end
io.new_line

-- Change the first character of string str1 and then compare
-- str1 and message once again
str1.mirror
io.putstring ("str1 = ")
io.putstring (str1)
io.new_line

-- Reverse the sequence of characters in string str1
str1.mirror
str1.to_upper
io.putstring ("str1 = ")
io.putstring (str1)
io.new_line

-- Obtain the first occurrence of the letter 'G'
io.putstring ("First occurrence of 'G%' = ")
io.putint (str1.index_of ('G', 1))
io.new_line

- Obtain the first occurrence of the substring "ING"
io.putstring ("First occurrence of 'ING%' = ")
io.putint (str1.substring_index ("ING", 1))
io.new_line

-- Output the value of the string true_constant
io.putstring (str1.true_constant)
io.new_line

-- Assign the substring of str1 from index locations
-- 24 to 27 to string str2
str2 := str1.substring (24, 27)
io.putstring ("str2 = ")
io.putstring (str2)
io.new_line

-- Assign str2 to real value r after converting the string to real
r := str2.to_real
io.putstring ("r = ")
```

```
io.putreal (r)
io.new_line

-- Add the string ".More testing" to the string message
message.append (". More testing ")
message.append_real (12345.6)
io.putstring ("message = ")
io.putstring (message)
io.new_line

-- Remove all but the first four characters of string str1
str1.head (4)
io.putstring ("str1 = ")
io.putstring (str1)
io.new_line

-- Remove all but the last two characters of string str1
str1.tail (2)
io.putstring ("str1 = ")
io.putstring (str1)
io.new_line

-- Remove all occurrences of character 'T' from message
message.prune_all ('T')
io.putstring ("message = ")
io.putstring (message)
io.new_line

-- Output various properties of str2
io.putstring ("str2.capacity = ")
io.putint (str2.capacity)
io.new_line
io.putstring ("str2.count = ")
io.putint (str2.count)
io.new_line

-- Dynamically change the size of string str2
str2.resize (100)
io.putstring ("str2.capacity = ")
io.putint (str2.capacity)
io.new_line

-- Output various properties of str1
io.putstring ("str1.capacity = ")
```

```
            io.putint (str1.capacity)
            io.new_line
            io.putstring ("str1.count = ")
            io.putint (str1.count)
            io.new_line
        end

end -- class STRING_APPLICATION
```

The output of the program is

```
message = Testing, testing, 123, 1234
str1 = message
str1/= message
str1 = 4321 ,321 ,gnitset ,gnitset
str1 = TESTING, TESTING, 123, 1234
First occurrence of 'G' = 7
First occurrence of 'ING' = 5
true
str2 = 1234
r = 1234
message = Testing, testing, 123, 1234. More testing 12345.6
str1 = TEST
str1 = ST
message = Testing, testing, 123, 1234. More testing 12345.6
str2.capacity = 9
str2.count = 4
str2.capacity = 100
str1.capacity = 40
str1.count = 2
```

3.14 Basic input and output

In earlier programs you have seen commands like

```
io.putstring ("The current balance in the checking account is: ")
io.putint (my_account.balance)
io.new_line
```

There are three output commands in the above code: *putstring, putint,* and *new_line.* Each is transmitted through the standard I/O object *io.* As indicated earlier, this object is available to an Eiffel program by default and does not have to be explicitly declared or initialized.

How is input obtained in a program?

The standard input device is the keyboard. The following segment of code illustrates how one could input a real value, an integer value, and a character value.

```
my_int :    INTEGER
my_char : CHARACTER
my_real :   REAL
io.readint              -- input command
io.readchar             -- input command
io.readreal             -- input command

my_int := io.lastint            -- query
my_char := io.lastchar          -- query
my_real := io.lastreal          -- query
```

The input commands used are *readint*, *readchar*, and *readreal*. Each is transmitted through the standard I/O object *io*. The values that were input (by typing information from the keyboard) are obtained through the queries *lastint*, *lastchar*, and *lastreal*, again transmitted through the standard I/O object *io*. The strict protocol of separating commands from queries is observed here. Although it might be tempting to have *readint* return an integer, the viewpoint taken here is that command *readint* changes the internal state of the *io* object and the query *lastint* accesses part of the internal state.

There are many input and output commands and queries defined in the Eiffel class STD_FILES that standardize input and output. A portion of the interface to this class is given in Listing 3.9.

Listing 3.9 Portion of interface to class STD_FILES

```
class interface STD_FILES

    feature -- Element change

        new_line
            -- Write line feed at end of default output.

        putchar (c: CHARACTER)
            -- Write 'c' at end of default output.
```

putdouble (d: DOUBLE)
    -- Write 'd' at end of default output.

putint (i: INTEGER)
    -- Write 'i' at end of default output.

putreal (r: REAL)
    -- Write 'r' at end of default output.

putstring (s: STRING)
    -- Write 's' at end of default output.

feature -- Input

next_line
    -- Move to next input line on standard input.

readchar
    -- Read a new character from standard input.
    -- Make result available in 'lastchar'.

readdouble
    -- Read a new double from standard input.
    -- Make result available in 'lastdouble'.

readint
    -- Read a new integer from standard input.
    -- Make result available in 'lastint'.

readline
    -- Read a line from standard input.
    -- Make result available in 'laststring'.

readreal
    -- Read a new real from standard input.
    -- Make result available in 'lastreal'.

readstream (nb_char: INTEGER)
    -- Read a string of at most 'nb_char' bound characters
    -- from standard input.
    -- Make result available in 'laststring'.

readword
    -- Read a new word from standard input.
    -- Make result available in 'laststring'.

feature -- Status report

```
        lastchar: CHARACTER
            -- Last character read by readchar

        lastdouble: DOUBLE

        lastint: INTEGER
            -- Last integer read by readint

        lastreal: REAL
            -- Last real read by readreal

        laststring: STRING
            -- Last string read by readline,
            -- readstream, or readword

    end -- class STD_FILES
```

In order to gain a better understanding of standard input and output several test programs are presented.

The routines *new_line, putbool, putchar, putdouble, putint, putreal,* and *putstring* are illustrated in a simple test program given in Listing 3.10.

Listing 3.10 Test program for STD_FILES output routines

```
    class APPLICATION

    creation
        start

    feature

        start is
            local
                b: BOOLEAN
                d: DOUBLE
                r: REAL
                c: CHARACTER
                i: INTEGER
                s: STRING
            do
                io.putstring ("Output routines%N")
                b := False
                d := 1.23456789
                r := 1.23456
                c := 'A'
```

```
            i := 15
            s := "Hello"
            io.putstring (s)
            io.new_line
            io.putbool (b)
            io.new_line
            io.putdouble (d)
            io.new_line
            io.putreal (r)
            io.new_line
            io.putint (i)
            io.new_line
            io.putstring ("This is the end of program%N")
        end

end -- class APPLICATION
```

The output to the program in Listing 3.10 is

```
Hello
false
1.2345678899999999
1.23456
15
```

In operating systems such as DOS and UNIX output can be redirected to a file instead of appearing on the standard output device, the output video terminal. This may be accomplished by typing the name of the program followed by a greater than symbol ("＞") followed by the name of the output file. As an example, suppose you wish to output a program called *my_prog* to a file *my_output*. You would accomplish this using the command

$$my\_prog > my\_output.$$

Listing 3.11 exercises some input commands and queries.

Listing 3.11 Input and status report routines from class STD_FILES

```
class APPLICATION

creation
        start

feature
```

```
start is
    local
        d: DOUBLE
        r: REAL
        c: CHARACTER
        i: INTEGER
        s: STRING
    do
        io.putstring ("Input routines")
        io.new_line
        io.putstring ("Enter a character: ")
        io.readchar
        io.new_line
        io.putstring ("Enter an integer: ")
        io.readint
        io.new_line
        io.putstring ("Enter a double: ")
        io.readdouble
        io.new_line
        io.putstring ("Enter a real: ")
        io.readreal
        io.new_line
        io.putstring ("Enter a string: ")
        io.readline
        io.new_line
        io.putstring ("The string entered was: ")
        io.putstring (io.laststring)
        io.new_line
        io.putstring ("The character entered earlier was: ")
        io.putchar (io.lastchar)
        io.new_line
        io.putstring ("The integer entered earlier was: ")
        io.putint (io.lastint)
        io.new_line
        io.putstring ("The double entered earlier was: ")
        io.putdouble (io.lastdouble)
        io.new_line
    end

end -- class APPLICATION
```

3.15 Mathematical routines and "number crunching"

One of the first high-level programming languages, FORTRAN (an acronym for Formula Translator), was originally developed to support mathematical computation for science and engineering. The IBM Scientific Programming Library was developed in the early years of FORTRAN to provide many important functions that support mathematical computation. In these early days of computing almost all programming activity centered around what is now called "number crunching." Today it is estimated that less than 10 percent of computing is related to numerical analysis or "number crunching." Yet it is interesting that the word "computing" is still used. Are we "computing" when we run a word processing application? Are we computing when we access information from a database? Clearly the answer is no. The legacy of our early computation still haunts us.

Suppose we need to do some mathematical analysis as part of some application. Suppose we wish to write a program to solve the following problem:

A surveyor wishes to estimate the height of a tall office building. The distance, d, is measured with an optical instrument and so is the angle of the line with respect to the horizontal. The given information, *distance* and *angle*, is shown in Figure 3.13. We wish to compute the *height* of the building.

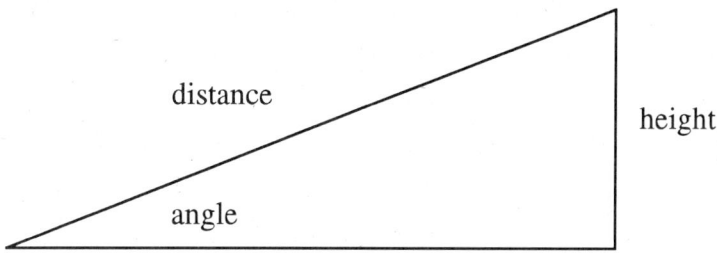

Figure 3.13 Computing the Height of a Building

One can perform this computation for a given set of values of *distance* and *angle* using a scientific calculator. Suppose one wishes to write an interactive program that allows the user to input the two values of *distance* and *angle* and then the value of *height* is computed and displayed.

Some elementary trigonometry suggests that *height = distance * sin(angle)*, where *sin* is the sine function.

The challenge here, in terms of programming, lies in being able to access and compute the sine of an angle. Most programming languages, including Eiffel, do not include this or other mathematical functions in the language itself. Instead such functions are supplied through an external library.

In an object-oriented language such as Eiffel, functions can be invoked only through an object. Therefore the key to using an external math library is to declare a math object whose type is the class containing the desired mathematical functions. All mathematical functions are then invoked through this math object.

Listing 3.12 shows the solution to the above problem using such a math object. An attribute *math_object* is declared. In the *start* routine of class APPLICATION, this object is initialized. Following this, all mathematical functions such as *sin* or *arc_tangent* are invoked through this *math_object*. The class APPLICATION may be thought of as "containing" a math object that is used to access the various mathematical functions needed for the application.

Listing 3.12 Using a mathematical object

```
class APPLICATION

creation
    start

feature

    math_object:  SINGLE_MATH   -- Used to access trigonometric functions
    distance:     REAL
    angle:        REAL
    pi:           REAL

    start is
        do
            !! math_object
            pi := 4.0 * math_object.arc_tangent (1.0)
            from
                distance := 1.0
            until
                distance = 0.0
            loop
```

```
        get_input
        io.putstring ("height = ")
        io.putreal (compute_height (distance, angle))
        io.new_line
      end
    end

  get_input is
  -- Input the values distance and angle
    do
      io.putstring ("Enter distance (0.0 to quit): ")
      io.readreal
      distance := io.lastreal
      io.new_line
      io.putstring ("Enter angle: ")
      io.readreal
      angle := io.lastreal
    end

  compute_height (dist: REAL; ang: REAL): REAL is
  -- Return the height of a triangle when given the hypotonuse and angle
    do
      Result := dist * math_object.sine (pi * ang / 180.0)
    end

end -- class APPLICATION
```

In Listing 3.12, the attribute queries of class APPLICATION include the geometric variables *distance, angle,* the *math_object* of class SINGLE_MATH, and the real number *pi*, computed later. All of the routines in class APPLICATION need access to these attributes so they cannot be declared as local entities within a given routine.

The attribute *pi* is computed using the mathematical fact that it is *4 * arctan(1)*, since the inverse tangent of 1 equals π divided by 4. The inverse tangent function is accessed through the *math_object*.

Other basic mathematical routines are also available from class SINGLE_MATH. The interface showing a portion of this class is given in Listing 3.13.

Listing 3.13 Portion of interface to class SINGLE_MATH

```
class interface SINGLE_MATH
```

feature -- Access

    arc_tangent (v: REAL): REAL
        -- Trigonometric arctangent of 'v'

    cosine (v: REAL): REAL
        -- Trigonometric cosine of radian 'v' approximated
        -- in the range [-pi/4, +pi/4]

    log (v: REAL): REAL
        -- Natural logarithm of 'v'

    sine (v: REAL): REAL
        -- Trigonometric sine of radian 'v' approximated
        -- in range [-pi/4, +pi/4]

    sqrt (v: REAL): REAL
        -- Square root of 'v'

    tangent (v: REAL): REAL
        -- Trigonometric tangent of radian 'v' approximated
        -- in range [-pi/4, +pi/4]

end -- class SINGLE_MATH

3.16 Files and secondary storage

In section 3.14 we examined the behavior of class STD_FILES. The input/output routines of this class are most useful when input is taken from the keyboard and output is sent to a video terminal. It is often necessary to take input from and send output directly to a file. This is the case when the results of a computation must be saved and perhaps reused the next time an application is run.

A file is an information structure that resides on a disk, tape, or some secondary storage device. The information stored on the secondary storage device persists after the program that generated the data terminates. When a file is created, it is assigned a file name. This name appears in the directory listing. When a file is opened, the name of the file is used to distinguish one file from another.

Information can be stored or accessed from a file in either a sequential manner or random access manner. Each byte of information stored in a file is saved at an offset from the starting location in the file which has an offset of 0.

When sequential access is used, information is written or read contiguously starting from the current offset in the file. With random access, the programmer can specify the byte offset for either reading or writing information to the file.

In Eiffel, a file object must be created, as for any Eiffel object. When a file object is created, there are several creation options. A physical file with a directory listing can be associated with the file object being created. This is the *open* operation. A new physical file can be generated (or an existing file with the same name overwritten) and associated with the file object. This new file can be opened for write-only, read-only, read/write, and several other options. This is the *create* operation.

The lengthy but important interface to class PLAIN_TEXT_FILE is presented in Appendix 2. Only a small portion of this interface is shown in Listing 3.14.

Listing 3.14 Small portion of interface to class PLAIN_TEXT_FILE

```
class interface PLAIN_TEXT_FILE
-- See Appendix 2 for the complete interface

creation
        make,
        make_open_read,
        make_open_write,
        make_open_append,
        make_open_read_write,
        make_create_read_write,
        make_open_read_append

feature

        item: CHARACTER
                -- Current item

        name: STRING
                -- File name

        back
                -- Go back one position.

        finish
                -- Go to last position.
```

forth
> -- Go to next position.

go (abs_position: INTEGER)
> -- Go to the absolute position.

move (offset: INTEGER)
> -- Advance by offset from current location.

next_line
> -- Move to next input line.

start
> -- Go to first position.

new_line
> -- Write a new line character at current position.

putchar (c: CHARACTER)
> -- Write c at current position.

putdouble (d: DOUBLE)
> -- Write ASCII value d at current position.

putint (i: INTEGER)
> -- Write ASCII value of i at current position.

putreal (r: REAL)
> -- Write ASCII value of r at current position.

putstring (s: STRING)
> -- Write s at current position.

readchar
> -- Read a new character.
> -- Make result available in last_character.

readdouble
> -- Read the ASCII representation of a new double
>   from file. Make result available in last_double.

readint
> -- Read the ASCII representation of a new integer
>   from file. Make result available in last_integer.

readline
> -- Read a string until new line or end of file.

```
                -- Make result available in last_string.
                -- New line will be consumed but not part of last_string.

        readreal
                -- Read the ASCII representation of a new real
                    from file. Make result available in last_real.

        count: INTEGER
                -- Size in bytes (0 if no associated physical file)

        last_character: CHARACTER
                -- Last character read by read_character

        last_double: DOUBLE
                -- Last double read by read_double

        last_integer: INTEGER
                -- Last integer read by read_integer

        last_real: REAL
                -- Last real read by read_real

        last_string: STRING
                -- Last string read

end -- class PLAIN_TEXT_FILE
```

There are seven creation routines specified in the interface to class PLAIN_TEXT_FILE given in Listing 3.14. The user must choose an appropriate mechanism for creating a file based on the intended usage and whether a physical file already exists.

A test program that uses only a small subset of the resources available in class PLAIN_TEXT_FILE is presented in Listing 3.15 and discussed below the listing.

Listing 3.15 A test program for class PLAIN_TEXT_FILE

```
class FILE_APPLICATION

creation
    start

feature

    my_file:        PLAIN_TEXT_FILE
    math_object:    SINGLE_MATH
```

```
start is
  do
    !! math_object

    -- Open an existing file, "richard", for writing only
    !! my_file.make_open_write ("richard")
    -- Write some data into this file
    my_file.putstring ("My name is Richard Wiener%N")
    my_file.putstring ("I have ")
    my_file.putint (3)
    my_file.putstring (" children.%N")
    my_file.putstring ("The value of sqrt( 2 ) = ")
    my_file.putreal (math_object.sqrt (2))
    my_file.new_line
    my_file.close

    -- Open my_file for read-only
    my_file.open_read
    from
      my_file.readline
    until
      my_file.end_of_file
    loop
      io.putstring (my_file.laststring)
      io.new_line
      my_file.readline
    end
    io.new_line

    -- Move cursor to the beginning of my_file
    my_file.start
    my_file.readchar
    io.putchar (my_file.lastchar)
    my_file.forth
    io.putchar (my_file.lastchar)
    my_file.go (5)
    my_file.readchar
    io.putchar (my_file.lastchar)
    my_file.move (3)
    my_file.readchar
    io.putchar (my_file.lastchar)
    io.new_line
```

```
    -- Open file "richard" so that data can be appended
    my_file.make_open_append ("richard")
    my_file.putstring ("%NThis is the final sentence%N")

    -- Open file "richard" for read-only
    my_file.make_open_read ("richard")
    from
        my_file.readline
    until
        my_file.end_of_file
    loop
        io.putstring (my_file.laststring)
        io.new_line
        my_file.readline
    end
    io.new_line
    end

end -- class FILE_APPLICATION
```

The output of the program is

My name is Richard Wiener.
I have 3 children.
The value of sqrt(2) = 1.41421.

MMms
My name is Richard Wiener.
I have 3 children.
The value of sqrt(2) = 1.41421.

This is the final sentence

In Listing 3.15 the APPLICATION class contains two attributes, *my_file* and *math_object*. The *math_object* is used to compute the square root of 2.

The object *my_file* is created and initialized. An empty physical file with this name is already in existence before executing the program. Input into the file is accomplished by invoking a series of *putstring, putint,* and *putreal* routines through the object *my_file*. The file is then closed.

Following these actions, *my_file* is reopened using the *open_read* routine. It is not necessary to create the object *my_file* a second time. The *open_read* routine attaches the *my_file* object to this existing physical file and opens it for read-only purposes.

The *from-until-loop* structure invokes the input routine *readline* while testing *my_file* for the end of file symbol. In the body of the loop entire lines of *my_file* are read and output to the video terminal.

Later in the program *my_file* is reopened. Then one additional line of input is sent to *my_file*.

Finally, *my_file* is reopened and traversed line by line while outputing its contents.

3.17 Summary

This chapter introduced the basic elements of Eiffel programming. Important features of the language and external classes were introduced. Some of the important ideas presented include:

- A software system is an interconnected collection of units sometimes called modules. Each module contains a logically coherent set of operations and an underlying data model.

- In an object-oriented context a module is the same as a class—a unification of a data model and behavioral model (set of functions called methods or routines that can access and manipulate the information contained in the data model).

- Using the "systems" approach, each module is responsible for only a small but well-focused portion of the desired behavior of the software. Most modern programming languages including Eiffel favor a "systems" approach to software construction.

- All Eiffel software systems must have an Ace specified creation routine in one of its classes to "trigger" an application.

- An Ace file must be supplied in the directory containing the Eiffel files that comprise an application. See the User's Guide that accompanies your Eiffel compiler for more information about Ace files.

- The Eiffel language was "born" in the late 1980s. It is a pure object-oriented language. This implies that functions can be invoked only through objects and not as stand-alone logical entities.

- As a pure object-oriented language, the class in Eiffel is the basic logical unit of encapsulation as well as the basic physical unit, a module. Eiffel software is organized as a set of interrelated and cooperating classes.

- Programs consist of objects. These objects are created during program execution, perform their tasks, and then are typically destroyed.

- An object in Eiffel and in other object-oriented languages is an instance of a class. Its attributes are given by the data model of its class. The messages that it can respond to (i.e., the routines that one can invoke through the object) are specified by the behavioral model of the class (the set of routines given in the class description).

- Before an object can be created in Eiffel it must be declared to be of a given type. Its type is the name of the class that the object will be an instance of (after it is created).

- Objects must be explicitly created either using the creation operator (!!) in front of the variable or using a specified creation routine in conjunction with the creation operator.

- Eiffel systems provide for "automatic garbage collection." As an Eiffel application runs, a garbage collection process is running in the background and detecting when storage is no longer connected to a variable name. At an opportune moment the garbage collection process recycles (effectively destroys) the unneeded storage.

- There are several basic object types that do not require explicit creation in order to be used. These are INTEGER, CHARACTER, REAL, and BOOLEAN.

- Objects of type INTEGER have a default value of 0. Objects of type CHARACTER have a default value of the NULL character (ASCII value 0). Objects of type REAL have a default value of 0.0. Finally, objects of type BOOLEAN have a default value of *false*.

- Ordinary objects (non-basic type objects) have "reference" semantics. This implies that the programmer is responsible for explictly allocating storage using a creation operator possibly in conjunction with a creation routine. The initial value of an ordinary object is Void. After the programmer creates storage for such an object, the object name is attached to the storage.

- In order for the *copy* routine to work, it is essential that the target object (object being copied to) be already created.

- Two objects are equal if they are attached (bound) to the same storage. If one wishes to test whether the objects x and y are equal, an expression of the form *if $x = y$* would be used.

- Within the body of a routine there are times when a choice must be made among several alternative blocks of code to be executed. This choice is usually based on the value of some expression that may assume a value *true* or a value *false*.

- It is often necessary to carry out a sequence of statements repeatedly until some condition is met. The construct *from-until-loop* may be used in this situation.

- An Eiffel routine specifies both interface information as well as implementation details. The user of a class (consumer) needs access to only the interface portion of a routine. The producer of the class needs access to the implementation details when performing maintenance on the routine.

- Classes contain queries and commands. Commands do not return a value whereas queries do. Commands are used to change the internal state of an object (the values of its attributes). Queries are used to access state information from the object (the value of one or more of its attributes) or perform some computation that may involve the current state of the object without changing the internal state of the object.

- For a command, a verb name should be used. For a query, a noun that is descriptive of what is returned should be used.

- The Eiffel language, like many other modern programming languages, relegates important tasks such as keyboard input and terminal output, mathematical functions, arrays, strings, and secondary storage input and output to routines available in standard libraries. These external routines become a typical and basic element of Eiffel programs.

- It is usually foolish and often unproductive to reinvent the wheel by creating your own basic software components, especially when the language you are using already provides a fully tested and highly rationalized set of classes through several class libraries. It is important that you learn to browse and then utilize these available resources. You must become an intelligent consumer before you can become a competent producer.

- The routines that support the keyboard input and terminal output come from a class called STD_FILES.

- In the business of programming, a string is an array of characters.

- A file is an information structure that physically resides on a disk, tape, or some secondary storage device. The information stored on the secondary storage device persists after the program that generated the data terminates. When a file is created, it is assigned a file name. This name appears in the directory listing. When a file is opened, the name of the file is used to distinguish one file from another.

3.18 Exercises

1. Write your first Eiffel program. Its purpose is to display your name and address on the video terminal. Build an Ace file for your program, compile and link it, and show its output.

2. Write a program that uses the four basic types: INTEGER, REAL, CHARACTER, and BOOLEAN. Put comments in your program to indicate the purpose of each block of code.

3. Carefully state the difference in meaning between assignment, copy, and clone.

4. Write a program that computes the sum of the square of the integers from 1 to 1000.

5. Write a program that prompts the user for the radius of a circle and outputs its area.

6. Write a program that prompts the user for the temperature in Fahrenheit and returns the equivalent temperature in centigrade.

7. Write a program that outputs to the video terminal two columns of numbers, the first column labeled Degrees Fahrenheit, the second labeled Degrees Centigrade, as the temperature is varied from 0 degrees Fahrenheit to 212 degrees Fahrenheit.

8. Write a test program that exercises at least ten routines from class ARRAY.

9. Write a program that creates an array called *family* and then inserts the names of your parents, grandparents (if you can remember this information), wife (if you have one), and children (if you have them) into this array. Then iterate through *family* and output each of its elements.

10. Write a function routine called *average_value* that computes the mean value of the numbers in an array that is input. The interface to this routine is the following:

average_value (data: ARRAY [REAL]) : REAL. Test your routine by loading your array with the square root of the integers from 1 to 10,000 (i.e., the first index in your array contains the square root of 1, the second index the square root of 2, the third index the square root of 3, ..., up to the last index that contains the square root of 10,000).

11. Show how you would use a routine from class STRING to extract the substring "Rich" from the string, "My name is Richard Wiener".

12. Show how you would use routine(s) from class STRING to extract all occurrences of the character 'e' from the string, "My name is Richard Wiener".

13. Write a simple program that uses the infix "<" operator in class STRING.

14. Using a text editor, type in the following text file and assign it the disk filename, "words.txt": "Eiffel is a pure and elegant object-oriented programming language." Write a program that opens the file containing this sentence (i.e., opens "words.txt") and counts the number of occurrences of each character (from 'a' to 'z') in that file. There is no need to distinguish upper-case characters from lower-case characters.

15. Using a text editor, create a file called "number." In this file write a single integer from 1 to 10. Write an application program called GUESS. In the application prompt the user to guess a number from 1 to 10. Open the file "number" and compare the number in this file to the number that the user has guessed. Allow many users to run this program. Each time the program is run, update a file called "statistics" that keeps track of the number of correct guesses and the number of incorrect guesses. Using a text editor this information should always be available. You may wish to initialize this file by hand using a text editor. Your program should access this file and update the guessing statistics after each user has made his or her guess.

Chapter
4

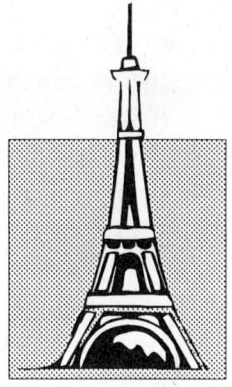

Algorithms

4.1 Introduction

An **algorithm** is a formal sequence of instructions for performing a computation. An algorithm is the computational abstraction or schema required to solve some well-specified problem. Algorithms can sometimes be expressed in a natural language such as English but are most often expressed in either a pseudo-code (a made-up language without a formal grammar or syntax that is usually a bastardized version of some programming language) or a code segment from an actual programming language. An algorithm usually expresses only the barest skeletal structure of the computational process required to obtain a solution. The important details associated with the input and output of information are usually ignored when expressing an algorithm. Even a moderate-sized software system typically requires many algorithms. Each algorithm focuses on a particular portion of the overall mission of the software system. The algorithm is usually implemented as a routine in a given class.

The study of algorithms helps to justify the "science" in "computer science." Algorithm design is concerned with correctness and efficiency. Correctness is concerned with establishing that the algorithm works for all instances of a problem, with no exceptions. Efficiency is concerned with the speed and memory requirements necessary to solve the problem.

A problem has many instances, usually an infinite number of instances. The difference between a problem and its instances is discussed in the next section.

4.2   Problems versus their instances

Consider the specific requirement of writing a function that can rearrange the five numbers, 5, 3, 4, 1, and 7 so that they become ordered from smallest to largest. Of course for such a small data set you may well wonder why one needs a computer program to perform this computation. The numbers can be rearranged by inspection! Small instances of problems can usually be solved by inspection.

The requirement of sorting the five numbers 5, 3, 4, 1, and 7 is an instance of a much more general problem called the sorting problem. The general sorting problem can be stated as follows:

Given an array of n numbers (the particular type of numbers are not important), where n is an integer. Write a function that outputs an array that contains the original numbers in ascending order.

Since an array can be of any size, n, and contain an arbitrary collection of numbers, there are an infinite number of instances of the sorting problem. The particular sequence of five numbers 5, 3, 4, 1, and 7 is merely one instance from among the infinite collection of sorting problems.

A sorting algorithm must be able to correctly order an arbitrary sequence of numbers. Although the computation time or computational effort will increase as the size, n, of the data set increases, the algorithm should work successfully for any n and any set of numbers. If such an algorithm can be found, it represents a "solution" to the "problem."

Sorting is a basic and well understood problem. Because of the practical importance of the sorting problem (the need to order a collection of information is quite fundamental), many sorting algorithms have been designed. Each correctly orders an arbitrary set of numbers. How do these sorting algorithms differ? They differ in their efficiency, the speed and memory resources required to perform their task. Efficiency is the subject of section 4.4.

Before returning to a discussion of algorithm efficiency, let us sample the flavor of algorithms by considering two simple examples.

4.3 A taste of algorithms—some simple examples

4.3.1 Algorithms for finding smallest and largest array values

Suppose we wish to compute the smallest and largest values of data stored in an array. For now, assume that the "data" consists of an array of numbers. The size of the array, n, although specified, is arbitrary. The sequence of values stored in the array is also arbitrary. How can we solve this general problem? We design an algorithm that solves this problem.

First we express the algorithm in words as a logical sequence of actions that will guarantee a correct solution. Then we will more formally express the algorithm using the syntax and semantics of an Eiffel command. By expressing the algorithm in this way, we can actually test the algorithm on sample data sets (instances of the problem) to obtain a better "feel" of the computational process and to gain confidence in the correctness of the algorithm.

Algorithm for finding smallest value in an array of n numbers

1. Assume tentatively that the first number in the array (number at index 1) is the smallest.

2. Consecutively compare this tentative smallest value to each of the remaining numbers in index locations 2 up to n.

3. If a particular number in this sequence is smaller than the tentative smallest value, replace the tentative smallest value with this particular number.

4. When all of the numbers in the index locations 2 up to n have been exhausted, return the tentative smallest number as the solution to the problem.

The correctness of the algorithm follows from the observation that we are comparing the best solution to date (smallest among the first k numbers) with the next available number in the sequence until the next available number is the nth number. The transitivity relationship that asserts that if number a is less than b and b is less than c, it follows that a is less than c serves as the final logical link in the proof.

The algorithm for finding the largest value in an array of n numbers is almost the same. All occurrences of smallest become largest. The basic logic is the same.

Listing 4.1 presents the algorithms for finding the smallest and largest values in an array in the form of two queries written in Eiffel.

Listing 4.1 Routines for finding the smallest and largest number in an array

```
smallest (data: ARRAY [REAL]): REAL is
    local
        tentative:      REAL
        index:          INTEGER
    do
        tentative := data.item (1)
        from
            index := data.lower
        until
            index = data.upper
        loop
            index := index + 1
            if data.item (index) < tentative then
                tentative := data.item (index)
            end
        end
        Result := tentative
    end

largest (data: ARRAY [REAL]): REAL is
    local
        tentative: REAL
        index: INTEGER
    do
        tentative := data.item (1)
        from
            index := data.lower
        until
            index = data.upper
        loop
            index := index + 1
            if data.item (index) > tentative then
                tentative := data.item (index)
            end
        end
        Result := tentative
    end
```

The routines *smallest* and *largest* given in Listing 4.1 are solutions to the problems. They work correctly for any *data* of any *size*.

We consider a slight variation on this problem. Suppose we wish to compute the array index that contains the smallest value in the array between the limits *lower_limit* and *upper_limit*. Let us call this algorithm *smallest_index_in_range*.

An Eiffel query (function) that implements this algorithm is given in Listing 4.2.

Listing 4.2 Algorithm smallest_index_in_range

```
smallest_index (data: ARRAY [REAL]; lower: INTEGER;
                upper: INTEGER): INTEGER is
    local
        tentative: REAL
        tentative_index: INTEGER
        index: INTEGER
    do
        tentative := data.item (lower)
        tentative_index := lower
        from
            index := lower
        until
            index = upper
        loop
            index := index + 1
            if data.item (index) < tentative then
                tentative := data.item (index)
                tentative_index := index
            end
        end
        Result := tentative_index
    end
```

The result returned is the index associated with the smallest value in the range *lower* to *upper* in the *data* array.

4.3.2 Simple sorting algorithm

We return to the problem of sorting and present a particularly simple solution to the problem. The algorithm is called **selection sort**. The algorithm works as follows:

Selection Sort Algorithm for Sorting Numbers in an Array

1. In a loop that iterates the index k from 1 to n,

2. Compute the smallest element and its index among the elements from k to n.

3. Interchange this smallest element with the element at index k.

4. When the loop is completed, the elements are sorted.

Step 2 of the selection sort algorithm requires that the smallest element among a subset of elements in an array be computed. This is the algorithm presented in Listing 4.2.

In Listing 4.3, an Eiffel routine for sorting numbers using the selection sort algorithm in conjunction with function *smallest_index_in_range* is presented. This Eiffel function represents a solution to the sorting problem.

Listing 4.3 Routine for sorting an array using selection sort

```
selection_sort (data: ARRAY [REAL]) is
    local
        index: INTEGER
        smallest: REAL
        s_index: INTEGER
        temp: REAL
    do
        from
            index := 0
        until
            index = data.upper - 1
        loop
            index := index + 1
            s_index := smallest_index_in_range (data, index, data.upper)
            smallest := data.item (s_index)
            temp := data.item (index)
            data.put (smallest, index)
            data.put (temp, s_index)
        end
    end
```

We illustrate the details of selection_sort by "walking" through an example containing four numbers. Figure 4.1 shows the initial array to be sorted.

8	5	3	7

Figure 4.1 Initial Array to Be Sorted with Selection Sort

The function *smallest_index_in_range (data, 1, 4)* returns 3. The value *smallest* is 3. The values 8 and 3 are swapped. The new array following the first iteration is shown in Figure 4.2.

3	5	8	7

Figure 4.2 Array after First Iteration of Selection Sort

In the second iteration, the function *smallest_index_in_range (data, 2, 4)* returns 2. The value *smallest* is 5. The value 5 is swapped with itself. There is no change in the array following the second iteration.

In the third and final iteration, the function *smallest_index_in_range (data, 2, 4)* returns 7. The value of smallest is 7. The values 8 and 7 are swapped. The array following this third iteration is shown in Figure 4.3.

3	5	7	8

Figure 4.3 Array after Third and Final Iteration of Selection Sort

The array is sorted.

Let us return now to a discussion about algorithm efficiency.

4.4   The efficiency of algorithms

The efficiency of an algorithm is related to the speed with which it performs its work and the memory that is required to do this work. Often there are a set of distinct algorithms independently constructed to solve a given problem. The computer scientist is usually concerned with determining and then using the most efficient algorithm for solving a problem since computation time is valuable. It is often the case that a "brute-force" approach to solving a problem (i.e., one that is relatively easy to construct and prove correct) is significantly less efficient than a more clever approach.

Various measures have been devised to indicate the computational efficiency of an algorithm. These include worst-case asymptotic complexity and average-case asymptotic complexity. By asymptotic complexity is meant the growth in computation time as a function of the growth in problem size as the problem size approaches infinity. The worst-case complexity measure deals with a guaranteed upper bound in performance. That is, the algorithm is guaranteed to perform equal or better than this result. Such a complexity measure is quite useful. The average-case complexity measure deals with an "average" configuration of data. That is, things may sometimes be better or worse but the average-case complexity provides an indication of typical performance.

The "big O" notation is often used to express the asymptotic complexity of an algorithm. Suppose, for example, an algorithm has a worst-case asymptotic complexity given by $O(n^2)$. This implies that if it takes t units of time to perform a computation of size n, where this size is quite large (approaching infinity), then it would take $4 * t$ units of time to perform a computation of size $2 * n$. If the algorithm were of complexity $O(n)$, then doubling the size of the problem would double the computational effort required to solve the problem. If the complexity were $O(n^3)$, then doubling the size of the problem would cause the computational effort to increase by a factor of 8. It is assumed throughout that the original size of the problem is large.

Let us consider the algorithmic complexity of each of the algorithms presented in section 4.3.

The algorithm for computing either the smallest or largest value in an array of size n given in section 4.3.1 is $O(n)$. The *from-until* loop single iteration structure that is central to the algorithm suggests that if the size of the array is doubled (even for small size), the number of comparison operations also doubles. This establishes the linear complexity structure of this algorithm.

The selection sort algorithm given in section 4.3.2 is more complicated to analyze. The first iteration requires n comparison operations (since the smallest value among n values is being sought). The second iteration requires $n-1$ comparison operations (since the smallest value among $n-1$ values is being sought). Subsequent iterations require n - 2, n - 3, ..., 2, and 1 comparison operations respectively. The total number of comparison operations is therefore given by: $n + (n-1) + (n-2) + (n-3) + ... + 2 + 1$. This is the sum of the well-known arithmetic series: $1 + 2 + ... + n$. From elementary algebra it is known that such a series sums to: $n*(n+1)/2$. This is a polynomial of second degree in n. For large values of n the linear term is dominated by the second-order term and is therefore considered insignificant and thus the selection sort algorithm is $O(n^2)$.

If one doubles the size of the array of numbers being sorted (for a large size), the sorting time will increase by approximately a factor of four for selection sort. This quadratic complexity is not very good and makes this algorithm relatively inefficient for sorting large data sets.

4.5 Computing faster

How can we increase the speed of computation for a given problem? One fairly certain way of doing this is to use a faster hardware processor (a faster computer). The speed of processors has been doubling roughly every two years for the past ten years.

We can often apply intellectual effort to improve the speed of computation for a given problem. In other words we can design a more efficient algorithm to solve the problem. This is of course not always possible but when it is, the dividends can be much more dramatic than the increase resulting from better hardware over the past ten years.

4.5.1 Illustrative example—subvector problem for arrays

A dramatic example (and in all honesty, an unusual example) of the improvement in efficiency that is sometimes attainable through creative and successful intellectual effort is presented next. This new problem, like the two before it, concerns arrays. Although it may not be obvious, the problem actually has some practical applications in signal processing.

We define a subvector as containing the values associated with a contiguous collection of successive index locations in the array. Each element of the array by itself is a subvector. Any two consecutive elements represent a subvector. Any three consecutive elements represent a subvector.

This pattern can be continued until we have the entire array which is also a subvector. Clearly, a large array contains many subvectors.

Suppose we associate a number with each subvector. This number is computed by taking the sum of the elements in the subvector. Suppose that we further stipulate that a given array contains at least one positive and at least one negative number. The problem is to find an algorithm that determines the largest sum among all the subvector sums for such an array. If all the numbers were positive, the solution would be the whole vector.

It would seem that the number of subvectors grows rapidly with the size of the array. Therefore, it would seem that the complexity of the algorithm (solution to the problem) that computes the largest sum associated with a subvector would be of complexity greater than linear.

We examine first a "brute-force" method for computing this maximum sum. We define three indices, *first, second*, and *third*. The index *first* is assigned consecutive values from 1 to the size of the array. Index *second* is assigned consecutive values from 1 to *size*. Finally, index *third* is assigned consecutive values from *first* to *second*. We compute the sum of every possible subvector since the index values *first* and *second* range over all the possibilities.

The code in Listing 4.4 presents this "brute-force" approach.

Listing 4.4 Brute force method for computing largest array sum of subvector

```
sum_subvectors1 (values: ARRAY [INTEGER]; size: INTEGER): INTEGER is
    local
        first, second, third: INTEGER
        total, max: INTEGER
    do
        max := - - 429654015
        from
            first := 1
        until
            first > size
        loop
            from
                second := 1
            until
                second > size
            loop
```

```
        total := 0
        from
            third := first
        until
            third > second
        loop
            total := total + values.item (third)
            if total > max then
                max := total
            end
            third := third + 1
        end
        second := second + 1
    end
    first := first + 1
  end
  Result := max
end
```

Because of the triple nested *from-until* loop structures, the complexity of the algorithm in Listing 4.4 is $O(n^3)$. This is evident in some timing calculations in which the execution time of the algorithm is determined for several array sizes. This timing information is given in Table 4.1.

Table 4.1 Computation Time versus Array Size for Listing 4.4

Array Size	Computation Time
50	0.983 seconds
100	7.45 seconds
200	58.55 seconds
400	8 minutes (estimate)
800	1 hour(estimate)
1600	8 hours (estimate)
3200	64 hours (estimate)
6400	21 days (estimate)
12800	5 months(estimate)

The first three actual execution times show the $O(n^3)$ complexity. Each successive computation time is roughly eight times greater than the previous computation time. The remaining six computation times are only estimates obtained by extrapolating the multiplicative factor of 8. The estimate of five months of computational effort to solve a problem of size 12,800 elements is quite discouraging.

It appears that we must bring a much faster machine to the rescue. Although this may help for problems of this size, sooner or later the multiplicative factor of 8 will make the computational effort prohibitive for even the fastest machine if the array size is allowed to grow. Instead of a faster machine, what we really need is a more clever algorithm!

Much work was done on this problem because of its application in digital signal processing. After some time several very clever and quite complicated algorithms were designed, each of complexity $O(n \log n)$. As the story goes (and this story is true to the best of the author's knowledge) one of the $O(n \log n)$ solutions was being presented at a research conference on algorithm design. A graduate student who had never seen the problem before humbly raised his hand after the 30-minute presentation of the $O(n \log n)$ solution was concluded and suggested that he had just devised (while listening to the lecture) a simple algorithm of $O(n)$. The algorithm (dutifully translated to Eiffel syntax) that the graduate student presented on the back of a napkin is presented in Listing 4.5.

Listing 4.5 Fast algorithm for computing maximum sum of subvectors of an array

```
sum_subvectors2 (values: ARRAY [INTEGER]; size: INTEGER): INTEGER is
    local
        max_so_far, max_ending_here: INTEGER
        index: INTEGER
    do
        max_so_far := - -1
        max_ending_here := 0
        from
            index := 0
        until
            index = size
        loop
            index := index + 1
            if max_ending_here + values.item (index) > 0 then
                max_ending_here := max_ending_here + values.item (index)
```

```
    else
        max_ending_here := 0
    end
    if max_ending_here > max_so_far then
        max_so_far := max_ending_here
    end
end
Result := max_so_far
end
```

Can you verify that this algorithm is correct? You may wish to "walk" through a simple example and think about each step. Although such a "walk-through" does not serve as a proof of correctness, it should at least raise your comfort level and confidence that the algorithm is indeed correct. That is, it produces the maximum sum of subvectors for an arbitrary array of integers. The algorithm is linear in complexity, $O(n)$, since its key steps are enclosed by a single iteration structure.

To show how dramatically faster this algorithm performs compared to the previous "brute-force" algorithm, consider the output given in Table 4.2. This data was obtained using the same computer and compiler as the original data.

Table 4.2 Computation Time versus Array Size for Listing 4.5

Array Size	Computation Time (seconds)
50	0 (below granularity of clock)
100	0 (below granularity of clock)
200	0.017
400	0.033
800	0.05
1600	0.1
3200	0.2
6400	0.42
12800	0.82
25600	1.65
52200	3.33

The linear character of the fast algorithm of Listing 4.5 is quite evident. Every time the problem size doubles, the computation time roughly doubles.

It is rarely possible to redesign a "brute-force" algorithm and obtain the dramatic improvement just seen. Modest improvements are always welcome. The discipline of algorithm design seeks to better understand and improve existing algorithms.

4.6 Some more sorting

In section 4.3 an algorithm for selection sort was discussed. It was shown to be of complexity $O(n^2)$. As indicated before, sorting is an important task and therefore important problem in algorithm design. In this section we discuss two more sorting algorithms. The first is another well-known but relatively inefficient sorting algorithm called "bubble-sort." The second is a recently discovered algorithm that will be referred to here as "gap-sort." It is a minor variation on "bubble-sort," but as you will see much more efficient.

4.6.1 Bubble-sort

Bubble-sort involves a series of major iterations. During each iteration, the first element is compared to the second element and if in order (the first smaller than the second), they are left alone, if out of order they are interchanged. Then the second element is compared to the third element. Again, if they are already in order, they are left alone whereas if they are out of order they are interchanged. Then the third element is compared to the fourth using the same logic, then the fourth element is compared to the fifth. This pattern is continued until the n-1 element is compared to the nth element. When this first major iteration is completed, the largest element in the array will have been shifted to the nth index position in the array. What about the other elements? They are not necessarily sorted but clearly some movement in the direction of sorting will have occurred.

During the second major iteration of bubble-sort, the elements are again compared, two at a time, starting with the first and second elements. But this time the comparisons stop when the n-2 element has been compared with the n-1 element. The nth element is not touched since it is already known to be the largest element in the array. When the second major iteration is completed, the second to the largest element in the array is guaranteed to be in the n-1 index location. Major iterations continue, each time involving one less element, until only the first two elements are compared. Then the algorithm ends and the numbers in the array will have been sorted.

To illustrate the workings of this algorithm, consider the following small data set of 10 integers:

Original data set: 4, 1, 5, 7, 10, 8, 2, 6, 3, 9.

During the first major iteration, the first element, 4, is compared to the second element 1. Since they are out of order they are interchanged. This produces

1, 4, 5, 7, 10, 8, 2, 6, 3, 9.

The second and third elements are in order so nothing is done. The third and fourth elements are in order so nothing is done. The fifth and sixth elements are out of order so they are interchanged. This produces

1, 4, 5, 7, 8, 10, 2, 6, 3, 9.

Next the sixth and seventh elements are compared and interchanged. This produces

1, 4, 5, 7, 8, 2, 10, 6, 3, 9.

Next the seventh and eighth elements are compared and interchanged. This produces

1, 4, 5, 7, 8, 2, 6, 10, 3, 9.

This process continues until the first major iteration concludes with the new array:

1, 4, 5, 7, 8, 2, 6, 3, 9, 10.

As stated earlier, the largest element in the array, the value 10, has been shifted to the right-most position in the array. Like a bubble, it has risen to the surface (if one rotates the array by 90 degrees so the largest element in the array is geometrically at the top of the array rather than on the right).

After the second major iteration (the same process repeated among the first nine elements), the new array is

1, 4, 5, 7, 2, 6, 3, 8, 9, 10.

After the third major iteration, the array looks like

1, 4, 5, 2, 6, 3, 7, 8, 9, 10.

After the fourth major iteration, the array looks like

1, 4, 2, 5, 3, 6, 7, 8, 9, 10.

After the fifth major iteration, the array looks like

1, 2, 4, 3, 5, 6, 7, 8, 9, 10.

After the sixth major iteration, the array looks like

1, 2, 3, 4, 5, 6, 7, 8, 9, 10.

The array is completely sorted. In the general case of sorting an array of size 10, three more major iterations may have been required. We got lucky this time. Of course the algorithm should detect when no further iterations are required and not perform any additional iterations once this is determined.

In Listing 4.6, we present the bubble-sort algorithm using Eiffel syntax. In fact, the algorithm is implemented as an Eiffel routine.

Listing 4.6 Bubble-sort algorithm

```
bubble_sort (values: ARRAY [REAL]; size: INTEGER) is
    local
        interchanged:              BOOLEAN
        i, j, major_iteration, top: INTEGER
        temp:                      REAL
    do
        interchanged := true
        from
            major_iteration := 1
        until
            not interchanged or major_iteration = size - 1
        loop
            interchanged := false
            top := size - major_iteration
            from
                i := 0
            until
                i = top
            loop
                i := i + 1
                j := i + 1
                if values.item (i) > values.item (j) then
```

```
            temp := values.item (i)
            values.put (values.item (j), i)
            values.put (temp, j)
            interchanged := true
         end
      end
      major_iteration := major_iteration + 1
   end
end
```

Can the reader explain why it is essential to assign interchanged to *true* above the first *from-until* loop in Listing 4.6? What would happen if this statement were omitted?

The results of some timing runs for instances of various sizes are presented in Table 4.3. For each timing run an array of reverse ordered data was used as input. This is the worst case data set for the bubble-sort algorithm.

Table 4.3 Computation Time versus Array Size for Listing 4.6

Array Size	Computation Time (seconds)
25	0.099
50	0.333
100	1.383
200	5.460
400	22.08
800	Estimated time of 1.25 minutes
1600	Estimated time of 6 minutes
3200	Estimated time of 24 minutes
6400	Estimated time of 1.6 hours

The computation time appears to increase according to an $O(n^2)$ law. This is indeed the algorithmic complexity of bubble-sort as evident from the doubly nested *from-until* loops.

The estimated time of 1.6 hours of computation to sort a data set of size 6400 is quite discouraging.

Once again, instead of looking for a more powerful computer to solve this problem, we instead look for a more efficient algorithm. There is an entire class of "super" sorting algorithms whose algorithmic complexity is

$O(\ n\ log n\ )$. It is not our goal in this section to explore this powerful set of sorting algorithms.

The "gap-sort" algorithm discussed in the next subsection is built on the idea of bubble-sort and is in fact, only a minor variation of bubble-sort. What is remarkable is how fast this minor variant performs. As you will soon see, what is even more remarkable is that no one, to date, fully understands why!

4.6.2 Gap-sort—a magic number and a fast variant of bubble-sort

Let us study the behavior of a small sorting problem using bubble-sort. This will set the stage for a discussion of an algorithm recently discovered that significantly improves the performance of bubble-sort.

Suppose the array we wish to sort contains the sequence 5, 4, 3, 2, 1.

After the first major iteration, the sequence becomes 4, 3, 2, 1, 5. After the second major iteration, the array contains the sequence 3, 2, 1, 4, 5. After the third major iteration, the array contains 2, 1, 3, 4, 5. After the fourth and final iteration the array contains the sequence 1, 2, 3, 4, 5.

No surprise. We already know how bubble-sort works. But, ..., observe the motion of the smallest element, the number 1. It migrates quite slowly, one unit to the left during each major iteration. Until this smallest number reaches the left most index of the array, the sorting process is not completed.

Suppose a way could be devised to speed up the motion of this and other slow moving elements as they migrate from the right of the array to its left. The gap-sort algorithm does exactly this. In rough terms, here is how it works.

A gap equal to the total size of the array divided by a constant in the neighborhood of 1.3, the *shrink_factor*, is defined. This gap is rounded down to an integer (the ratio is a decimal quantity). The first element is compared to the element in index 1 + gap, the second element is compared to the element in index 2 + gap, ..., until the size-gap element is compared to the element in the right most position (index equal to size) of the array. As with bubble-sort, the numbers are interchanged if they are out of order and left alone if they are in order.

During the next major iteration, the gap is divided by the *shrink_factor* and the process continued. Eventually, the gap will become a fraction less than one. Instead of rounding down to 0 (which would make no sense), the gap is set equal to 1. When the gap reaches a value of 1, the algorithm becomes identical to ordinary bubble-sort.

In order to appreciate the effect the gap has on the sorting process, we consider another sorting problem containing ten numbers that is similar to the one given above. The original sequence of numbers to be sorted is 10, 9, 8, 7, 6, 5, 4, 3, 2, 1. The size of the array is 10 so the initial value for the gap is 7 (i.e., 10.0 / 1.3 rounded down to the nearest integer).

The number in the first index is compared to the number in index 8, the number in index 2 is compared with the number in index 9, and the number in index 3 compared with the number in index 10. This causes the following changes to occur in the array after the first major iteration: 3, 2, 1, 7, 6, 5, 4, 10, 9, 8. The smallest value of 1 has already been shifted to index 3 after just one iteration.

The gap is reduced to 7.0 / 1.3 rounded down to the nearest integer or 5. During the second major iteration, the number in index 1 is compared to the number in index 6, and this pattern continues until the number in index 5 is compared to that in index 10. The result of these comparisons and required interchanges after the second major iteration is 3, 2, 1, 9, 6, 5, 4, 10, 7, 8.

The gap is reduced to 5.0 / 1.3 rounded down to the nearest integer or 3. The next iteration proceeds by comparing the number in index 1 with the number in index 4, ..., the number in index 7 with the number in index 10. This third major iteration produces the result 3, 2, 1, 4, 6, 5, 9, 10, 7, 8.

The gap is reduced to 3.0 / 1.3 rounded down to the nearest integer, or 2. The fourth major iteration using the gap of 2 produces the result 1, 2, 3, 4, 6, 5, 7, 8, 9, 10.

The gap is reduced to 2.0 / 1.3 rounded down to 1. The fifth major iteration produces the sorted sequence 1, 2, 3, 4, 5, 6, 7, 8, 9, 10.

Not only did gap-sort require only half the number of major iterations as bubble-sort, but the number of computations required in most of the iterations were considerably less than in bubble-sort.

Listing 4.7 presents the algorithm for gap-sort as an Eiffel routine.

Listing 4.7 Algorithm gap-sort

```
gap_sort (values: ARRAY [REAL]; size: INTEGER) is
    -- This algorithm is much more efficient than bubble-sort when the shrink_factor
    -- is near 1.3
    local
        interchanged: BOOLEAN
        i, j, top, gap: INTEGER
        temp, shrink_factor, rgap: REAL
    do
        shrink_factor := 1.3
```

```
interchanged := true
gap := size
from
until interchanged = false and gap = 1
loop
    interchanged := false
    rgap := gap
    gap := (rgap / shrink_factor).truncated_to_integer
    if gap = 0 then
        gap := 1
    end
    top := size - gap
    from
        i := 0
    until
        i = top
    loop
        i := i + 1
        j := i + gap
        if values.item (i) > values.item (j) then
            temp := values.item (i)
            values.put (values.item (j), i)
            values.put (temp, j)
            interchanged := true
        end
    end
end
end
```

The results of some timing runs for instances of various sizes are presented in Table 4.4. For each timing run an array of reverse ordered data was used as input.

Table 4.4 Computation Time versus Array Size for Listing 4.7

Array Size	Computation Time (seconds)
25	0.0166
50	0.050
100	0.117
200	0.300

400	0.717
800	1.56
1600	3.65
3200	8.97
6400	19.09

If you compare the computation time in Table 4.4 using gap-sort with the computation time given in Table 4.3 using bubble-sort, you have to agree that the results are dramatic. For a problem of size 6400 we are comparing approximately 1.6 hours with 19 seconds. The computation time appears to be growing at a rate given by $O(n \log n)$. Of course to verify this more rigorously, the points need to be plotted on semi-log paper. The reader is encouraged to do this as an exercise.

The title of this subsection is "Gap-sort—a magic number and a fast variant of bubble-sort." What is the magic number? The answer is 1.3. This is the *shrink_factor* used in the gap-sort algorithm. You may properly be asking yourself, "Is there anything magical or special about the number 1.3?" Glad you asked!

In the context of gap-sort, the answer is yes. If the *shrink_factor* were set to any number greater than or less than 0.5 from 1.3, the performance of gap-sort would degrade substantially. Only when the *shrink_factor* is a decimal value close to 1.3 does the algorithm provide a significant performance boost compared to bubble-sort. Why?

Unfortunately, there is currently no clear explanation. It is relatively easy to understand why the structure of gap-sort works. A careful review of the sorting example presented above involving ten numbers reveals the structural reasons for gap-sort's success. But why is this success dependent on a *shrink_factor* that must be so carefully tuned? The magic of numbers!

In the final subsection concerning sorting, another important and widely used algorithm is presented, insertion-sort.

4.6.3 Insertion-sort

For this final sorting algorithm in this section the insertion-sort algorithm is first presented formally as an Eiffel routine. Then from this description we will attempt to reverse engineer or explain the algorithm. It is important for computer scientists to learn to do this since the computer science literature does not always provide gentle or lucid explanations of algorithms but often expects the reader to engage in this reverse engineering process.

Listing 4.8 presents the insertion-sort algorithm.

Listing 4.8 Algorithm for insertion-sort

```
insertion_sort (values:  ARRAY [REAL]) is
   local
      index1, index2:  INTEGER
      x:               REAL
   do
     from
        index1 := values.lower
     until
        index1 = values.upper
     loop
        index1 := index1 + 1
        x := values.item (index1)
        index2 := index1 - 1
        from
        until
           index2 < 1 or x >= values.item (index2)
        loop
           values.put (values.item (index2), index2 + 1)
           index2 := index2 - 1
        end
        values.put (x, index2 + 1)
     end
   end
```

The results of some timing runs using insertion-sort are presented in Table 4.5. Once again, for each timing run an array of reverse ordered data was used as input.

Table 4.5 Computation Time versus Array Size for Listing 4.8

Array Size	Computation Time (seconds)
25	0.00
50	0.166
100	0.645
200	2.633
400	10.73

The data appears to follow an $O(n^2)$ law for its growth.

How does one reverse engineer an algorithm to gain an understanding of how it works? The most reliable method is to "walk" through an example of sufficient size to reveal the underlying structure of the algorithm but not a size so great that the hand computation becomes unwieldy. We consider an array of size 5 with its numbers loaded in reverse sorted order. The original data set is 5, 4, 3, 2, 1.

When index1 = 2 and index2 = 1, and x = 4, the algorithm assigns 5 to index location 2 and then the inner loop terminates. Then the value 4 is put at index 1. The new array is 4, 5, 3, 2, 1.

When index1 = 3, and index2 = 2, the value of x is 3. The value of 5 is assigned to the location 3 and index2 is set to 1. The value of 4 is assigned to location 2 and then the inner loop terminates. Then the value 3 is put at index 1. The new array is 3, 4, 5, 2, 1.

When index1 = 4, and index2 = 3, the value of x is 2. The value of 5 is assigned to location 4 and index2 is set to 2. The value of 4 is assigned to location 3 and index2 is set to 1. The value of 3 is set to location 2 and then the inner loop terminates. Then the value of 2 is put at index 1. The new array is 2, 3, 4, 5, 1.

When index1 = 5, and index2 = 4, the value of x is 1. The value of 5 is assigned to location 5 and index2 is set to 3. The value of 4 is set to location 4 and index2 is set to 2. The value of 3 is set to 3 and index2 is set to 1. The value of 2 is set to location 3 and then the inner loop terminates. Then the value of 1 is put at index 1. The final sorted array is 1, 2, 3, 4, 5.

4.7 Hard problems

A problem is considered to be a "hard" problem not because it is difficult to design or to understand the algorithm but because the algorithm produces a computationally intractable solution. An algorithm is considered to be computationally intractable if its complexity is slower than all polynomial solutions. Examples of intractable complexity would be algorithms of $O(2^n)$ or $O(n!)$. The computation time or memory requirements for such an algorithm rapidly consumes all available resources for even modest sized problems.

We outline two hard problems, both believed to be intractable.

4.7.1 Traveling salesperson problem

This classic problem, considered to be intractable, is stated as follows:
Given: A collection of n cities and a distance matrix that specifies the positive dis-

tance between every pair of cities. A salesperson must choose a tour that starts at city 1, visits the other cities exactly once, and then returns from the last city visited to city 1. The problem is to determine the tour that minimizes the total distance traveled.

Using a "brute-force" solution, one can simply enumerate all possible tours, compute the distance of each tour, and choose the tour with the smallest distance. This is a correct algorithm. How many tours would have to be enumerated if there are n cities? There are $(n-1)!$ (i.e., $n(n-1)(n-2)\ldots 2 \times 1$) permutations of the cities not including city 1. So, for a 50-city problem there would be 49! different tours. Do you know how large the number 49! is? It is larger than the estimated number of molecules in the universe! The fastest computer on earth would take millions of years to perform such a computation.

We can do better than $O(n!)$. But not too much better. Using a method of algorithm design discovered in the 1960s and called dynamic programming, we can design an algorithm that solves the traveling salesperson problem in time $O(n2^n)$. This algorithm is beyond the scope of this book.

In the last chapter of the book *Software Development Using Eiffel: There Can Be Life Other Than C++* [1], an approximate or heuristic solution to this problem is presented that generally produces solutions that are within 1 percent of optimum in a tractable manner.

4.7.2 Knapsack problem

Another classic problem, also considered to be intractable, is the knapsack problem. This problem is stated as follows: *A set of n objects are given each with a specified weight and value (profit). That is, object i has a known p_i and w_i (profit and weight). Suppose we wish to load the objects into a knapsack that has a specified weight limit, W. Further assume that the summation of all the weights exceeds this weight limit. The problem is to choose a subset of the objects that satisfies the weight constraint and maximizes the profit (the total value of the objects contained in the knapsack).*

The knapsack problem involves making a yes/no choice regarding each potential object that may be put into the knapsack. If there are n objects, there are 2^n different combinations of objects that can be put into the knapsack. A brute-force algorithm that simply enumerates all these possible combinations of object insertions would be of $O(2^n)$. This solution is of course intractable.

You may be thinking that certainly over the years creative computer scientists would have come up with a better solution than the brute-force solution. Unfortunately, this problem, like the traveling salesperson problem, does not have a known polynomial complexity solution. Even more frustrating, no one has been able to prove that such a polynomial solution is impossible. At this time we just do not know!

4.8 Concluding remarks

Hopefully you can now appreciate the excitement, challenge, and yes, mystery of algorithm design. We have seen in the sum of subvector problem and the sorting problem the dramatic and significant benefits that are possible through human intellect. In these two problems a clever algorithm reduces the computational effort by orders of magnitude for a large sized problem compared with a "brute-force" approach. We have also seen that there exist problems for which no efficient solutions are known. In such cases we typically must use approximation techniques that provide solutions close to optimal in an efficient manner.

Algorithms form the computational fabric of software systems. In combination with the data structures that are typically used to support them, algorithms and data structures, as Niklaus Wirth indicated on the cover of his famous book, equal programs.

4.9 Summary

- An **algorithm** is a formal sequence of instructions for performing a computation.

- The study of algorithms helps to justify the "science" in "computer science."

- Algorithm design is concerned with correctness and efficiency. Correctness is concerned with establishing that the algorithm works for all instances of a problem.

- The efficiency of an algorithm is related to the speed with which it performs its work and the memory that is required to do this work.

- A problem has many instances, usually an infinite number of instances.

- It is often the case that a computation must be done in conjunction with a supporting data structure. The design of algorithms is closely related to the design of information structures or data structures.

- Various measures have been devised to indicate the computational efficiency of an algorithm. These include worst-case asymptotic complexity and average-case asymptotic complexity.

- By asymptotic complexity is meant the growth in computation time as a function of the growth in problem size as the problem size approaches infinity.

- The "big O" notation is often used to express the asymptotic complexity of an algorithm.

- A problem is considered to be a "hard" problem not because it is difficult to design or understand the algorithm but because the algorithm produces a computationally intractable solution. An algorithm is considered to be computationally intractable if its complexity is slower than all polynomial solutions.

- Examples of intractable complexity would be algorithms of $O(2^n)$ or $O(n!)$. The computation time or memory requirements for such an algorithm rapidly consume all available resources for even modest sized problems.

4.10 Exercises

16. Describe three problems and for each problem state three instances.

17. Write an algorithm for converting a given month and day to the day number in a year. Please take leap years into account. Express your algorithm as an Eiffel routine.

18. Write an algorithm for displaying all the prime numbers that exist in the range from 1 to 10,000. A prime number is a whole number that is not divisible by any smaller whole number except 1. Express your algorithm as an Eiffel routine.

19. Write an algorithm for computing the average of a set of numbers in an array. Express your algorithm as an Eiffel routine.

20. Write an algorithm for computing the median of a set of numbers in an array. Express your algorithm as an Eiffel routine.

21. Write an algorithm for computing the kth largest value in a set of numbers in an array. Assume that the array contains n numbers where $n > k$. Express your algorithm as an Eiffel routine.

22. Write an Eiffel routine for computing the roots of the quadratic equation, $ax^2 + bx + c$, where a, b, and c are real numbers. Express your algorithm as an Eiffel routine.

23. Given a string of characters, *a_string* and another string *search_string*. Write an algorithm that determines whether one or more occurrences of the *search_string* is contained within *a_string*. Express your algorithm as an Eiffel routine that returns TRUE if the *search_string* is found within *a_string* and FALSE otherwise.

24. Write an algorithm that approximates the square root of a number. Hint: You wish to approximate the solution to the equation, $x^2 - n = 0$, where n is the number whose square root you desire. Use the Newton iterative approximation technique that involves moving down a line tangent to the quadratic curve.

25. Using semi-log paper, verify that the data given in Table 4.4 (the sort times associated with gap-sort) grow according to $n \log n$.

26. Can the reader explain why it is essential to assign *interchanged* to TRUE in the bubble-sort algorithm? What would happen if this statement were omitted?

27. Verify that the clever $O(n)$ sum of subvectors algorithm is correct.

28. Change the *shrink_factor* in gap-sort and observe the effect it has on sorting time.

4.11 References

1. *Software Development Using Eiffel: There Can Be Life Other Than C++*, R. S. Wiener, Prentice Hall, Englewood Cliffs, NJ, 1995.

month - 1
2
3
4
5
6
7
8
9
10
11
12

Find the month
sum the days in proceding months
add value of date

If year # 4 = 0
then month ~~register~~ (3) = 29
Else

Chapter

5

Building Some
Simple Eiffel Systems

In this chapter some relatively simple, but complete, Eiffel software components and systems are constructed. This is in contrast to the two previous chapters in which the examples were designed to illustrate some Eiffel language feature or represent an algorithm. Typically in these previous chapters only small segments of total systems were discussed.

After completing this chapter the reader should feel much more comfortable with the notion of a complete Eiffel software system and its software components.

5.1 Dice

Dice, six-sided cubes with each face containing a pattern of black dots that represent a distinct integer from 1 to 6, are an important ingredient in many games of chance. If we wish to build software systems that simulate games of chance, dice may be an important reusable software component. In this section we construct a DIE class (a pair of dice contain two DIE objects). Later in the chapter we use the dice in a game of chance.

We will ignore the interesting and challenging issue of creating a fancy display of our dice. We do not wish to get involved in discussions of graphic subsystems in this book especially since they are machine and operating system dependent. Instead we will focus on the computational aspects of the problem.

For each die comprising the dice we must compute a random integer from 1 to 6. Each of the six possible outcomes must be equally likely in order for us to be able to call the dice "fair." We will be content for our present purposes in requiring only the computation of this "random" integer from 1 to 6 for each die. Therefore, the "behavior" of each die will be characterized by the creation routine *initialize*, that "warms up" a random number generator, the command *throw* that generates a new random outcome and a query *value* that returns a random integer from 1 to 6.

5.1.1 Random number generators

Computer scientists employ random numbers to simulate uncertainty in "real-world" systems. These random numbers are generated algebraically and therefore in principle can be predicted in advance. For this reason the numbers are often referred to as "pseudo-random." The sequence of numbers produced from a typical random number generator display statistical characteristics that are similar to a sequence of numbers that are really produced in a random manner (e.g., such as the sequence of actual values produced from a real physical die). Various mathematical algorithms have been studied and tested for producing pseudo-random numbers.

Typically a "seed" value (the first number in the sequence) is selected either by the user or the program. This seed value is used to generate the next number in the sequence according to an algebraic relationship. Each succeeding number in the sequence is generated from the previous number. The choice of the initial seed number is quite important. If different sequences of random numbers are desired for successive experiments (runs of a simulation program), the initial seed is usually derived from the current clock time on the computer system's clock. This assures a different sequence of random values for each separate run of the program. If the programmer wishes to use the same sequence of random values in repeated experiments then the same initial seed must be used each time.

The mathematical properties of random number generators will not be discussed in this book. The interested reader may wish to consult the excellent book, *System Simulation* by Geoffrey Gordon [1] or any other book that deals with computer simulation theory for a detailed discussion of random number generators.

A good random number generator in addition to possessing good statistical characteristics should have a long cycle length. This means that the pattern of numbers should not repeat itself for a long period. This enables a huge set of numbers to be used without concern that the same numbers are being reused.

In the spirit of first learning to effectively reuse standard components without necessarily understanding all of their details, an effective random number generator designed by the author is presented in Appendix 3. Class, RANDOM_NUMBER uses several external "C" language routines to support its work. It is not appropriate here to attempt an explanation of this Eiffel capability or to explain the implementation details of class RANDOM_NUMBER. The goal is to provide the reader with an effective reusable software component. The interface to class RANDOM_NUMBER appears in Listing 5.1.

Listing 5.1 Interface to class RANDOM_NUMBER

```
class interface RANDOM_NUMBER

creation
        initialize

feature -- public
        initialize -- Chooses random seed and "warms up" generator
        next -- Command to advance random number to next value

        next_value : REAL -- query returning uniformly distributed
                                random real between 0.0 and 1.0

        value_between (low: INTEGER; high: INTEGER): INTEGER
        -- query returning uniformly distributed random integer between low and high

end -- class RANDOM_NUMBER
```

A recent release of the ISE Eiffel libraries includes a class RANDOM. Readers who have access to this ISE library may wish to use this class instead of the one presented in Appendix 3.

5.1.2 Implementation of die class

The principal method of the die class is to compute a random integer between 1 and 6. Although this could be accomplished directly using the RANDOM_NUMBER class presented in section 5.1.1, it is better to hide the low-level details of this RANDOM_NUMBER class and present only the simple abstraction of a die in the new class DIE.

Class DIE is a client of class RANDOM_NUMBER (i.e., it uses some of the resources of class RANDOM_NUMBER). This layering of abstractions provides a simple interface to any clients of class DIE (users who wish to construct a die in their application software). It enforces the data abstraction that the only thing you can "do" to a die is throw it and obtain its value, a uniformly distributed random integer from 1 to 6.

Listing 5.2 shows the implementation details of class DIE.

Listing 5.2 Class DIE

```
class DIE

creation
    initialize

feature {NONE} -- Protected section

    r: RANDOM_NUMBER

feature

    initialize is
        do
            !! r.initialize
        end

    throw is
    -- Advance die to next value
        do
            r.next
        end

    value: INTEGER is
        do
            Result := r.value_between (1, 6)
        end

end -- class DIE
```

There are two feature sections in class DIE. The first section has an export clause, { NONE } following the key word *feature*. This implies that no client classes can read the data or invoke the methods contained within this section. The data and methods contained in this section are for internal use only. The second feature section is the normal public section that provides read-only access to any data and the ability to invoke any of the methods from a client class.

The user (client) of class DIE is completely insulated from class RANDOM_NUMBER since attribute *r* is in the protected section of the class and is for internal use only.

The method *initialize* causes the hidden attribute *r* to be initialized and warmed up. The command throw and query function value are defined in the public section.

Before constructing any applications that use dice, it is useful to test the die. In this test program, a pair of dice are "thrown" (simulated) 10,000 times. Statistics are kept regarding the number of outcomes of 2, 3, 4, 5, 6, 7, 8, 9, 10, 11, and 12.

On the average the numbers 2 and 12 should occur roughly 1/ 36 x 10,000 or 278 times. The numbers 3 and 11 should occur roughly 2 / 36 of the time or 556 times. The numbers 4 and 10 should occur 3/ 36 of the time or 833 times. The numbers 5 and 9 should occur 4/ 36 of the time or 1111 times. The numbers 6 and 8 should occur 5 / 36 of the time or 1389 times. Finally, the number 7, the most likely outcome, should occur 6 / 36 of the time or 1667 times.

Listing 5.3 shows a test program that simulates the throw of 10,000 dice.

Listing 5.3 Test program for dice

```
class TEST_DICE

creation
    start

feature
    Number_experiments: INTEGER is 10000
    -- Constant attribute explained in the next section

    start is
        local
            die1, die2: DIE
            dice: INTEGER
            index: INTEGER
            results: ARRAY [INTEGER]
        do
            !! die1.initialize
            !! die2.initialize
            !! results.make (2, 12)
            from
```

```
          index := 0
      until
          index = number_experiments
      loop
          index := index + 1
          die1.throw
          die2.throw
          dice := die1.value + die2.value
          results.put (results.item (dice) + 1, dice)
      end
      display_results (results)
  end

  display_results (results: ARRAY [INTEGER]) is
      local
          index: INTEGER
      do
          io.new_line
          from
              index := 1
          until
              index = 12
          loop
              index := index + 1
              io.putint (index)
              io.putstring (": ")
              io.putint (results.item (index))
              io.new_line
          end
      end

end -- class TEST_DICE
```

The output of the program is compared to predicted results below.

Outcome	Theoretical	Actual
2	278	243
3	556	583
4	883	812
5	1111	1162

6	1389	1378
7	1667	1691
8	1389	1373
9	1111	1079
10	883	835
11	556	561
12	278	283

The actual results are fairly close to the theoretical predictions.

5.2 Constant attributes

Listing 5.3 introduces a feature of Eiffel not previously encountered, the constant attribute. The attribute, *number_experiments*, is declared:

Number_experiments: INTEGER is 10000

Constant attributes such as this one are useful in parameterizing a class with respect to certain features. If one wishes to change the number of experiments, only one value needs to be changed (10000).

Other attribute types that may be assigned constant values are REAL, BOOLEAN, CHARACTER, and STRING. The following code segment illustrates some typical cases:

my_string	*: STRING is "This is my favorite string"*
my_real	*: REAL is 1.34*
my_bool	*: BOOLEAN is FALSE*
my_char	*: CHAR is 'A'*

5.3 A horse race using unusual dice

The statistician Bradley Efrom from Stanford University created an unusual and most interesting set of four dice. Instead of labeling each of the six faces with either 1, 2, 3, 4, 5, or 6 dots (representing the integers 1 to 6) as with the ordinary dice discussed in section 5.1, he instead allowed arbitrary integers to be assigned to each face of the cube. Furthermore he imposed no restriction that each face contain a unique integer. This allows the possibility of one or more repeated integers on a given die. Using these rules, Efrom produced a specific set of four dice. Their configurations are displayed later.

Suppose we label the Efrom die 1, 2, 3, and 4. A human player is to play against the computer. Each will choose one of the four Efrom die. The two die chosen will be used to drive a horse in a horse race simulation.

The game is played as follows:

Choice of die: The human player gets to choose first (to provide every advantage possible). She selects any one of the four Efrom die after carefully inspecting and evaluating each of them. The computer then chooses one of the remaining three Efrom die.

Horse race: The human player throws her die (the computer will help in this regard by accurately simulating the throw of the player's die). Next, the computer will accurately simulate the throw of its die. If the player's die has a higher value than the computer's die, her horse advances one unit toward the finish line; otherwise the computer's horse advances one unit toward the finish line. This pattern is repeated until either the player's horse or the computer's horse reaches the finish line which is 100 units away from the starting line. The computer then displays the two scores and announces the winner of the game.

Clearly the human player will attempt to choose the strongest of the four Efrom die. In this context "strongest" means the die with the highest probability of returning a high score. Each of the four Efrom die are assumed to be balanced ("fair") with each of its 6 sides having an equal probability of occurring. Only the distribution of integer values on each die determines the "strength" of the die. We allow the human player the advantage of making the first choice with the computer making a choice among the three remaining die.

The four Efrom die are shown below.

Die 1:   4, 4, 4, 4, 0, 0

Die 2:   3, 3, 3, 3, 3, 3

Die 3:   6, 6, 2, 2, 2, 2

Die 4:   5, 5, 5, 1, 1, 1

Our goal is to write an Eiffel software system that allows the horse race game to be simulated. The game must interact with a user and allow the user to make the first choice of either die 1, 2, 3, or 4. The computer will then display its choice of die on the screen. The horse race will then proceed according to the rules given above.

The computer program must construct each of the Efrom die so that a statistically accurate and fair "throw" of the die can be simulated. The program must also control the flow of events and display the final scores and the winner at the end of the race.

One of the algorithmic challenges in constructing this software system is defining the logic (algorithm) that allows the computer to choose one of the 3 remaining Efrom die after the human player has made his or her choice. The computer also wishes to "win" the race and therefore wishes to make an intelligent choice of die.

After we construct this horse race simulation, we will document the output of several games between the author and his computer. The reader might wish to speculate how he or she would play this game. Which of the four Efrom die would you choose? What fraction of the time would you expect to "win" the race? These are interesting questions that you should ponder as we proceed with the construction of the software system.

5.3.1 Analysis and design of horse race game

From the game description the key domain objects are the four Efrom die, whose classes are DIE1, DIE2, DIE3, and DIE4. In addition there is the HORSE_RACE class that starts and controls the overall system.

Should each of the Efrom die classes, DIE1, DIE2, DIE3, and DIE4, be modeled as separate classes or are they subclasses of a common ancestor class? Both are legitimate possibilities and there is no absolute right and wrong in these matters.

An ancestor class EFROM_DIE is constructed. Its only attribute is *ordinary_die* of type DIE. The only effective routine in this class is the routine, *make*. This class is an abstract class. No instances of type EFROM_DIE can actually be created; only subclass instances can be created. The key word *deferred* in front of the class name causes the compiler to prohibit instances from being created. The query *value* has a deferred implementation. Effective implementations of this routine are provided in each subclass. In the next chapter, abstract classes are discussed in more detail.

The source listing for class EFROM_DIE is given in Listing 5.4.

Listing 5.4 Class EFROM_DIE

```
deferred class EFROM_DIE

feature {NONE} -- Protected section

    ordinary_die: DIE
```

```
feature
    throw is
            -- Command to obtain a new value for die
        do
            ordinary_die.throw
        end

    value: INTEGER is
            -- Outcome of a throw
        deferred
        end

    make is
        do
            !! ordinary_die.initialize
        end

end -- class EFROM_DIE
```

Since the attribute *ordinary_die* is in the protected section, clients have no knowledge that an EFROM_DIE is composed of an ordinary die.

Each of the four specialized types of EFROM_DIE are constructed as subclasses of EFROM_DIE (they satisfy the "is a kind of" EFROM_DIE relationship).

The Booch diagram in Figure 5.1 shows the relationships among the classes.

These four classes are presented in Listing 5.5.

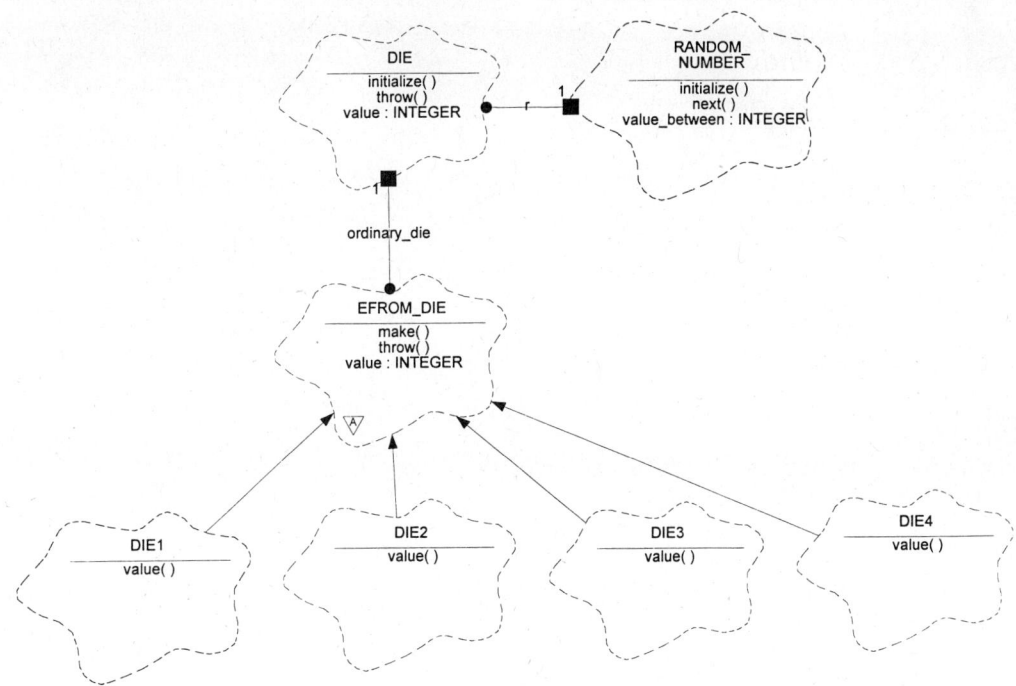

Figure 5.1 Key Classes in Horse Race Game

Listing 5.5 Four specialized EFROM die classes

```
class DIE1

inherit
    EFROM_DIE

creation
    make

feature

    value: INTEGER is
        local
            a_value: INTEGER
        do
            a_value := ordinary_die.value
            if a_value <= 4 then
                Result := 4
            else
```

```
                    Result := 0
                end
            end

end -- class DIE1


class DIE2

inherit
    EFROM_DIE

creation
    make

feature

    value: INTEGER is
        do
            Result := 3
        end

end -- class DIE2


class DIE3

inherit
    EFROM_DIE

creation
    make

feature

    value: INTEGER is
        local
            a_value: INTEGER
        do
            a_value := ordinary_die.value
            if a_value <= 4 then
                Result := 2
            else
                Result := 6
            end
        end

end -- class DIE3
```

```
class DIE4

inherit
    EFROM_DIE

creation
    make

feature

    value: INTEGER is
        local
            a_value: INTEGER
        do
            a_value := ordinary_die.value
            if a_value <= 3 then
                Result := 5
            else
                Result := 1
            end
        end

end -- class DIE4
```

In Chapter 6 the details of Eiffel class construction and the inheritance mechanism are presented. But for now it is important to mention that when a routine from an ancestor class (e.g., query *value* from class EFROM_DIE) is made effective in a descendant class (e.g., classes DIE1, DIE2, DIE3, and DIE4), the run-time system will bind to the correct version of *value* based on the type of object receiving the *value* message. This **late-binding** capability of Eiffel and all object-oriented languages is a fundamental part of object-oriented programming. It is the subject of Chapter 9.

Now we are ready to examine the HORSE_RACE class that starts and controls the application. The late-binding nature of the design will be evident in the implementation of this class.

Listing 5.6 presents the details of this class.

Listing 5.6 Class HORSE_RACE

```
class HORSE_RACE

creation
    start

feature
```

```
d1:                 DIE1
d2:                 DIE2
d3:                 DIE3
d4:                 DIE4

players_horse:      INTEGER
computers_horse:    INTEGER
players_die:        EFROM_DIE
computers_die:      EFROM_DIE
player_score:       INTEGER
computer_score:     INTEGER
player_throw:       INTEGER
computer_throw:     INTEGER

start is
    do
        display_die
        io.putstring ("Enter your choice of horse (1, 2, 3 or 4): ")
        io.readint
        if io.lastint = 1 or io.lastint = 2 or io.lastint = 3 or io.lastint = 4 then
            choose_horses (io.lastint)
            play_game
        end
    end

display_die is
    do
        io.new_line
        io.new_line
        io.putstring ("Die 1: 4, 4, 4, 4, 0, 0")
        io.new_line
        io.putstring ("Die 2: 3, 3, 3, 3, 3, 3")
        io.new_line
        io.putstring ("Die 3: 6, 6, 2, 2, 2, 2")
        io.new_line
        io.putstring ("Die 4: 5, 5, 5, 1, 1, 1")
        io.new_line
        io.new_line
    end

choose_horses (player_horse: INTEGER) is
    require
        legal_horse: player_horse >= 1 and player_horse <= 4
```

```
        do
            if player_horse = 4 then
                !! d4.make
                players_die := d4
                computers_horse := 3
                !! d3.make
                computers_die := d3
            elseif player_horse = 3 then
                !! d3.make
                players_die := d3
                computers_horse := 2
                !! d2.make
                computers_die := d2
            elseif player_horse = 2 then
                !! d2.make
                players_die := d2
                computers_horse := 1
                !! d1.make
                computers_die := d1
            else
                !! d1.make
                players_die := d1
                computers_horse := 4
                !! d4.make
                computers_die := d4
            end
        end

    play_game is
        do
            io.new_line
            io.putstring ("Computer chooses horse ")
            io.putint (computers_horse)
            io.new_line
            from
            until
                player_score = 100 or computer_score = 100
            loop
                players_die.throw
                player_throw := players_die.value
                computers_die.throw
```

```
        computer_throw := computers_die.value
        if player_throw > computer_throw then
            player_score := player_score + 1
        else
            computer_score := computer_score + 1
        end
    end
    io.putstring ("Final scores: Player: ")
    io.putint (player_score)
    io.putstring (" Computer: ")
    io.putint (computer_score)
    io.new_line
    if player_score > computer_score then
        io.putstring ("The player is the winner")
    else
        io.putstring ("The computer is the winner")
    end
    io.new_line
end
```

end -- class *HORSE_RACE*

The various objects that comprise the horse race domain are listed as attributes in the application class HORSE_RACE. These include *d1, d2, d3, d4* (of types DIE1, DIE2, DIE3, and DIE4), *players_horse* and *computers_horse* (of type INTEGER), *players_die* and *computers_die* (of type EFROM_DIE), and other integer types.

In the *start* routine the first task is to display the four die for the user. This task is carried out by the routine *display_die*. The user is then prompted to enter his or her horse (by number). The routine *choose_horses* is invoked with the player's horse number serving as input.

The *require* clause is a **precondition**. This logical assertion indicates the responsibility of all clients, namely to make sure that the value of the input number (*player_horse*) is between 1 and 4. If the client fails to do this, an exception in the client's routine will be raised. If the client's routine does not handle this exception, the program will be halted with an error message indicating that the *legal_horse* assertion was violated. In Chapter 6, the details of assertion and exception handling are presented.

Let us now closely examine the algorithm (logic) that the *choose_horses* routine uses to assign the computer's die (horse) after the player has made his or her choice. You may be surprised!

If the player has chosen horse 4, the object *d4* is initialized. The object *players_die* is assigned to this initialized object. That is the easy part. If one inspects the four Efrom die carefully, it should be evident that die 3 has a 2:1 chance to score higher than die 4. This is because 24 of the 36 possible outcomes favor die 3. The two 6's of die 3 beat all six numbers of die 4 (12 favorable outcomes for die 3) and the four 2's of die 3 beat the three 1's of die 4 (12 more favorable outcomes for die 3). Therefore 24 of the 36 possible outcomes favor die 3. Die 3 is twice as strong as 4. The object *d3* is therefore initialized and the *computers_die* object is assigned to this initialized object.

If the player has chosen horse 3, the object *d3* is initialized and *players_die* is assigned to this object. The computer chooses horse 2 and die *d2* (which is initialized and assigned to the object *players_die*). A careful inspection of the four die reveals that 24 of the 36 possible outcomes favor die 2 over 3 (the six 3's of die 2 beat the four 2's of die 3 for 24 favorable outcomes). Die 2 is twice as strong as die 3.

If the player has chosen horse 2, the object *d2* is initialized and *players_die* is assigned to this object. The computer chooses horse 1 and die *d1*. Die 1 is twice as strong as die 2 since the four 4's of die 1 beat the six 3's of die 2 (24 favorable outcomes).

So far it does not look too good for the player if he or she has chosen die 2, 3, or 4. The computer is able to choose a die that is twice as strong. In a game involving 100 points the computer is almost sure to win.

But alas, the player can always choose die 1, clearly the best of the four die. After all, we have shown that die 1 is better than die 2 (by 2:1), die 2 is better than die 3 (by 2:1), and die 3 is better than die 4 (by 2:1). Using the principle of transitivity, it would certainly follow that die 1 must be the best of the four die.

So what happens if the player choose die 1? The computer can still choose a die that beats die 1 by a 2:1 margin! This in fact is the whole point of these Efrom dice. They are non-transitive. They violate the most basic and deeply ingrained intuitive notion—that of transitivity (if $a > b$ and $b > c$ and $c > d$ then $a > d$).

If the player chooses die 1, the computer chooses die 4. An inspection of these two die reveals that die 4 beats die 1 by a 2:1 margin. Die 4's three 5's beat the six values of die 1 (18 favorable outcomes) and in addition die 4's three 1's beat die 1's two 0's (for 6 more favorable outcomes) for a total of 24 favorable outcomes of die 4 against die 1.

So using the ring logic shown, the computer can pretty much lock up the game and win almost all of the time.

The output of a typical game confirms this point. This output is the following:

Die 1: 4, 4, 4, 4, 0, 0
Die 2: 3, 3, 3, 3, 3, 3
Die 3: 6, 6, 2, 2, 2, 2
Die 4: 5, 5, 5, 1, 1, 1

Enter your choice of horse (1, 2, 3 or 4): 1

Computer chooses horse 4

Final scores: Player: 60 Computer: 100
The computer is the winner

Let us continue our examination of Listing 5.6. When one is learning software development, the means are sometimes more important than the ends!

What makes it legal for statements such as *computer_die := d1*, or *computers_die := d2*, or *computers_die := d3*, or *computers_die := d4* as given in routine *choose_horses*? The **principle of conformance** provides the answer. This principle states that an object of some class on the left side of an assignment (target of the assignment) can be assigned to a descendant type of the target. A class can be its own descendant. The type of *computers_die* is EFROM_DIE. The type DIE1, DIE2, DIE3, and DIE4 are all descendants of type EFROM_DIE.

In routine *play_game* the player's die is evaluated using the expression, *player_throw := players_die.value*. At compile time there is no way to bind the message *value* to one of the four effective *value* methods. The principle of **late-binding polymorphism** (literally to change shapes) states that the system performs its binding based on the *actual type* of the object *players_die, not the formal type*. If binding were to the formal type, then the *value* method of class DIE would always be used and the four specialized types of die would become irrelevant.

Stated another way, each of the four specialized types of EFROM_DIE objects are allowed to define the behavior associated with computing a value. The system uses the correct computational scheme at run time and bases its decision on the actual type of object that is asked to return its value.

The remaining code of Listing 5.6 is straightforward and requires no further comments.

5.3.2 A four-way race

What if we declare a four-way race between the four Efrom dice? Which horse would you put your money on? This is left as an exercise for you.

5.4 Summary

In this chapter several small but complete Eiffel software systems were constructed. Some inheritance and late-binding were used in some of the examples providing the reader with a preview of these important language capabilities. Some limited use of preconditions was also employed providing an additional preview of this important language feature.

One of the examples, the non-transitive Efrom die, demonstrates the subtlety of understanding and modeling the problem domain.

5.5 Exercises

1. What would be the outcome of a four-way race using the Efrom dice? Why? Confirm your answer by performing a simulation of such a race. Show your Eiffel code.

5.6 References

1. Gordon, Geoffrey, *System Simulation*, Prentice Hall, Englewood Cliffs, NJ, 1969.

Chapter 6

The Construction of Eiffel Classes

The class is the basic logical and physical unit of software construction in Eiffel. As a logical unit, a class represents an abstract data type—a unification of an underlying data model with a set of operations (routines) that manipulate this data model. As a physical unit a class is a module—a file with suffix ".e". An Eiffel compiler with its static type checking mechanism and rules for "conformance" (to be explored in this chapter) is able to enforce the correct usage of objects by examining the definitions for attributes and routines specified in the various classes that define a software system.

This chapter focuses on some of the technical details and issues associated with the most important elements of class construction in Eiffel. Because of the introductory nature of this book, some aspects of Eiffel classes are not discussed at all and no attempt is made to provide a totally rigorous explanation of the features that are discussed. The reader is encouraged to read a reference manual such as *Eiffel: The Language* or *Software Development Using Eiffel: There Can Be Life Other Than C++* for more details.

6.1   An overview of the components of an Eiffel class

The major components of an Eiffel class are displayed in Figure 6.1. Some of the components have already been used in previous chapters while others will be introduced in this chapter. Not all of the components of an Eiffel class will be discussed because their application lies outside the scope of this book. In later chapters if other class components are needed, they will be defined in the appropriate context.

```
class SOME_DESCRIPTIVE_NAME

    inherit
        rename -- optional subclause
            -- List of inherited routines and their new names
        export -- optional subclause
            -- Used to control the scope of one or more inherited routines
        undefine -- optional subclause
            -- Will not be discussed in this book
        redefine -- optional subclause
            -- List of inherited routines to be redefined
        select -- optional subclause
            -- Used with multiple inheritance in conjunction with rename
    end
    creation { export scope }
        -- List of routines that can create and initialize objects of this class

    feature { export scope }
        an_attribute : SOME_TYPE
        -- Other attributes in feature section
        a_routine (a_possible_parameter_list) [ : a_possible_return_type ] is
        require
            -- Preconditions
        local
            -- Temporary objects
        do
            -- Algorithmic details of routine
        ensure
            -- Postconditions
        end

        -- Other routines in feature section

    invariant
        -- class invariants

end
```

Figure 6.1 Some Major Components of an Eiffel Class

6.2 Creation

"Let there be light." Creation routines provide a mechanism to dynamically allocate storage for new objects and initialize the attributes of the new objects at the time they are created. It must be recalled that an Eiffel object is not created by virtue of its declaration (a default value of VOID is assigned to an object before it is created). An Eiffel object must be created before it can be used for any practical purpose.

Creation routines may also be used as ordinary routines typically to update the values of attributes for an existing object. Only if the creation operator, "!!", is used in front of a creation routine will a new object be brought to life.

If a class does not include any creation routines, instances can be created merely by using the creation operator in front of the name of an object. In such a case the attributes contained within the object assume their default values.

Creation clauses may contain an export section bounded by curly braces, "{" and "}". Objects of the given class may be created only in the classes and their descendants specified in the export section, if present. If no export section is present, a default export section of ANY is implied. Since all Eiffel classes are descendants of ANY, the absence of an explicit export section implies that objects of the given class may be created from within any other class (i.e., universal export).

Listing 6.1 demonstrates the use of a creation routine that can be used for object creation but not as an ordinary routine. It would not be desirable to allow this creation routine to be used as an ordinary "mutator" (a routine that can change the internal state of an object once it exists) because this would violate the protocol that an account balance can be modified only through deposit or withdrawal. We do not want to allow a client to set the balance on an existing account once it is created.

By making the export scope of the creation routine universal (by the absence of an export scope) and then placing the creation routine in a protected section (a feature section with export scope {NONE}), objects may be created anywhere but not modified using the creation routine.

Listing 6.1 Creation routine that cannot be used as an ordinary routine

```
class ACCOUNT

creation
    open
```

```
feature

    balance: REAL

    deposit (amount: REAL) is
        do
            balance := balance + amount
        end

    withdraw (amount: REAL) is
        do
            balance := balance - amount
        end

feature {NONE} -- For internal use only

    open (initial_deposit: REAL) is
            -- Can be used only to create an account
        do
            balance := initial_deposit
        end

end -- class ACCOUNT
```

6.2.1 Subclass creation

A subclass often contains more attributes than its parent. The creation routine of the parent class can often be invoked to assist in the implementation of the creation routine of the subclass. This is illustrated in the next example.

A class JET is defined as a subclass of AIRPLANE. It inherits the attributes *wingspan*, *weight*, and *cost* from AIRPLANE and in addition has the attribute *thrust*. As evident in Listing 6.2, the creation routine *build* in JET uses the *make* routine of AIRPLANE. It is important to emphasize that *make* is invoked as an ordinary routine inside of *build*. An AIRPLANE object is not being created by *build*; a JET object is.

Listing 6.2 Classes AIRPLANE and JET

```
class AIRPLANE

creation
    make

feature
```

```
    wingspan: REAL

    weight: REAL

    cost: REAL

    make (wing_size: REAL; the_weight: REAL; the_cost: REAL) is
        do
            wingspan := wing_size
            weight := the_weight
            cost := the_cost
        end

    -- Other features not shown

end -- class AIRPLANE


class JET

inherit
    AIRPLANE

creation
    build

feature

    thrust: REAL

    build (wing_size: REAL; the_weight: REAL; the_cost: REAL; the_thrust: REAL) is
        do
            make (wing_size, the_weight, the_cost)
            thrust := the_thrust
        end

    -- Other features not shown

end -- class JET
```

6.2.2 More advanced subclass creation

A descendant of a given class can be created by enclosing the name of the descendant class between each "!" operator. This is illustrated in Listing 6.3. Here a subclass CHECKING of ACCOUNT is introduced. Its creation routine, *open*, is inherited from its parent class ACCOUNT. An object *my_checking_account* is produced by using the expression, *!CHECKING!my_checking_account.open (500.0)*.

It is essential to declare *open* in the *creation* clause of class CHECK-ING. Its status as a *creation* routine in class ACCOUNT does not automatically make it a creation routine in the descendant class CHECKING. This must be accomplished explicitly.

Listing 6.3 Creating subclass objects

```
class CHECKING

inherit
        ACCOUNT -- See Listing 6.1 for definition of class ACCOUNT

creation
        open -- This routine is inherited from class ACCOUNT

feature
        monthly_fee: REAL

        set_monthly_fee (amount: REAL) is
            do
                monthly_fee := amount
            end

        apply_fee is
            do
                balance := balance - monthly_fee
            end

end -- class CHECKING


class APPLICATION

creation
        start

feature
        start is
            local
                my_checking_account: ACCOUNT
                my_account: ACCOUNT
            do
                !CHECKING! my_checking_account.open (500.0)
                my_checking_account.deposit (300.0)
                my_checking_account.withdraw (100.0)
```

```
        io.putstring ("Balance in checking = ")
        io.putreal (my_checking_account.balance)
        io.new_line
        !! my_account.open (200.0)
        my_account.deposit (50.0)
        my_account.withdraw (10.0)
        io.putstring ("Balance in account = ")
        io.putreal (my_account.balance)
        io.new_line
    end

end -- class APPLICATION
```

In class APPLICATION in Listing 6.3, one would normally not declare *my_checking_account* to be of type ACCOUNT when its intended use is that of type CHECKING. This was done in Listing 6.3 purely for tutorial reasons. It is noted that the effect produced is identical to the following statements:

```
check        : CHECKING
my_checking  : ACCOUNT

!!check.open (500.0)
my_checking := check
```

If a class has one or more creation routines, it is illegal to create a new object using just the creation operator, "!!", followed by the object name. One of the creation routines must be used. So, for example, it would be illegal to write *!!my_account*, if *my_account* were declared to be of type ACCOUNT.

6.3   Inheritance

(Conversation overheard between a three-year-old and her friend while pointing to her grandmother: "That's my ancestor Mary.")

Inheritance is an architectural property of object-oriented systems used for establishing a decomposition of a software system into classes and subclasses. Inheritance also provides the basis for software reuse. The accepted practice is for classes at the top of a hierarchy to encapsulate general properties of some domain and for classes lower in the hierarchy to extend and to encapsulate more specialized properties of the domain. As one moves down a class hierarchy, the "is-a" or "is a kind of" relationship should hold between child class and parent class. Attributes and methods defined in a parent class should make sense in all descendant classes.

In going from a parent class to its child, **specialization** involves redefining one or more of the parent's routines or attributes, **extension** involves adding routines or attributes not present in the parent, and **restriction** involves blocking one or more routines of the parent. All three may be used simultaneously, but it is most common to use only specialization and extension in going down a class hierarchy.

If only extension is involved in going from a class to its child, the child is considered to be a **subtype** of its parent. Its behavior can be characterized by the sum of the parent's behavior and the additional behavior given by the routines and attributes present only in the child.

6.3.1 Extension—subtypes

An example of extension may be found in classes ACCOUNT and CHECKING, given in Listings 6.1 and 6.3. Class CHECKING is a subtype or pure extension of class ACCOUNT. The behavior of CHECKING objects includes the behavior of ACCOUNT objects as a proper subset. For example, the operations that can be performed on CHECKING objects include the following subset inherited from class ACCOUNT: *open* (for class creation only), *balance* (a read-only attribute), *deposit* (for adding funds to an account), *withdraw* (for subtracting funds from an account). The following additional behavior is associated with CHECKING objects only: *monthly_fee* (a read-only attribute), and the mutator routines *set_monthly_fee* (set the value of the attribute monthly_fee) and *apply_fee* (change the current balance by subtracting the value of *monthly_fee*).

Once the behavior of parent class instances (such as objects of type ACCOUNT) are understood, it is quite easy to understand the behavior of subtype instances (such as objects of type CHECKING). In a subtype hierarchy behaviors are additive. That is, the behavior of a descendant subtype is the strict addition of the behaviors of all its ancestor types and the immediate additions in the descendant type.

Unfortunately, subtyping is much more rare in practice than specialization, considered in the next subsection.

6.3.2 Specialization—the *redefine* subclause

In many practical class hierarchies, subclasses typically redefine as well as add to the protocol of their ancestors. When either an attribute or method of an ancestor class is redefined, this must be indicated explicitly using a *redefine* subclause. Although the name of the inherited attribute or method is unchanged, the behavior associated with the inherited feature is changed.

We consider a simple example of redefinition here. Suppose class CORPORATE_CHECKING is created as a specialized type of CHECKING_ACCOUNT. This subclass of CHECKING is presented in Listing 6.4.

Listing 6.4 Class CORPORATE_CHECKING

```
class CORPORATE_CHECKING

inherit
    CHECKING
        redefine
            apply_fee
        end

creation
    open

feature

    apply_fee is
            -- Monthly fee structure is changed
        do
            balance := 0.99 * balance - 2 * monthly_fee
        end

end -- class CORPORATE_CHECKING
```

6.3.3 Selective export—the *export* subclause

The *export* subclause may be used to block or redefine the scope in which one or more routines inherited from an ancestor are visible to instances and descendants of the child class.

To continue the account classes example a bit further, suppose we wish to create another specialized class, a NO_FEE_CHECKING account, inherited from CHECKING. One way of accomplishing this is to simply use the existing CHECKING class and set the *monthly_fee* to 0. Another way would be to create the subclass NO_FEE_CHECKING and block access to the *set_monthly_fee* and *apply_fee* commands in all clients of NO_FEE_CHECKING.

Listing 6.5 shows how this can be accomplished.

Listing 6.5 Class NO_FEE_CHECKING

class NO_FEE_CHECKING

inherit
    CHECKING
        export
            {NONE} set_monthly_fee, apply_fee
        end

creation
    open

end -- class NO_FEE_CHECKING

The routines *set_monthly_fee* and *apply_fee* are not available to any clients of class NO_FEE_CHECKING. If an attempt is made to invoke these commands through any objects type NO_FEE_CHECKING, the compiler will emit an error message indicating that these commands are not exported to the client class.

6.3.4 Renaming inherited routines—the *rename* subclause

It is often the case that the designer of a subclass wishes to utilize the behavior of a routine inherited from an ancestor class, but the name given to the routine by the designer of the ancestor class may not be appropriate, suitable, or just plain liked by the subclass designer. The *rename* subclause allows the subclass designer the freedom to reuse the behavior of the inherited routine while giving it a new name. This new name, unless changed again by the designer of a descendant class, remains in force for all descendant classes.

As an example, suppose a class designer creates a FLOWER class partially given as follows:

class FLOWER

    feature
        smell : STRING

    -- Other features not shown
end -- FLOWER

Suppose a subclass designer is building a ROSE subclass that inherits from FLOWER (certainly a rose "is a kind of" flower). The designer of the

ROSE class does not like the choice of name given to the attribute that characterizes how the flower smells. So she renames this attribute *fragrance* as follows:

```
class ROSE
    inherit
        FLOWER
            rename
                smell as fragrance   -- all clients of ROSE and its descendants must use
                                     -- the name fragrance
        end

    -- Other features not shown

end -- ROSE
```

Another example of renaming is shown in another revision to class CORPORATE_CHECKING given in Listing 6.6.

Listing 6.6 Another revision of class CORPORATE_CHECKING

```
class CORPORATE_CHECKING

inherit
    CHECKING
        rename
            apply_fee as pay_monthly_fee
        redefine
            pay_monthly_fee
        end

creation
    open

feature

    pay_monthly_fee is
        do
            balance := 0.99 * balance - 2 * monthly_fee
        end

end -- class CORPORATE_CHECKING
```

The combination of rename and redefine subclauses in Listing 6.6 demonstrates how the name of the inherited *apply_fee* command has been changed while at the same time redefining its meaning (compared to the parent class). In all instances of subclasses and clients of CORPORATE_CHECKING, the command *pay_monthly_fee* must be used. Only for instance of class CHECKING would the name *apply_fee* be used.

6.3.5 The *select* subclause

It might appear that renaming is strictly a cosmetic issue. Even if that were true, the *rename* subclause would still be a most useful artifact. Renaming has a deeper purpose, primarily when multiple inheritance is employed in a design.

In this section a relatively simple but important use of renaming is discussed. Suppose a method is defined in a parent class. In a subclass the method is redefined. In redefining the subclass method, the designer wishes to reuse the behavior of the parent class method but add to this behavior. That is, the subclass routine needs to be able to invoke the parent class routine. But they both have the same name. The use of the *rename* and *select* subclauses provides a way to do this. An example, given in Listing 6.7, illustrates the technique.

Class PARENT defines two attributes. The *display* routine outputs these attributes. Class CHILD introduces a third attribute. Its *display* routine calls the parent class version and then adds output for the third attribute. Although this example does nothing useful, it illustrates a common situation that occurs in many real applications.

Class CHILD inherits from class PARENT twice using the multiple inheritance capability of Eiffel in a unique way. In the first inheritance, the parent routine *display* has its name changed to *parent_display*. In the second inheritance, the parent routine *display* is redefined. In the implementation of this redefinition, the parent version of *display* can be called directly using its new and unique name, *parent_display*. The purpose of the *select* subclause is to inform the run-time system that an object of type CHILD should use the redefined version of *display* rather than the original PARENT version of *display* when the formal type of the object is PARENT and the actual type is CHILD. This situation will be discussed in detail in Chapter 9 when late-binding and polymorphism are presented.

Listing 6.7 Use of the *select* subclause

```
class PARENT

creation
    make
```

```
feature

      attribute1: INTEGER

      attribute2: REAL

      make (value1: INTEGER; value2: REAL) is
          do
             attribute1 := value1
             attribute2 := value2
          end

      display is
          do
             io.putstring ("Attribute1 = ")
             io.putint (attribute1)
             io.new_line
             io.putstring ("Attribute2 = ")
             io.putreal (attribute2)
             io.new_line
          end

end -- class PARENT


class CHILD

inherit
      PARENT
          rename
             display as parent_display
          end
      PARENT
          redefine
             display
          select
             display
          end

creation
      make_child

feature

      attribute3: DOUBLE
```

```
        make_child (value1: INTEGER; value2: REAL; value3: DOUBLE) is
            do
                make (value1, value2)
                attribute3 := value3
            end

        display is
            do
                parent_display
                io.putstring ("Attribute3 = ")
                io.putdouble (attribute3)
                io.new_line
            end

end -- class CHILD


class APPLICATION

creation
        start

feature

        start is
            local
                p: PARENT
                c: CHILD
            do
                !! p.make (10, 20.0)
                !! c.make_child (50, 60.0, 70.0)
                p.display
                c.display
            end

end -- class APPLICATION
```

6.4   Abstract classes using Eiffel's deferred class facility

To motivate the need for abstract classes (to be defined shortly), the small hierarchy of two ACCOUNT classes introduced in section 6.2 is continued a little further. This will provide a most natural setting in which to introduce the concept of abstract classes, implemented in Eiffel as **deferred** classes.

Suppose we wish to add several additional saving account classes. Specifically we wish to add (1) a non-interest bearing savings account, (2) a savings account in which monthly interest is based on the end of month or final balance, (3) a savings account in which monthly interest is based on the maximum balance that was achieved anytime during the month, and (4) a savings account whose interest is computed on a daily basis.

Each of the specialized types of savings accounts given above share some protocol. They all have a monthly interest rate given by the attribute *monthly_interest_rate* and behavior given by *apply_interest*. This latter routine is implemented differently in each of the savings account classes.

The common features of all the savings accounts can be factored into an abstract class, SAVINGS. The class is called abstract because no actual instances (objects) of this type will ever be created. In fact it would be illegal to attempt the creation of such an instance. Only the common properties associated with the data model and methods of the more specialized types of savings accounts are specified in the abstract class, SAVINGS.

In Eiffel a class is abstract and can produce no actual instances if the implementation details of one or more of its methods is *deferred*. Then the entire class is *deferred*.

The code for abstract class SAVINGS is given in Listing 6.8.

Listing 6.8 Abstract class SAVINGS

```
deferred class SAVINGS

inherit
    ACCOUNT

feature

    monthly_interest: REAL

    set_interest_rate (value: REAL) is
        do
            monthly_interest := value
        end

    apply_interest is
        deferred
        end

end -- class SAVINGS
```

The routine *apply_interest*, given as *deferred* in Listing 6.8, must be made effective in all non-abstract descendant classes (concrete classes). Any subclass that does not define this method is considered a *deferred* class and must be tagged as such.

Listing 6.9 shows the details of class NON_INTEREST, the first of our four specialized types of savings account classes.

Listing 6.9 Class NON_INTEREST

```
class NON_INTEREST
inherit
      SAVINGS
creation
      open
feature
      apply_interest is
            -- Null routine needed to make class effective
      do
      end
end -- class NON_INTEREST
```

Listing 6.10 presents the details of class FINAL_BALANCE, the second of the four specialized savings account classes.

Listing 6.10 Class FINAL_BALANCE

```
class FINAL_BALANCE
inherit
      SAVINGS
creation
      open
feature
      apply_interest is
            -- Compute monthly interest from final balance
      do
            balance := (1 + monthly_interest) * balance
      end
end -- class FINAL_BALANCE
```

Class MAXIMUM_BALANCE is presented in Listing 6.11.

Listing 6.11 Class MAXIMUM_BALANCE

```
class MAXIMUM_BALANCE
inherit
    SAVINGS
        redefine
            deposit, open
        end

creation
    open

feature -- largest monthly balance

    maximum_balance: REAL

    reset_maximum_balance (value: REAL) is
            -- Used at the beginning of every month
        do
            maximum_balance := value
        end

    apply_interest is
            -- Compute monthly interest from maximum balance
        do
            balance := (1 + monthly_interest) * maximum_balance
        end

    deposit (amount: REAL) is
        do
            balance := balance + amount
            if balance > maximum_balance then
                maximum_balance := balance
            end
        end

    open (initial_deposit: REAL) is
        do
            balance := initial_deposit
            maximum_balance := balance
        end

end -- class MAXIMUM_BALANCE
```

The additional attribute, *maximum_balance*, is introduced in class MAXIMUM_BALANCE. The *deposit* routine, inherited from class ACCOUNT (through class SAVINGS), updates *maximum_balance* whenever appropriate.

Finally class DAILY_BALANCE, the most complex of the four specialized savings account classes is shown in Listing 6.12.

Listing 6.12 Class DAILY_BALANCE

```
class DAILY_BALANCE

inherit
    SAVINGS
        export
            {NONE} deposit, withdraw
        end

creation
    open_daily

feature -- day of month of last deposit

    last_deposit: INTEGER

    cumulative_interest: REAL

    deposit_daily (amount: REAL; day_of_month: INTEGER) is
        local
            daily_interest: REAL
        do
            daily_interest := monthly_interest / 30.0
            cumulative_interest := cumulative_interest + balance *
                (day_of_month - last_deposit) * daily_interest
            balance := balance + amount
            last_deposit := day_of_month
        end

    withdraw_daily (amount: REAL; day_of_month: INTEGER) is
        local
            daily_interest: REAL
        do
            daily_interest := monthly_interest / 30.0
            cumulative_interest := cumulative_interest + balance *
                (day_of_month - last_deposit) * daily_interest
```

```
        balance := balance - amount
        last_deposit := day_of_month
    end

  apply_interest is
      do
        balance := balance + cumulative_interest
      end
```

feature {NONE}

```
    open_daily (initial_deposit: REAL; day_of_month: INTEGER) is
      do
        balance := initial_deposit
        last_deposit := day_of_month
        cumulative_interest := 0.0
      end
```

end -- class *DAILY_BALANCE*

Class DAILY_BALANCE adds two attributes, *last_deposit* and *cumulative_interest*, to the data model inherited from SAVINGS.

The *deposit* and *withdraw* methods, inherited from ACCOUNT (through SAVINGS) are blocked. They are no longer applicable for adding or subtracting funds from a DAILY_BALANCE account. These methods are replaced with the routines *deposit_daily* and *withdraw_daily*. In each of these new methods, the *cumulative_interest* is incremented based on the current balance and the number of days it has been in force (of course multiplied by the daily interest rate).

The creation routine, *open_daily*, like its counterpart *open* in class ACCOUNT, is placed in a protected section in order to prevent the routine from being used as a mutator. Method *open*, inherited from ACCOUNT (through SAVINGS), is inaccessible to instances of class DAILY_BALANCE because it is not declared as a creation routine and appears in a protected section in class ACCOUNT. The only way to create an instance of class DAILY_BALANCE is through the creation routine *open_daily*.

You may be wondering why none of the descendants of class SAVINGS (i.e., the four specialized savings account classes) needed to specify the routine *apply_interest* in a *redefine* subclause. The answer is that the four definitions of this method are not redefinitions but original definitions since the abstract class SAVINGS provides no effective definition. A *rede-*

fine subclause is required only when an effective version of a routine is changed in a descendant class.

In general, abstract (*deferred*) classes are key components of highly evolved class hierarchies such as the core Eiffel libraries. The information contained within an abstract class represents a generalization of the behavior of many more specialized classes. It is fairly typical in mature libraries to find many layers of abstract classes sitting above the concrete or effective classes that represent the actual objects of the system. Since one of the major purposes of a class hierarchy is to provide an "intellectual" decomposition of the features that represent a particular problem domain in order to manage the complexity of the domain, it should be evident that abstract classes are an important ingredient in the management of complexity.

6.5 Storage versus computation: Attributes versus routines

A client of a class such as ACCOUNT (see Listing 6.1) does not need to know whether the query *balance*, in an expression such as *current_amount := my_account.balance,* is an attribute (obtained through storage) or a routine (obtained through computation). From the client's viewpoint this information is irrelevant. Only when one or more parameters are required in a routine does the syntax make it obvious that information is being obtained through computation (the invocation of a routine).

As an example, suppose one is interested in designing a VECTOR class. Figure 6.2 shows a typical vector, *v.*

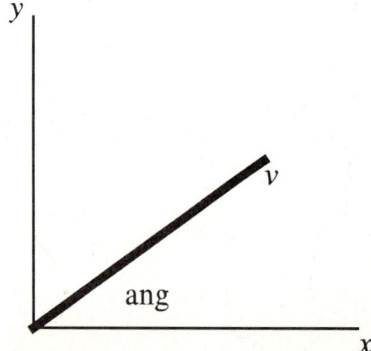

Figure 6.2 Vector

The vector shown in Figure 6.2 is characterized by either its x coordinate and y coordinate (Cartesian form) or by its angle and length or magnitude (polar form). It is of course easy to convert from one form to the other. For example, if the vector were given in its Cartesian form, its magnitude v is computed by taking the square root of the sum of the squares of x and y. If the vector were given in its polar form, its x and y values are computed by taking $v *$ cosine (ang) and $v *$ sine (ang).

There would be three alternative ways to represent the data model of such a class. In the first, featuring a Cartesian representation, the data model would be represented as

```
class VECTOR
    feature
        x, y : REAL

        magnitude : REAL is
            do
                Result := -- details not shown
            end -- magnitude

        angle : REAL is
            do
                Result := -- details not shown
            end
end
```

In the second featuring a polar representation, the data model would be represented as

```
class VECTOR
    feature
        magnitude, angle : REAL

        x : REAL is
            do
                Result := -- details not shown
            end

        y : REAL is
            do
                Result := -- details not shown
            end
end
```

Finally in the third, featuring both a Cartesian and polar representation, the data model would be represented as

class *VECTOR*

>**feature**
>>*magnitude, angle, x, y : REAL*
>>*-- Other details not shown*

end

In all three cases, a client module that declares and appropriately initializes a vector, *my_vector*, could access the angle using the expression *my_vector.angle*.

If the class were represented in the first way (Cartesian form), *angle* would refer to a routine (computation) that computes the inverse tangent of *y* divided by *x*. If the class were represented in the second way (polar form), *angle* would refer to an attribute (storage). Finally, if the class were represented in the third way (combination of Cartesian and polar), *angle* would again refer to an attribute (storage).

The only motivation for the client to "look under the hood" and determine whether the *angle* is obtained through storage or computation would be if the client needed to determine performance information in a computation in which every machine cycle needed to be accounted for (such computations are rare). Then it would be comforting to learn that the angle was obtained through storage rather than through computation.

6.6 Protecting and documenting routines—assertions and programming by contract

The routines of a class specify the behavior of the class (i.e., the behavior of the objects spawned by the class). For each routine this behavior is affected by the values of input parameters, if present, the current values of the object's attributes, and the algorithm specified in the routine.

An important issue concerns whose responsibility it is to ensure that legal values are passed to a routine? An associated question is, whose responsibility is it to handle the error that results if one or more illegal values are passed to a routine? Is it the user's or class designer's responsibility to handle errors? That is should the producer (routine itself) or consumer (client module using the routine) be responsible for handling the errors?

Clearly it is the user's responsibility to ensure that legal values are provided to the routine. The designer of the routine has no control over the use of the routine. Some readers may be inclined to think that the designer of the routine has the responsibility to deal with errors committed by the user. After all, it is he or she who intimately knows the requirements of the routine and indeed "owns" and controls the routine.

The designer of the routine does not typically know the best way to handle an error produced by the client. An error message emitted from the failed routine may destroy the user's carefully designed screen display. Halting program execution may bring a real-time system such as an avionic system on a Boeing 757 to a dangerous state. In fact there is no appropriate general error handling that the class designer (the author of the routine) can devise that would be satisfactory to all users. Indeed, all the routine can and should do on behalf of the user is to raise an exception (a signal that triggers an exception handling section in the user's code) so that the user may respond appropriately to the error condition. If the user chooses to ignore the error, program execution must be halted since it would be imprudent to continue program execution when the system is in an unsafe state.

The assertion handling mechanism for Eiffel routines provides the basis for this division of responsibility between the producer and consumer, that is, the class designer and user.

The preconditions section of a routine, specified by a *require* clause, precisely specifies the conditions that must be satisfied in order for the routine to successfully perform its function. The user of a routine can inspect the preconditions. They are available in both the long (full source code) or short (only attributes, routine signatures, and assertions) forms that can be inspected by the user. It is the user's responsibility to ensure that every precondition required of the routine is satisfied upon entry into the routine.

In exchange, the routine may provide one or more postconditions, given by an *ensure* clause. Such an *ensure* clause specifies the state the system is guaranteed to be in as a result of executing the routine. In other words, if the user complies with all the preconditions, the routine (class designer) guarantees the postconditions. This compact between the producer and consumer is called "programming by contract" by its originator Bertrand Meyer, the creator of the Eiffel language. It has emerged over the years as a highly respected design tool.

Preconditions and postconditions provide a powerful, precise, and extremely useful type of self-documentation for a routine. The semantics of the routine, that is its purpose, may often be clarified by the preconditions and postconditions. To an inexperienced user, the preconditions provide the basis for accelerating the learning process associated with using features from a class. Whenever a precondition is violated, in the absence of a user-defined exception handler (to be introduced later in this section), program execution is halted with an exception trace output to the user. This exception trace indicates the exception that was violated and the errant routine that engaged in the violation. This allows the user to re-examine his or her code and make appropriate modifications so that the routine that was violated may be used legally and properly.

Listing 6.13 demonstrates the use of preconditions and exception handling in a class called MATH and a short test program in class APPLICATION.

The routine *silly* contains a precondition with the tag, *value_not_five*. If a client passes the value 5 to this routine, an exception will be raised.

The routine *load_value* contains an exception handler that begins with the keyword *rescue*. If an exception is raised while in this routine, the code in the *rescue* section is activated.

In routine *load_value*, the user is prompted to enter an integer value. This value is input to the *silly* routine. If the *value* parameter does not equal 5, the *silly* function returns 5 minus the *value*.

If the user enters 5, this triggers an exception in routine *load_value* (the exception is raised in routine *silly*). Business as usual ceases. Instead of outputting the value of *r*, as would normally be done, the code in the *rescue* clause is activated. An error count, *num_errors*, is incremented by 1. The output message, *"Error: Cannot enter the value of 5"*, is sent to the user's screen. If the error count equals 3, the error message, *"Three strikes and you are out"*, is put on the user's screen and the program terminates. Otherwise the *retry* function causes routine *load_value* to be called again while preserving the current state of the variables *r* and *num_errors*.

Listing 6.13 Demonstration of preconditions and exception handling

```
class MATH

feature

    silly (value: INTEGER): INTEGER is
        require
            value_not_five: value /= 5
        do
            Result := 5 - value
        end
```

```
load_value is
    local
        r: INTEGER
        num_errors: INTEGER
    do
        io.putstring ("%NEnter value: ")
        io.readint
        r := silly (io.lastint)
        io.putstring ("r = ")
        io.putint (r)
        io.new_line
    rescue
        num_errors := num_errors + 1
        io.putstring ("Error: Cannot enter the value 5%N")
        if num_errors = 3 then
            io.putstring ("Three strikes and you are out!%N")
        else
            retry
        end
    end

    -- Other features not shown

end -- class MATH


class APPLICATION

creation
    start

feature

    start is
        local
            m: MATH
        do
            !! m
            m.load_value
        end

end -- class APPLICATION
```

Portions of the program output when 5 is entered three times are shown below.

```
Enter value: 5
Error: Cannot enter the value 5

Enter value: 5
Error: Cannot enter the value 5

Enter value: 5
Error: Cannot enter the value 5
Three strikes and you are out!

test: system execution failed.
Following is the set of recorded exceptions:

-------------------------------------------------------------------
Class / Object Routine Nature of exception Effect
-------------------------------------------------------------------
MATH silly value_not_five:
<001D1BB0> Precondition violated. Fail
-------------------------------------------------------------------
MATH load_value
<001D1BB0> Resumption attempt failed. Rescue
-------------------------------------------------------------------
APPLICATION start
<001D1BA8> Routine failure. Fail
-------------------------------------------------------------------
APPLICATION root's creation
<001D1BA8> Routine failure. Exit
```

6.6.1 Account classes revisited with assertions

In order to illustrate the use of preconditions and postconditions in a more meaningful context, we revisit all of the ACCOUNT classes presented earlier in this chapter and add assertions to key routines.

The short/flat form for the revised class ACCOUNT is shown in Listing 6.14.

Listing 6.14 Short/flat form for revised class ACCOUNT with assertions

class interface ACCOUNT

creation
    open

```
feature
    balance: REAL

    deposit (amount: REAL)
        require
            non_negative_amount: amount >= 0.0
        ensure
            balance = old balance + amount

    withdraw (amount: REAL)
        require
            funds_available: amount <= balance
        ensure
            balance = old balance - amount

end -- class ACCOUNT
```

The precondition for the *deposit* routine specifies that the parameter *amount* must be non-negative. The tag *non_negative_amount* is used to indicate this condition. The postcondition in this routine specifies that the balance upon exit from the routine equals the balance upon entry (*old balance*) plus the *amount* deposited. Although the postcondition provides information that would obviously be available by directly inspecting the code of the routine, this code is not printed in an Eiffel short form. It is therefore highly desirable to include this obvious postcondition in a postcondition.

The pre- and postconditions of the *withdraw* routine are similar.

Listing 6.15 presents the short/flat forms of the remaining classes.

Listing 6.15 Short/flat forms for remaining ACCOUNT classes with assertions

```
class interface CHECKING

creation
    open

feature
    apply_fee
        ensure
            balance <= old balance

    monthly_fee: REAL

    set_monthly_fee (amount: REAL)
        require
```

```
            non_negative: amount >= 0.0
end -- class CHECKING

deferred class interface SAVINGS

feature

    apply_interest
        ensure
            balance >= old balance

    monthly_interest: REAL

    set_interest_rate (value: REAL)
        require
            positive_rate: value > 0.0

end -- class SAVINGS


class interface NON_INTEREST

creation
    open

feature

    apply_interest
            -- Null routine needed to make class effective
        ensure
            balance = old balance

end -- class NON_INTEREST


class interface MAXIMUM_BALANCE

creation
    open

feature -- largest monthly balance

    apply_interest
            -- Compute monthly interest from maximum balance

    deposit (amount: REAL)

    maximum_balance: REAL

    open (initial_deposit: REAL)
```

reset_maximum_balance (value: REAL)
    -- Used at the beginning of every month

end -- class MAXIMUM_BALANCE

class interface FINAL_BALANCE

creation
    open

feature

    apply_interest
        -- Compute monthly interest from final balance

end -- class FINAL_BALANCE

class interface DAILY_BALANCE

creation
    open_daily

feature -- day of month of last deposit

    apply_interest
        -- Compute monthly interest from maximum balance

    cumulative_interest: REAL

    deposit_daily (amount: REAL; day_of_month: INTEGER)
        require
           positive_deposit: amount > 0.0
           legal_day: day_of_month >= 0 and day_of_month <= 31

    last_deposit: INTEGER

    withdraw_daily (amount: REAL; day_of_month: INTEGER)
        require
           positive_withdrawal: amount > 0.0
           legal_day: day_of_month >= 0 and day_of_month <= 31

end -- class DAILY_BALANCE

In class CHECKING, routine *apply_fee* contains only a postcondition that specifies that the value of the *balance* attribute upon leaving the routine is equal or less than the value of the *balance* attribute upon exiting the routine. This information summarizes essential information about the semantics of the routine. In routine *set_monthly_fee*, the precondition specifies that the parameter *amount* must be non-negative.

In deferred class SAVINGS there are two assertions. In the routine *apply_interest*, the postcondition specifies that the *balance* attribute upon leaving the routine must be equal or greater than the *balance* attribute upon entering the routine. The precondition of routine *set_interest_rate* specifies that the parameter *value* must be positive.

6.6.2 Propagation of assertions through inheritance

A fundamental question that has not been discussed so far concerns the propagation of assertions through inheritance. Specifically, how do the assertions (both pre- and postconditions) in class ACCOUNT affect descendant classes? The same question may be asked of the assertions just discussed in the deferred class SAVINGS.

If a descendant routine redefines an effective routine in a parent class or makes effective a deferred routine in an abstract class, its preconditions are logically connected to those of all ancestor routines of the same name by the logical "or" operation. This implies that the precondition of a redefined or effective descendant routine may be weaker than that of its ancestor (i.e., the "or" condition can create a weaker condition than those inherited). This is a subtle issue. In fact, it is sensible that if a redefined descendant routine can accomplish the same task by requiring less on the part of the input parameters (a weaker condition imposed in the redefined routine's *require* clause), this implies the descendant routine is stronger than its ancestor. It should of course be legal to strengthen a routine through redefinition in a class hierarchy. The *require* clause in a redefined descendant routine must now be called a *require else* clause. This notifies a person performing maintenance on the redefined routine to examine the preconditions in all ancestor routines with the same name.

On the other hand, if a descendant routine redefines an effective routine in a parent class or makes effective a deferred routine in an abstract class, its postconditions are logically connected to those of all ancestor routines with the same name by the logical "and" operation. This implies that the postcondition of such a routine is stronger than that of its ancestor. This is because more conditions must be satisfied upon exit from the routine (i.e., all of the conditions given in the ancestor postconditions "and" those given in the redefined class). The *ensure* clause in a redefined descendant routine must be called an *ensure then* clause.

Class NON_INTEREST makes effective the routine *apply_interest* since this routine was *deferred* in the parent class SAVINGS. In class SAV-

INGS the postcondition specifies that the *balance* upon exit is equal or greater than the *balance* upon entry to the routine. In class NON_INTEREST the postcondition (which in the actual code is given by an *ensure then* clause) specifies that the *balance* upon exit equals the *balance* upon entry to the routine. This condition when combined with its parent condition through the logical "and" operation yields the same condition (i.e., *balance >= old balance AND balance = old balance -> balance = old balance*). Had the postcondition in the parent class SAVINGS been *balance > old balance*, the postcondition in the child class NON_INTEREST could never be satisfied.

In class DAILY_BALANCE given in Listing 6.15, routine *deposit_daily* specifies two preconditions. The first, with tag *positive_deposit_amount*, requires the parameter *amount* to be positive. The second, with tag *legal_day*, requires the *day_of_month* parameter to be equal or greater than 0 and less than or equal to 31. The *withdraw_daily* routine specifies similar preconditions.

Pre- and postconditions when used in abstract (deferred) classes provide a useful tool for imposing logical constraints on the postconditions of all descendant classes. So in addition to providing documentation about the semantics of a routine, postconditions establish constraints on the semantics of all redefined versions of the routine that may be produced in the future.

Consider again the class AIRPLANE in Listing 6.16, this time defined as an abstract class (deferred class). There is no creation routine because deferred classes cannot have instances. The *make* routine would probably be declared to be a creation routine in one of the subclasses. Its preconditions require 6000 pounds of initial fuel. This guarantees sufficient fuel to become airborne, fly for a prescribed period, and make a safe landing.

The takeoff routine, which is deferred (actually defined in subclasses) imposes the precondition that the fuel be greater than 6000 pounds (for the same reason as above). The postconditions require that upon completing takeoff the fuel remaining is greater than 5000 pounds (to provide a margin of safety for flying and landing), the altitude greater than 1000 feet (to provide sufficient glide for an emergency landing), and the speed greater than 220 knots (to prevent stall).

A subclass of AIRPLANE may weaken the preconditions (e.g., require less than 6000 pounds of fuel on takeoff if at least 5000 pounds remain after takeoff and the other postconditions are either met or exceeded - a more efficient plane might be able to achieve the same postconditions with weaker preconditions).

So the pre- and postconditions in the abstract class AIRPLANE have profoundly affected the semantics of all subclasses.

Listing 6.16 Abstract class with pre- and postconditions

```
deferred class AIRPLANE

feature

        fuel:      REAL
        -- pounds of fuel

        weight:   REAL

        position: COMPASS_SETTING

        speed:   REAL

        altitude:  REAL

        -- other attributes not shown

feature {NONE}

        make (initial_fuel: REAL; initial_weight: REAL) is
            require
                sufficient_fuel: initial_fuel > 6000.0
                positive_weight: initial_weight > 0.0
            do
                fuel := initial_fuel
                weight := initial_weight
            end

        takeoff is
            require
                sufficient_fuel: fuel > 6000.0
            deferred
            ensure
                fuel > 5000
                altitude > 1000
                speed > 220
            end

end -- class AIRPLANE
```

6.7 Summary

- The class is the basic logical and physical unit of software construction in Eiffel.

- As a logical unit, a class represents an abstract data type—a unification of an underlying data model with a set of operations (routines) that manipulate this data model.

- As a physical unit a class is a module—a file with suffix ".e".

- Creation routines provide a mechanism to dynamically allocate storage for new objects and initialize the attributes of the new objects at the time they are created.

- Before an Eiffel object may be used for any practical purpose it must be created.

- Creation routines may also be used as ordinary routines typically to update the values of attributes for an existing object. Only if the creation operator, "!!", is used in front of a creation routine will a new object be brought to life.

- If a class does not include any creation routines, instances can be created merely by using the creation operator in front of the name of an object. In such a case the attributes contained within the object assume their default values.

- Creation clauses may contain an export section bounded by curly braces, "{" and "}". Objects of the given class may be created only in the classes and their descendants specified in the export section, if present.

- If no export section is present, a default export section of ANY is implied. Since all Eiffel classes are descendants of ANY, the absence of an explicit export section implies that objects of the given class may be created from within any other class (i.e., universal export).

- Creation routines may be used on objects formally declared to be of a given parent class to produce objects of a child class.

- If a class has one or more creation routines, it is illegal to create a new object using just the creation operator, "!!", followed by the object name. One of the creation routines must be used.

- Inheritance is an architectural property of object-oriented systems used for establishing a decomposition of a software system into classes and subclasses.

- Inheritance also provides the basis for software reuse. The accepted practice is for classes at the top of a hierarchy to encapsulate general properties of some domain and for classes lower in the hierarchy to extend and to encapsulate more specialized properties of the domain.

- As one moves down a class hierarchy, the "is-a" or "is a kind of" relationship should hold between child class and parent class. Attributes and methods defined in a parent class should make sense in all descendant classes in which they are not redefined.

- In going from a parent class to its child, **specialization** involves redefining one or more of the parent's routines or attributes.

- **Extension** involves adding routines or attributes not present in the parent.

- **Restriction** involves blocking one or more routines of the parent. All three may be used simultaneously, but it is most common to use only specialization and extension in going down a class hierarchy.

- If only extension is involved in going from a class to its child, the child is considered to be a **subtype** of its parent. Its behavior can be characterized by the sum of the parent's behavior and the additional behavior given by the routines and attributes present only in the child.

- If even a single method is redefined in a subclass, that subclass cannot be considered to be a subtype of its parent. This is a most common situation.

- When either an attribute or method of an ancestor class is redefined, this must be indicated explicitly using a *redefine* subclause. Although the name of the inherited attribute or method is unchanged, the behavior associated with the inherited feature is changed.

- The rules of conformance require that if an attribute is redefined in a descendant class that its new type be a descendant of the original type.

- The *export* subclause may be used to block or redefine the scope in which one or more routines inherited from an ancestor are visible to instances and descendants of the child class.

- It is often the case that the designer of a subclass wishes to utilize the behavior of a routine inherited from an ancestor class, but the name given to the routine by the designer of the ancestor class may not be appropriate, suitable, or just plain liked by the subclass designer.

- The rename subclause allows the subclass designer the freedom to reuse the behavior of the inherited routine while giving it a new name. This new name, unless changed again by the designer of a descendant class, remains in force for all descendant classes.

- In Eiffel a class is abstract and can produce no actual instances, if the implementation details of one or more of its methods is *deferred*. Then the entire class is *deferred*.

- A *redefine* subclause is required only when an effective version of a routine is changed in a descendant class.

- In general, abstract (*deferred*) classes are key components of highly evolved class hierarchies such as the core Eiffel libraries.

- The information contained within an abstract class represents a generalization of the behavior of many more specialized classes.

- It is fairly typical in mature libraries to find many layers of abstract classes sitting above the concrete or effective classes that represent the actual objects of the system.

- Since one of the major purposes of a class hierarchy is to provide an "intellectual" decomposition of the features that represent a particular problem domain in order to manage the complexity of the domain, it should be evident that abstract classes are an important ingredient in the management of complexity.

- Only when one or more parameters are required in a routine does the syntax make it obvious that information is being obtained through computation (the invocation of a routine).

- The preconditions section of a routine, specified by a *require* clause, precisely specifies the conditions that must be satisfied in order for the routine to successfully perform its function.

- It is the user's responsibility to ensure that legal values are provided to a routine. The designer of the routine has no control over the use of the routine.

- All a routine can and should do on behalf of a user in the event that a precondition is violated is to raise an exception (a signal that triggers an exception handling section in the user's code) so that the user may respond appropriately to the error condition.

- If the user chooses to ignore the error, program execution must be halted since it would be imprudent to continue program execution when the system is in an unsafe state.

- The assertion handling mechanism for Eiffel routines provides the basis for this division of responsibility between the producer and consumer, that is, the class designer and user.

- It is the user's responsibility to ensure that every precondition required of the routine is satisfied upon entry into the routine.

- In exchange, the routine may provide one or more postconditions, given by an *ensure* clause. Such an *ensure* clause specifies the state the system is guaranteed to be in as a result of executing the routine.

- If the user complies with all the preconditions, the routine (class designer) guarantees the postconditions. This compact between the producer and consumer is called "programming by contract" by its originator Bertrand Meyer, the creator of the Eiffel language. It has emerged over the years as a highly respected language tool.

- Preconditions and postconditions provide a powerful, precise, and extremely useful type of self-documentation for a routine. The semantics of the routine, that is its purpose, may often be clarified by the preconditions and postconditions.

- If a descendant routine redefines an effective routine in a parent class or makes effective a deferred routine in an abstract class, its preconditions are logically connected to those of all ancestor routines of the same name by the logical "or" operation.

- The precondition of a redefined or effective descendant routine may be weaker than that of its ancestor (i.e., the "or" condition can create a weaker condition than those inherited).

- The *require* clause in a redefined descendant routine must be called a *require else* clause.

- If a descendant routine redefines an effective routine in a parent class or makes effective a deferred routine in an abstract class, its postconditions are logically connected to those of all ancestor routines with the same name by the logical "and" operation.

- The postcondition of such a routine is stronger than that of its ancestor. This is because more conditions must be satisfied upon exit from the routine (i.e., all of the conditions given in the ancestor postconditions "and" those given in the redefined class).

- The *ensure* clause in a redefined descendant routine must be called an *ensure then* clause.

6.8   Exercises

1. Add an additional subclass to the ACCOUNT hierarchy. Specify pre- and postconditions for each of its routines, if appropriate.

2. Add pre- and postconditions to appropriate routines of the RANDOM_NUMBER class whose interface is given in Listing 5.1.

3. Do the same for problem 2 for class DIE defined in Chapter 5.

4. Do the same for problem 2 for the four EFROM die classes defined in Chapter 5.

5. Design a small application in which it is appropriate to use one or two deferred classes (abstract classes). Explain why these abstract classes are used. Show all the implementation details in your application, some sample input, and the output.

6. Write a small example that illustrates the use of exception handling. Design the input in such a way that you demonstrate how the error handling is performed.

7. Complete the details of the query, magnitude, in the code of section 6.5.

8. Complete the details of the query, angle, in the code of section 6.5.

9. Complete the details of the query, x, in the code of section 6.5.

10. Complete the details of the query, y, in the code of section 6.5.

Chapter

7

Constructing Classes for Reuse— Generic Container Classes

A box of paper clips, a stack of trays in a cafeteria, a room full of desks, chairs, lamps, and other furniture, an array of integers, a bag of groceries, a set of lottery tickets, a dictionary of words, and a database of patient records are all examples of container objects. Some of the container objects such as the box of paper clips, stack of cafeteria trays, set of lottery tickets, and dictionary of words consist of identical types of objects (i.e., paper clip, cafeteria trays, integers, lottery tickets, dictionary words) whereas some of the container objects contain a diversity of objects (i.e., desks, chairs, lamps, and other furniture in a room, groceries, and patient records).

It is useful to make a distinction between the container object and the things that it contains. For example in the case of the cafeteria trays, we can distinguish the trays from the stack. This may seem quite artificial, but it is actually a useful abstraction. We can visualize an empty stack as being the physical location where the trays are piled one on top of another. We can identify an empty grocery sack (i.e., paper bag) as a legitimate object in its own right—one that becomes a useful artifact when it is filled with grocery or other objects. In short, containers have an existence separate from the things they contain.

This chapter examines several different types of container object classes. Such classes, once perfected, can be used in many software applications and are therefore ideal candidates for software reuse.

More formally, a container class is one that holds zero or more elements, each formally declared to be of a particular class type. The actual type inserted in the container must conform to (be a descendant of) the formal type. This allows a container to hold either a homogeneous or heterogeneous collection of elements.

There are many types of container classes. If the capacity of a container object, specified at the time of its creation, cannot be later modified, it is a static container; otherwise it is a dynamic container. The number of elements that can be inserted into a dynamic container is limited only by the memory space of the computer running the program. The capacity of a static container class is specified by the user or programmer.

In previous chapters we have already extensively used an important software container class, the ARRAY. An ARRAY object has an identity all its own, independent of the type or quantity of elements residing in the ARRAY. Each element in an ARRAY must be of a type that conforms to the formal type specified in the generic parameter representation for the ARRAY.

Arrays are most useful when direct access to individual index locations is essential. The order of insertion or deletion from an ARRAY class is arbitrary.

Some other important and potentially reusable container classes include STACK, QUEUE, UNORDERED_LIST, ORDERED_LIST, and SEARCH_TREE. All of these containers except the SEARCH_TREE are carefully examined in this chapter. The SEARCH_TREE is discussed in the next chapter.

A container class must specify protocol (a set of rules) for inserting, deleting, and accessing elements. This is what differentiates one type of container from another.

Before a given class, container or otherwise, can be considered "reusable," it typically has to meet the following conditions: (1) Each of its features has been extensively tested in many different applications over a reasonably long period of time, (2) it provides a range of services (implemented as routines) sufficient to meet the varied needs of many clients (applications that use the component), and (3) each of the services is efficiently implemented.

The most challenging issue related to the construction of a "reusable" class is the design of the class interface. Bertrand Meyer, in his classic book *Object-Oriented Software Construction*, states: "Few issues are more important in software development than the proper design of module interfaces...If there was just one issue on which to expect significant advances from object-oriented methods, then it would have to be this one." The class interface specifies the services and data model that are available to users.

The data structure libraries that are part of Eiffel provide definitions for the container types discussed in this chapter. It is highly recommended that one should utilize such highly tested and mature software components instead of writing one's own if one is building a commercial application. An important goal of this chapter is to explore some of the fundamental issues associated with the construction of "reusable" container classes. Therefore for some container classes we will construct our own whereas for others we will use and examine those present in the standard Eiffel library.

7.1 Stack

A stack is an important and widely used abstract data type. Many software applications require the logical equivalent of piling objects on top of each other. The only object that can be accessed in such a pile or stack is the last object put on the pile or the top object (assuming that gravity prevails and the stack is built vertically). An interior object can be accessed only by first removing all the objects on top of it.

Figure 7.1 shows a typical stack.

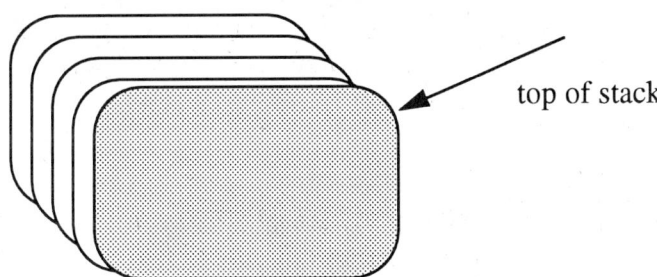

top of stack

Figure 7.1 A Stack of Objects

The protocol for insertion and deletion that defines the unique signature of a stack specifies that the last element inserted onto a stack is the first element that can be deleted from the stack. This is called a "last-in-first-out" (LIFO) protocol. If one inserts a sequence of objects onto a stack and then removes all of the objects, the sequence in which the objects are removed will be the reverse of the sequence in which they were inserted.

Therefore, stacks are useful containers for reversing the order of a collection of entities.

It is not legal to violate the strict LIFO protocol of a stack by, for example, accessing the next to the last item inserted before accessing the last item inserted. If this capability were needed, a container type other than a stack would have to be used.

The operations with their interface that define the behavior of a STACK class are

- *push (item : T)* - add item to stack

- *pop* - remove item from stack

- *top_element : T* - access first element that can be removed (top element)

- *empty : BOOLEAN* - True if no elements contained in stack; otherwise False

- *capacity : INTEGER* - The number of elements that can be held by the stack

- *num_elements : INTEGER* - The actual number of elements on the stack

As a reminder, we use verbs to name routines that perform an operation and do not return a value and we use nouns to name a routine that returns a value and yes/no questions.

The commands that change the configuration of the stack are *push* and *pop*. The queries that return information about the stack but do not change its configuration are *top_element, capacity, num_elements*, and *empty*. Some of these queries may be implemented through storage (as attributes) rather than as routines.

7.1.1 Static implementation of stack

Listing 7.1 presents a static implementation of the container class STACK.

Listing 7.1

```
class FIXED_STACK [T]

creation
    initialize

feature
```

```
capacity:        INTEGER

num_elements: INTEGER

push (item: T) is
    require
        under_capacity: num_elements < capacity
    do
        num_elements := num_elements + 1
        data.put (item, num_elements)
    ensure
        num_elements = old num_elements + 1
        not empty
        top_element = item
    end

pop is
    require
        non_empty: not empty
    do
        num_elements := num_elements - 1
    ensure
        num_elements = old num_elements - 1
    end

top_element: T is
    require
        non_empty: not empty ensure
        Result = true implies num_elements = capacity
    end

empty: BOOLEAN is
    do
        Result := num_elements = 0
    ensure
        Result = true implies num_elements = 0
    end

feature {NONE} -- Protected section for internal use only

data: ARRAY [T]

initialize (size: INTEGER) is
    require
        positive_size: size > 0
```

```
        do
            capacity := size
            !! data.make (1, size)
        ensure
            capacity = size
        do
            Result := data.item (num_elements)
        end

    at_capacity: BOOLEAN is
        do
            Result := num_elements = capacity
        ensure
            Result = true implies num_elements = capacity
        end

    empty: BOOLEAN is
        do
            Result := num_elements = 0
        ensure
            Result = true implies num_elements = 0
        end

feature {NONE} -- Protected section for internal use only

    data: ARRAY [T]

    initialize (size: INTEGER) is
        require
            positive_size: size > 0
        do
            capacity := size
            !! data.make (1, size)
        ensure
            capacity = size
            num_elements = 0
        end

invariant
    num_elements <= capacity
    num_elements >= 0

end -- class FIXED_STACK
```

In Listing 7.1, the creation routine *initialize* is implemented in the protected section of the class *(feature { NONE })*. This is to ensure that *initialize* can be used only for creation and not used as a mutator routine. We do not want to allow an existing STACK object to have its capacity changed once it is created.

The two attributes of STACK are *capacity* and *num_elements*. This latter attribute stores the last element to be removed from the STACK, if any.

Routine *push* requires for successful use that the attribute *num_elements* be less than the attribute *capacity* (see the precondition). Otherwise an overflow condition will result. The attribute *num_elements* is incremented by 1. The internal attribute *data* gets *item* at index *num_elements*. The postcondition specifies that when the routine exits, the *num_elements* equals the old value plus 1. Figure 7.2 shows the mechanism for routine *push*.

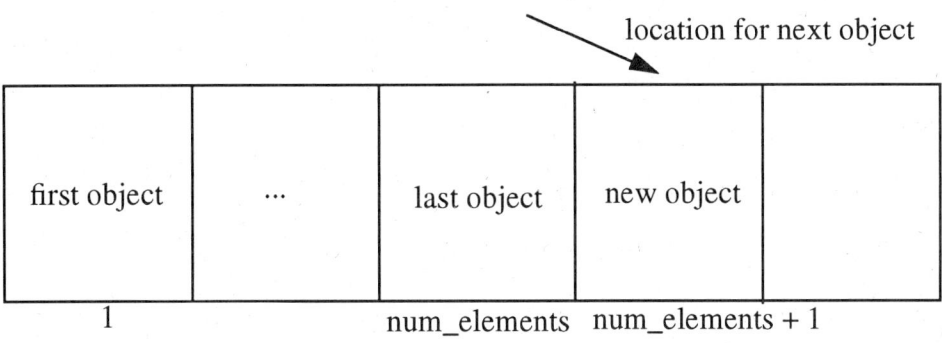

Figure 7.2 Mechanism of Push for Static Stack

The reader is urged to study the remaining routines with particular attention to the preconditions and postconditions of each routine.

A class invariant is specified in the last section of the class. The conditions *num_elements <= capacity* and *num_elements >= 0* are given. This indicates that upon exit from any routine of the class this condition must hold as well as on entry to every public routine except initialize.

Listing 7.2 presents a short form of the class. From this documentation all of the relevant module interface information is given. This includes pre- and postconditions.

Listing 7.2 Short form for class FIXED_STACK

class interface FIXED_STACK [T]

creation
    initialize

feature

    at_capacity: BOOLEAN
        ensure
           Result = **true implies** num_elements = capacity

    capacity: INTEGER

    empty: BOOLEAN
        ensure
           Result = **true implies** num_elements = 0

    num_elements: INTEGER

    pop
        require
           non_empty: **not** empty
        ensure
           num_elements = **old** num_elements - 1

    push (item: T)
        require
           under_capacity: num_elements < capacity
        ensure
           num_elements = **old** num_elements + 1
           not empty
           top_element = item

    top_element: T
        require
           non_empty: **not** empty

invariant
    num_elements <= capacity
    num_elements >= 0

end -- class FIXED_STACK

Listing 7.3 presents a small test program in class APPLICATION.

Listing 7.3 Test program for fixed stack

```
class APPLICATION

creation
     start

feature

     start is
        local
            my_stack: FIXED_STACK [INTEGER]
            index: INTEGER
        do
            !! my_stack.initialize (500)
            from
               index := 0
            until
               index = 1000
            loop
               index := index + 1
               if not my_stack.at_capacity then
                   my_stack.push (index)
               end
            end
            from
               index := 0
            until
               index = 1000
            loop
               index := index + 1
               if not my_stack.empty then
                   my_stack.pop
                   if index <= 20 then
                      io.putint (my_stack.top_element)
                      io.new_line
                   end
               end
            end
        end

end -- class APPLICATION
```

The user's code (in Listing 7.3) is protected. Before attempting to *push* onto *my_stack,* a test is performed using *my_stack.at_capacity.* Before attempting to *pop* from *my_stack,* a test is performed using *my_stack.empty.*

7.1.2 Dynamic implementation

The FIXED_STACK presented in Listing 7.1 imposes an artificial constraint on the user, namely a fixed and predetermined limit (the capacity) on the number of items that can be pushed onto the stack. This limitation is removed in another stack class, DYNAMIC_STACK presented in Listing 7.4.

Listing 7.4 Class DYNAMIC_STACK

```
class DYNAMIC_STACK [T]

feature

    num_elements: INTEGER

    push (item: T) is
        local
            new_node: NODE [T]
        do
            !! new_node.make (item, first)
            first := new_node
            num_elements := num_elements + 1
        ensure
            num_elements = old num_elements + 1
            not empty
            top = item
        end

    pop is
        require
            non_empty: not empty
        do
            first := first.next
            num_elements := num_elements - 1
        ensure
            num_elements = old num_elements - 1
        end
```

```
top: T is
    require
        non_empty: not empty
    do
        Result := first.item
    end

empty: BOOLEAN is
    do
        Result := num_elements = 0
    ensure
        Result = true implies num_elements = 0
    end

feature {NONE}

    first: NODE [T]

invariant
    num_elements >= 0

end -- class DYNAMIC_STACK
```

Listing 7.5 presents the details of class NODE.

Listing 7.5 Class NODE

```
class NODE [T]

creation {DYNAMIC_STACK}
    make

feature {DYNAMIC_STACK} -- Limited export scope

    item: T

    next: NODE [T]

    make (value: T  link: NODE [T]) is
        do
            item := value
            next := link
        end

end -- class NODE
```

As shown in Listing 7.4, a DYNAMIC_STACK has the attribute *num_elements* exported everywhere and the attribute *first* in a protected section. A client of DYNAMIC_STACK need not know about *first* but needs only the two public attributes.

The export section associated with the creation routine is DYNAMIC_STACK. This implies that it is only legal to create a node from within DYNAMIC_STACK or any of its descendants.

In Figures 7.3, 7.4, and 7.5 we examine graphically the three lines of code in routine *push*. Figure 7.3 shows an existing DYNAMIC_STACK containing two elements. Attribute *first* points to the NODE object containing *item1*. This NODE object points to the NODE object containing *item2*.

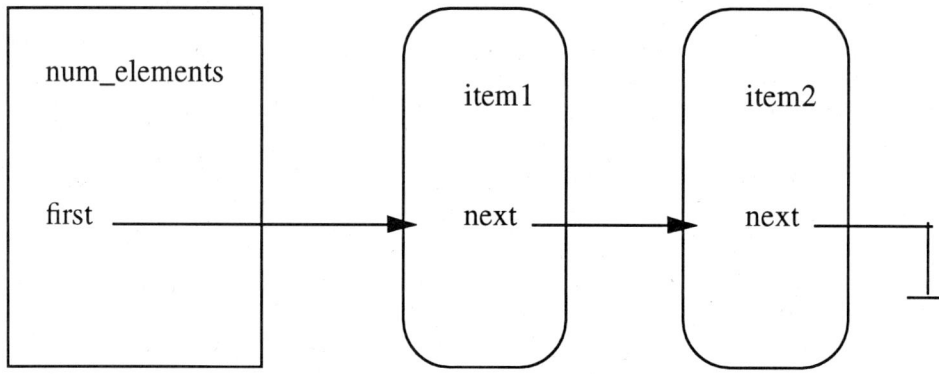

Figure 7.3 Initial Dynamic Stack

The first line of code creates and initializes a NODE object, *new_node*, with value equal to *item* and *next* equal to *first*. Figure 7.4 shows the results of this first line of code.

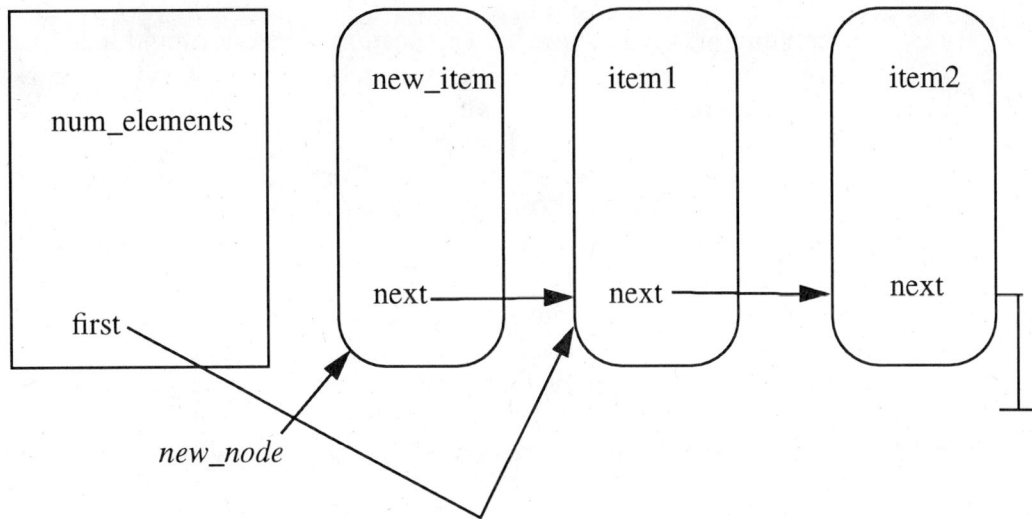

Figure 7.4 Dynamic Stack after New Node

Figure 7.5 shows the results after the second line of code, *first :=
new_node*.

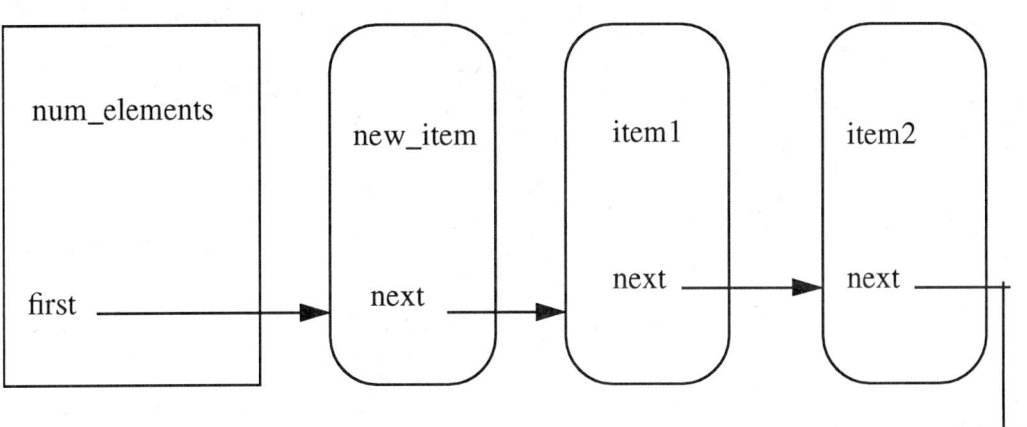

Figure 7.5 Completed Push Operation

7.2   Unordered list with duplicates not allowed

The container class examined in this section is an unordered list. This is a much more general and powerful abstraction than the simple stack considered in section 7.1. In fact as we will see later, the stack can be constructed in terms of an unordered list.

An unordered list is a linear sequence of arbitrary elements with no duplicate elements allowed. The unordered list is considered linear because its elements are stored in sequence, one after another. Such a list has a well defined "front" and "back."

In designing the class interface for UNORDERED_LIST we must identify the commands (the operations that modify the structure of the list) and queries (the operations that return information about the list but do not change its structure). We must ask ourselves the questions: (1) What do we wish to do to a list? and (2) What do we wish to find out about a list?

In designing an abstract data type as complex as an unordered list, it is useful to formulate the interface before worrying about any implementation details. The interface precisely specifies what a client can do with a list. Because of the powerful protection associated with encapsulation, only the operations (commands and queries) and features that are specified in the class interface can be used to modify or access information about the list.

As with any evolving software component, many clients (users) over time may and should influence the interface to such a class. Although the interface that will be presented for the UNORDERED_LIST is much more complex than that of any class discussed so far in this book, it is still much smaller than a commercial grade software component. We will in fact later compare the interface to the unordered list abstraction developed in this section with the commercial grade list abstraction that is part of the standard Eiffel class library.

7.2.1 Interface to UNORDERED_LIST class

Before we present the formal interface to this class, let us answer the two questions posed above: (1) What do we wish to do to a list? and (2) What do we wish to find out about a list?

Queries (What do we wish to find out about a list?)

- What is the first item on the list, if any?

- What is the last item on the list, if any?

- How many elements are in the list?

- Is a given item present in the list?

- What is the element just after a given item?

- What is the element just before a given item?

- Is the list empty?

- Is there an element directly to the right of the current element that a cursor points to?

- What is the element being pointed to by the cursor?

Commands (What do we wish to do with a list?)

- Insert an item into the front of the list

- Insert an item into the back of the list

- Insert an item just after a given item on the list

- Insert an item just before a given item on the list

- Remove a given item from the list

- Remove an item from the front of the list

- Remove an item from the back of the list

- Remove an item just after a given item on the list

- Remove an item just before a given item on the list

- Produce a list that contains the same elements in the reverse order from a given list

- Move a cursor so it points to the first element in the list

- Move the cursor forward so it points to the next element in the list

The notion of a cursor is mentioned in two queries and two commands. This is a pointer that enables a user to iterate through the elements of a list (i.e., access each element in sequence from the front to back) and perform some appropriate operation on each successive list element. Often this operation merely consists of displaying the element. Data hiding in the class ensures that a user cannot directly access this cursor but can only manipulate it using the two commands associated with the cursor (the last two bullets given above).

From the informal specifications given above, a more formal interface to class UNORDERED_LIST can be constructed. This interface contains the features that comprise the public data model of the class (some of these take care of required queries), and the routines that comprise the remaining queries and the commands.

For each routine, its parameters (if any) and return type (if any) are given. In addition, the semantics (desired behavior) of the routine are more completely specified if the preconditions and postconditions (if any) are given as well. It should be evident that the short form of the class comprises its formal interface. It contains exactly the ingredients specified above (i.e., the parameters, return type, preconditions, and postconditions for each routine in the public section of the class).

Listing 7.6 presents the short form for class UNORDERED_LIST. The features that are normally presented in alphabetical order have been rearranged into the categories of queries and commands.

Listing 7.6 Short form for class UNORDERED_LIST

```
class interface UNORDERED_LIST [T]

feature

        -- Data model queries
        front_item              : T
        back_item               : T
        number_elements         : INTEGER

        -- Query routines
        item_after (item: T): T
                -- Return the element just after item in the list
            require
                not_last_item: item /= back_item
                item_present: present (item)

        item_before (item: T): T
                -- Return the element just before item in the list
            require
                not_first_item: item /= front_item
                item_present: present (item)

        present (item: T): BOOLEAN
                -- Return TRUE if item is in list, otherwise FALSE
```

empty: BOOLEAN
*   -- Return TRUE if no elements in list, otherwise FALSE*

can_move: BOOLEAN
*   -- Returns TRUE if cursor can move forward, otherwise false*

get_item_at_cursor: T
*   -- Return the item under cursor*

-- Commands
insert_front (item: T)
*   -- Add item to the front of the list*
*   require*
*   no_duplicate: not present (item)*
*   ensure*
*   number_elements = old number_elements + 1*
*   front_item = item*
*   number_elements = 1 implies back_item = item*

insert_back (item: T)
*   -- Add item to the back of the list*
*   require*
*   no_duplicate: not present (item)*
*   ensure*
*   number_elements = old number_elements + 1*
*   back_item = item*
*   number_elements = 1 implies front_item = item*

insert_after (item: T; value: T)
*   -- Add item after element item in list*
*   require*
*   item_present: present (item)*
*   no_duplicate: not present (value)*
*   ensure*
*   number_elements = old number_elements + 1*

insert_before (item: T; value: T)
*   -- Add item before element item in list*
*   require*
*   item_present: present (item)*
*   no_duplicate: not present (value)*
*   ensure*
*   number_elements = old number_elements + 1*

remove (item: T)
    -- Remove the item from the list
  require
    item_present: present (item)
  ensure
    number_elements = old number_elements - 1
    number_elements = 1 implies front_item = back_item

remove_front
    -- Remove the first item in list
  require
    sufficient_elements: number_elements > 0
  ensure
    number_elements = old number_elements - 1
    number_elements = 1 implies front_item = back_item

remove_back
    -- Remove the last item in list
  require
    sufficient_elements: number_elements > 0
  ensure
    number_elements = old number_elements - 1
    number_elements = 1 implies front_item = back_item

remove_after (item: T)
    -- Remove the element after item on list
  require
    item_present: present (item)
    item_not_last: item /= back_item
  ensure
    number_elements = old number_elements - 1
    number_elements = 1 implies front_item = back_item

remove_before (item: T)
    -- Remove the element before item on list
  require
    item_present: present (item)
    item_not_first: item /= front_item
  ensure
    number_elements = old number_elements - 1
    number_elements = 1 implies front_item = back_item

reverse_sequence: UNORDERED_LIST

```
        -- Reverse the sequence of elements in the receiver and return new list
    require
        non_empty: number_elements > 0
    ensure
        Result.number_elements = number_elements

start
        -- Move cursor to the first element in list
    require
        not_empty: number_elements > 0

move_forward
        -- Move the cursor to the right one element
    require
        can_move_forward: can_move

invariant
    number_elements >= 0

end -- class UNORDERED_LIST
```

We discuss several of the routine specifications given in Listing 7.6. The reader is encouraged to study the others carefully.

The interface to the query routine, *item_after*, is

```
item_after (item: T): T
        -- Return the element just after item in the list
    require
        not_last_item: item /= back_item
        item_present: present (item)
```

A client must ensure before making this query on a list object that (1) the *item* is not the last item in the list, and (2) the *item* is present in the list. If any of these conditions are violated the *item_after* routine cannot do its job and an exception will be raised by the routine.

The interface to routine *remove_before* is

```
    remove_before (item: T)
        -- Remove the element before item on list
    require
        item_present: present (item)
        item_not_first: item /= front_item
    ensure
        number_elements = old number_elements - 1
        number_elements = 1 implies front_item = back_item
```

Before invoking this routine on a list object, the client must ensure that (1) the *item* is present in the object, and (2) the *item* is not the first object in the list. A list object must satisfy the two postconditions specified upon completion of this routine.

7.2.2 Implementation of class UNORDERED_LIST

The implementation details for the full class, UNORDERED_LIST, are given in Listing 7.7. The details of class NODE are given in Listing 7.8. The details of these listings are discussed in Section 7.2.3.

Listing 7.7 Class UNORDERED_LIST

```
class UNORDERED_LIST [T]

feature {NONE} -- Protected section
    front_node:  NODE [T]
    back_node:  NODE [T]
    cursor:      NODE [T]

feature -- Data model to support queries
    front_item:          T
    back_item:           T
    number_elements: INTEGER
            -- Queries

    item_after (item: T): T is
            -- Return the element just after item in the list
        require
            not_last_item: item /= back_item
            item_present: present (item)
        local
            item_node: NODE [T]
        do
            item_node := find (item)
            Result := item_node.next.value
        end

    item_before (item: T): T is
            -- Return the item just before element item in the list
```

```
require
    not_first_item: item /= front_item
    item_present: present (item)
local
    previous, curr: NODE [T]
do
    previous := front_node
    from
        curr := previous.next
    until
        curr.value = item
    loop
        previous := curr
        curr := curr.next
    end
    Result := previous.value
end

present (item: T): BOOLEAN is
        -- Return TRUE if item is in list, otherwise FALSE
    local
        item_node: NODE [T]
    do
        item_node := find (item)
        Result := item_node /= void
    end

empty: BOOLEAN is
        -- Return TRUE if no elements in list, otherwise FALSE
    do
        Result := number_elements = 0
    end

can_move: BOOLEAN is
        -- Returns TRUE if cursor can move forward, otherwise false
    do
        Result := cursor /= void
    end

get_item_at_cursor: T is
        -- Return the item under cursor
    do
```

```
        Result := cursor.value
    end

insert_front (item: T) is
        -- Add item to the front of the list
    require
        no_duplicate: not present (item)
    local
        old_front: NODE [T]
    do
        if front_node = void then
            !! front_node.make (item, void)
        else
            old_front := front_node
            !! front_node.make (item, old_front)
        end
        front_item := item
        if number_elements = 0 then
            back_node := front_node
            back_item := item
        end
        number_elements := number_elements + 1
    ensure
        number_elements = old number_elements + 1
        front_item = item
        number_elements = 1 implies back_item = item
    end

insert_back (item: T) is
        -- Add item to the back of the list
    require
        no_duplicate: not present (item)
    local
        new_node: NODE [T]
    do
        back_item := item
        if number_elements = 0 then
            !! back_node.make (item, void)
            front_node := back_node
            front_item := item
        else
            !! new_node.make (item, void)
```

```
      back_node.link (new_node)
      back_node := new_node
    end
    number_elements := number_elements + 1
  ensure
    number_elements = old number_elements + 1
    back_item = item
    number_elements = 1 implies front_item = item
  end

insert_after (item: T; value: T) is
    -- Add item after element item in list
  require
    item_present: present (item)
    no_duplicate: not present (value)
  local
    item_node: NODE [T]
    new_node: NODE [T]
  do
    item_node := find (item)
    !! new_node.make (value, item_node.next)
    item_node.link (new_node)
    if new_node.next = void then
      back_node := new_node
      back_item := value
    end
    number_elements := number_elements + 1
  ensure
    number_elements = old number_elements + 1
  end

insert_before (item: T; value: T) is
    -- Add item before element item in list
  require
    item_present: present (item)
    no_duplicate: not present (value)
  local
    curr, previous: NODE [T]
    new_node: NODE [T]
  do
    previous := void
    from
```

```
                curr := front_node
            until
                curr.value = item
            loop
                previous := curr
                curr := curr.next
            end
            !! new_node.make (value, curr)
            if previous = void then
                front_node := new_node
                front_item := value
            else
                previous.link (new_node)
            end
            number_elements := number_elements + 1
        ensure
            number_elements = old number_elements + 1
        end

    remove (item: T) is
            -- Remove the item from the list
        require
            item_present: present (item)
        local
            curr, previous: NODE [T]
        do
            previous := void
            from
                curr := front_node
            until
                curr.value = item
            loop
                previous := curr
                curr := curr.next
            end
            if previous = void then
                front_node := front_node.next
                if front_node = void then
                    back_node := front_node
                else
                    front_item := front_node.value
```

```
            end
        elseif curr = back_node then
            back_node := previous
            back_item := previous.value
            previous.link (void)
        else
            previous.link (curr.next)
        end
        number_elements := number_elements - 1
    ensure
        number_elements = old number_elements - 1
        number_elements = 1 implies front_item = back_item
    end

remove_front is
        -- Remove the first item in list
    require
        sufficient_elements: number_elements > 0
    do
        remove (front_item)
    ensure
        number_elements = old number_elements - 1
        number_elements = 1 implies front_item = back_item
    end

remove_back is
        -- Remove the last item in list
    require
        sufficient_elements: number_elements > 0
    do
        remove (back_item)
    ensure
        number_elements = old number_elements - 1
        number_elements = 1 implies front_item = back_item
    end

remove_after (item: T) is
        -- Remove the element after item on list
    require
        item_present: present (item)
        item_not_last: item /= back_item
    local
```

```
            value: T
        do
            value := item_after (item)
            remove (value)
        ensure
            number_elements = old number_elements - 1
            number_elements = 1 implies front_item = back_item
        end

    remove_before (item: T) is
            -- Remove the element before item on list
        require
            item_present: present (item)
            item_not_first: item /= front_item
        local
            value: T
        do
            value := item_before (item)
            remove (value)
        ensure
            number_elements = old number_elements - 1
            number_elements = 1 implies front_item = back_item
        end

    reverse_sequence: UNORDERED_LIST [T] is
            -- Reverse the sequence of elements in the receiver and return new list
        require
            non_empty: number_elements > 0
        local
            value: T
        do
            !! Result
            start
            from
                value := get_item_at_cursor
                Result.insert_front (value)
            until
                value = back_item
            loop
                move_forward
                value := get_item_at_cursor
                Result.insert_front (value)
```

```
        end
    ensure
        Result.number_elements = number_elements
    end

start is
        -- Move cursor to the first element in list
    require
        not_empty: number_elements > 0
    do
        cursor := front_node
    ensure
        cursor = front_node
    end

move_forward is
        -- Move the cursor to the right one element
    require
        can_move_forward: can_move
    do
        cursor := cursor.next
    end

feature {NONE} -- Protected section for internal use

    find (item: T): NODE [T] is
            -- Return the node containing item, if present
        local
            item_node: NODE [T]
        do
            from
                item_node := front_node
            until
                item_node = void or else item_node.value = item
            loop
                item_node := item_node.next
            end
            Result := item_node
        end

invariant
        number_elements >= 0

end -- class UNORDERED_LIST
```

Listing 7.8 Class NODE

```
class NODE [T]

creation {UNORDERED_LIST}
    make

feature {UNORDERED_LIST}

    value: T

    next: NODE [T]

    link (to: NODE [T]) is
        do
            next := to
        end

feature {NONE}

    make (item: T;  connected_to: NODE [T]) is
        do
            value := item
            next := connected_to
        end

end -- class NODE
```

7.2.3 Discussion of implementation

7.2.3.1 The data model

The attributes of a list containing three elements are shown in Figure 7.6.

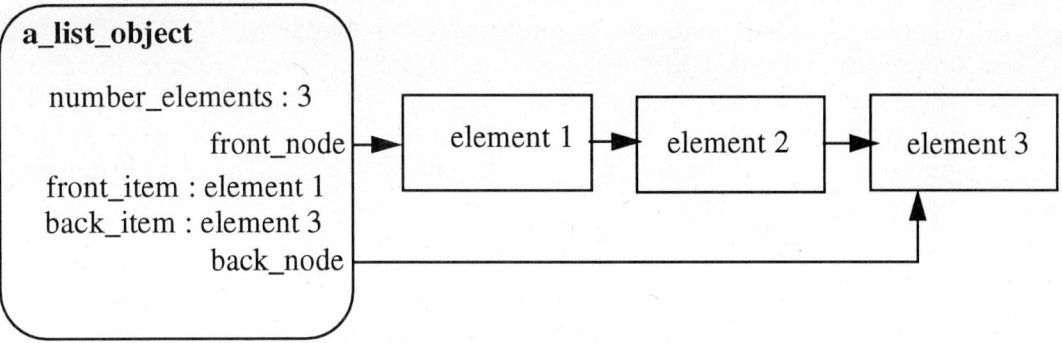

Figure 7.6 List Object with Three Elements

The "hidden" attributes *front_node* and *back_node* allow quick access to the front and back of the list. These attributes are for internal use only. A user cannot access these attributes. These internal attributes are most useful when either inserting an item at the front or at the back of the list.

The public attributes *front_item* and *back_item* are useful if the user makes a query about these elements. This query would be answered with storage (as opposed to computation).

7.2.3.2 Internal routine *find*

Routine *find*, in a feature section with export scope NONE, is used internally to return a node containing *item*, if *item* is present. If *item* is not present, find returns *Void*.

The loop is terminated when the condition, *item_node = Void or else item_node.value = item* is satisfied. The *or else* operator assures that only when *item_node* is not *Void* will its *value* be accessed. Either a *Void* node or the node containing *item* will be returned.

7.2.3.3 Public routine *item_before*

The body of routine *item_before* is

```
previous := front_node
from curr := previous.next
until curr.value = item
loop
        previous := curr
        curr := curr.next
end
Result := previous.value
```

The objects *previous* and *curr* are declared as type NODE [T]. The object *previous* is initially set to *front_node*. The object *curr* is initially set to *previous.next*. In the body of the loop, *previous* is advanced to *curr* and *curr* advanced to *curr.next* until *curr.value* = *item*. The reader might be wondering, what guarantee is there that *curr.value* will ever equal *item*? What guarantee is there that if *curr.value* equals *item* that *previous* will not be *Void*?

The preconditions of the routine assure that both conditions will occur. The element, *item*, is guaranteed to be present and the *item* is guaranteed not to be the first element. The presence of the preconditions permit the code to be much simpler than it otherwise would be because it does not need to test and protect against illegal input conditions.

7.2.3.4 Public routine *insert_front*

The body of code for this routine is

```
if front_node = Void then
      !!front_node.make (item, Void)
else
      old_front := front_node
      !!front_node.make (item, old_front)
end
front_item := item
if number_elements = 0 then
      back_node := front_node
      back_item := item
end
number_elements := number_elements + 1
```

A logical branch is introduced that links *front_node* to *Void* if the list is initially empty or to *old_front* if the list is non-empty.

Another logical test determines whether *back_node* and *back_item* must be set equal to *front_node* and *item* respectively in the case where *item* is the first element inserted in the list.

7.2.3.5 Public routine *insert_back*

The body of code for this routine is

```
back_item := item
if number_elements = 0 then
      !!back_node.make (item, Void)
```

```
        front_node := back_node
        front_item := item
else
        !!new_node.make (item, Void)
        back_node.link (new_node)
        back_node := new_node
end
number_elements := number_elements + 1
```

A logical branch separates the routine into two cases: an insertion into an empty list and an insertion into a non-empty list. For the first case, insertion into an empty list, a new *back_node* is created and linked to *Void*. The object *front_node* is set equal to *back_node* and *front_item* set equal to *item*. For the case when the list is not empty, a *new_node* is created and linked to *Void*. The existing *back_node* is linked to the *new_node* and then the value of *back_node* is set equal to the *new_node*.

7.2.3.6 Public routine *insert_before*

The body of code for this routine is

```
previous := Void
from curr := front_node
until curr.value = item
loop
        previous := curr
        curr := curr.next
end
!!new_node.make (value, curr)
if previous = Void then
        front_node := new_node
        front_item := value
else
        previous.link (new_node)
end
number_elements := number_elements + 1
```

The object *curr* is initialized to *front_node*. The loop advances *previous* and *curr* until the *value* field of *curr* equals *item*. A *new_node* is initialized with *value* and linked to *curr*. The precondition that requires *item* to be present assures that this loop will terminate. If the object *previous* is *Void*, then the objects *front_node* and *front_item* must be updated. If *previous* is not *Void*, then *previous* must be linked to *new_node* (it was formally linked to *curr*).

7.2.3.7 Public routine *remove*

The body of code for this routine is

```
previous := Void
from curr := front_node
until curr.value = item
loop
        previous := curr
        curr := curr.next
end
if previous = Void then -- removing front_node
        front_node := front_node.next
        if front_node = Void then
            back_node := front_node
        else
            front_item := front_node.value
        end
elseif curr = back_node then -- removing back_node
        back_node := previous
        back_item := previous.value
        previous.link (Void)
else
        previous.link (curr.next)
end
number_elements := number_elements - 1
```

The precondition of this routine requires the *item* being removed to be present. A loop advances *previous* and *curr* until the *value* field of *curr* equals *item*. If at the termination of this loop *previous* equals *Void*, this serves as an indicator that the front node (*front_node*) is being removed. In this case *front_node* is replaced by *front_node.next*. If at the termination of the loop *curr* equals *back_node*, *back_node* is set equal to *previous*. The object *back_item* is set equal to the *value* field of *previous* and *previous* is linked to *Void*. Finally, if at the termination of the loop *previous* does not equal *Void* and *curr* does not equal *back_node*, *previous* is linked to *curr.next* (this bypasses *curr*).

7.2.3.8 Public routines *remove_front* and *remove_back*

The bodies of code for these routines are *remove (front_item)* and *remove (back_item)*, respectively. This is an example where internal code reuse saves a great deal of programming effort.

7.2.3.9 Public routines *remove_after* and *remove_before*

The bodies of code for these routines are

```
value := item_after (item)
remove (value)
```

and

```
value := item_before (item)
remove (value)
```

respectively. Here the use of the existing routines *item_after* or *item_before* and *remove* provides other examples of internal code reuse.

7.2.3.10 Public routine *reverse_sequence*

The body of code for this routine is

```
!!Result
start
from value :=           get_item_at_cursor
                        Result.insert_front (value)
until value = back_item
loop
     move_forward
     value := get_item_at_cursor
     Result.insert_front (value)
end
```

The return type promised by this routine is of type UNORDERED_LIST. An object, *Result*, is constructed first by invoking a creation routine. The command *start* resets the *cursor* in the list to *front_node*. In the loop the elements of the list are inserted into the front of the *Result* object (like pushing the elements onto a stack). When this loop terminates (when the *value* field equals *back_item* of the list), the elements in the UNORDERED_LIST object *Result* will be in the reverse order of the elements in the original list. It is noted that there is no need to explicitly return the object *Result*. This is by default the object that is returned.

The reader is invited to dissect the remaining routines that were not discussed in this section.

7.3   Unordered list with duplicates allowed

An unordered list with duplicate elements allowed has exactly the same protocol as the unordered list presented in section 7.2 with the one important difference being that duplicate elements are allowed. The only routine that this significantly affects is *remove_back*.

In the section 7.2 version of *remove_back*, the one line of code is *remove (back_item)*. This code is sufficient because there can be only one element with the value *back_item*. In the revised version of UNORDERED_LIST, called UNORDERED_LIST_WITH_DUPLICATES, the modified routine *remove_back* is given in Listing 7.9 along with a few other sample routines. All of the preconditions that require no duplicates are absent.

Listing 7.9   Portions of class UNORDERED_LIST_WITH_DUPLICATES

```
class UNORDERED_LIST_WITH_DUPLICATES [ T ]
-- Duplicate values are allowed in list

-- Same data features as Listing 7.7 for UNORDERED_LIST

-- Queries
-- Same query routines as in Listing 7.7 except the first occurrence of item is used

-- Commands
-- Same command routines as in Listsing 7.7 except the precondition,
-- no_duplicate is absent and item means the first occurrence of item

    remove_back is
        -- Remove the last item in list
        require
            sufficient_elements: number_elements > 0
        local
            previous, curr : NODE [ T ]
        do
            from curr := front_node
            until curr = back_node
            loop
                previous := curr
                curr := curr.next
```

```
        end
      back_node := previous
      if back_node = Void then
          front_node := back_node
      else
          back_node.link (Void)
      end
    ensure
      number_elements = old number_elements - 1
      number_elements = 1 implies front_item = back_item
    end  -- remove_back
```

end -- *UNORDERED_LIST_WITH_DUPLICATES*

It is left as an exercise for the reader to complete and test the revised class UNORDERED_LIST_WITH_DUPLICATES.

7.4   The stack revisited

In section 7.1 the important stack container class was presented and implemented both statically and dynamically. In this section we revisit the stack abstraction and once again take advantage of code reuse, specifically from class UNORDERED_LIST_WITH_DUPLICATES presented in section 7.3.

The principle of composition is used in this case to reuse the code of the unordered list abstraction. Our new DYNAMIC_STACK class contains an instance of an UNORDERED_LIST_WITH_DUPLICATES. The implementation of this revised stack class is presented in Listing 7.10.

The layering of abstractions given by the DYNAMIC_STACK being composed of an UNORDERED_LIST_WITH_DUPLICATES allows only the limited number of routines required of the list to be used by the stack. Clients of the stack have access only to the public features of the stack and do not have access to the list.

A significant advantage of using composition in this design is that if the implementation of the list should be changed in the future, then as long as the interface to the two routines *insert_front* and *remove_front* remain unchanged, the stack class is unaffected. This would not be true if inheritance were used. In that case any changes made in the implementation of list would directly affect the stack.

Listing 7.10 Revised DYNAMIC_STACK class

```
class DYNAMIC_STACK [T]

creation
    make

feature {NONE} -- Protected section

    list: UNORDERED_LIST_WITH_DUPLICATES [T]

feature

    number_elements: INTEGER

    make is
        do
            !! list
        end

    push (item: T) is
        do
            list.insert_front (item)
            number_elements := number_elements + 1
        ensure
            number_elements = old number_elements + 1
        end

    pop is
        require
            non_empty: number_elements > 0
        do
            list.remove_front
            number_elements := number_elements - 1
        ensure
            number_elements = old number_elements - 1
        end

    top: T is
        require
            non_empty: number_elements > 0
        do
            Result := list.front_item
        end
```

```
empty: BOOLEAN is
    do
        Result := number_elements = 0
    end

invariant
    number_elements >= 0

end -- class DYNAMIC_STACK
```

7.5 The queue

A queue is a container abstraction that implements a "first-in-first-out" service mechanism. That is, elements may be removed in the same order as they are inserted. Access in a queue is limited to only one element, namely the oldest element that has been inserted (oldest meaning the element that has been in the queue the longest time).

The interface to a queue class contains the following queries and commands:

Queries

- *number_elements : INTEGER*

- *first_element : T*

- *empty : BOOLEAN*

Commands

- *make*

- *insert (item : T)*

- *remove*

The *first_element* query is implemented through storage and the last two through computation (as routines).

The implementation of the queue is accomplished using composition once again. The details are shown in Listing 7.11.

Listing 7.11 Class DYNAMIC_QUEUE

```
class DYNAMIC_QUEUE [T]

creation
    make

feature

    number_elements: INTEGER

    make is
        do
            !! list
        end

    insert (item: T) is
        do
            list.insert_back (item)
            number_elements := number_elements + 1
        ensure
            number_elements = old number_elements + 1
            number_elements = 1 implies first_element = item
        end

    remove is
        require
            non_empty: number_elements > 0
        do
            list.remove_front
            number_elements := number_elements - 1
        ensure
            number_elements = old number_elements - 1
        end

    first_element: T is
        require
            non_empty: number_elements > 0
        do
            Result := list.front_item
        end

    empty: BOOLEAN is
        do
            Result := number_elements = 0
```

ensure
    Result = **true implies** number_elements = 0
  end

feature {NONE}

    list: UNORDERED_LIST_WITH_DUPLICATES [T]

invariant
    number_elements >= 0

end -- class DYNAMIC_QUEUE

The list routines *insert_back* and *remove_front* are internally called by the queue routines *insert* and *remove*.

7.6 Summary

- It is useful to make a distinction between a container object and the things that it contains.

- A container class is one that holds zero or more elements, each formally declared to be of a particular class type.

- The actual type inserted in a container must conform to (be a descendant of) the formal type. This allows a container to hold either a homogeneous or heterogeneous collection of elements.

- A container class must specify protocol (a set of rules) for inserting, deleting and accessing elements. This is what differentiates one type of container from another.

- Before a given class, container, or otherwise can be considered "reusable," it typically has to meet the following conditions: (1) Each of its features has been extensively tested in many different applications over a reasonably long period of time, (2) it provides a range of services (implemented as routines) sufficient to meet the varied needs of many clients (applications that use the component), and (3) each of the services is efficiently implemented.

- Bertrand Meyer in his classic book *Object-Oriented Software Construction* states: "Few issues are more important in software development than the proper design of module interfaces."

- The protocol for insertion and deletion that defines the unique signature of a stack specifies that the last element inserted onto a stack is the first element that can be deleted from the stack. This is called a "last-in-first-out" (LIFO) protocol.

- The operations with their interface that define the behavior of a STACK class are
  push (item : T) - add item to stack
  pop - remove item from stack
  top_element : T - access first element that can be removed
  empty : BOOLEAN - True if no elements contained in stack, otherwise False

- An unordered list is a linear sequence of arbitrary elements with no duplicate elements allowed. The unordered list is considered linear because its elements are stored in sequence, one after another. Such a list has a well-defined "front" and "back."

- The queries and commands defined for an UNORDERED_LIST are

  Queries (What do we wish to find out about a list?)
  What is the first item on the list, if any?
  What is the last item on the list, if any?
  What is the last item removed from the list, if any?
  How many elements are in the list?
  Is a given item present in the list?
  What is the element just after a given item?
  What is the element just before a given item?
  Is the list empty?
  Is there an element directly to the right of the current element that a
     cursor points to?
  What is the element being pointed to by the cursor?

  Commands (What do we wish to do with a list?)
  Insert an item into the front of the list
  Insert an item into the back of the list
  Insert an item just after a given item on the list
  Insert an item just before a given item on the list
  Remove a given item from the list
  Remove an item from the front of the list
  Remove an item from the back of the list
  Remove an item just after a given item on the list
  Remove an item just before a given item on the list
  Produce a list that contains the same elements in the reverse order from
     a given list

Move a cursor so it points to the first element in the list
Move the cursor forward so it points to the next element in the list

- For an ORDERED_LIST, only a single insertion command, *insert*, is appropriate. The element being inserted must be placed after the element just smaller than it and before the element just larger than it.

- All of the other routines in an ORDERED_LIST are identical to those of either class UNORDERED_LIST or UNORDERED_LIST_WITH_DUPLICATES, depending on whether one wishes the ordered list to deny or allow duplicate elements.

- In an ORDERED_LIST the generic parameter *T* is constrained by the expression, *T -> COMPARABLE*. This is required because the implementation details of the *insert* routine require that the inserted *item* be compared to the *value* fields of some elements.

- A queue is a container abstraction that implements a "first-in-first-out" service mechanism. That is, elements may be removed in the same order as they are inserted. Access in a queue is limited to only one element, namely the oldest element that has been inserted.

- The interface to a queue class contains the following queries and commands:

Queries
number_elements : INTEGER
first_element : T
empty : BOOLEAN

Commands
make
insert (item : T)
remove

7.7   Exercises

1. Cite several examples of a stack that exist in the "real world."

2. Cite several examples of a queue that exist in the "real world."

3. Cite several examples of an UNORDERED_LIST that exist in the "real world."

4. Cite several examples of an UNORDERED_LIST_WITH_DUPLICATES that exist in the "real world."

5. Cite several examples of an ORDERED_LIST that exist in the "real world."

6. Implement class UNORDERED_LIST statically. Duplicate elements should not be allowed in your class. Discuss the advantages and disadvantages of the static versus dynamic implementation presented in the book.

7. Implement a stack class that does not allow duplicate elements by inheriting from class UNORDERED_LIST. Discuss the differences between this implementation and the implementation given in Listing 7.12.

8. Implement a queue class that does allow duplicate elements by inheriting from class UNORDERED_LIST_WITH_DUPLICATES. Discuss the differences between this implementation and the implementation given in Listing 7.13.

9. Write a test program that exercises all the queries and routines associated with class stack.

10. Write a test program that exercises all the queries and routines associated with class queue.

11. Explain why it is not desirable to include a method display in any of the container classes presented in this chapter.

7.8 References

1. *Reusable Software Components: The Base Object-Oriented Component Libraries*, Meyer, Bertrand, Prentice Hall, Englewood Cliffs, NJ, 1994.

Chapter 8

Recursion as a Design Principle

An Eiffel routine can invoke itself. This capability, supported by most modern programming languages, is called **recursion**. Although the capability of recursion might seem quite innocent and make you wonder why an entire chapter of this book is dedicated to the subject, recursion is actually a powerful and sometimes subtle design principle. Many important algorithms can be expressed recursively. Some of these will be explored in this chapter. In order to be able to use recursion successfully, one needs to learn how to think recursively. Many beginners to this subject find this at least initially challenging. Hopefully this chapter will get you on your way to using recursion intelligently and successfully.

8.1 The mechanics of recursion

As our first example of recursion consider the routine *do_it_recursively*, given in Listing 8.1. Assume that this routine is embedded in class APPLICATION and that from its creation routine the function *do_it_recursively ("Eiffel is a wonderful language", 5)* is invoked.

Listing 8.1 First example of recursion

```
do_it_recursively (str : STRING; number_times : INTEGER) is
    do
```

```
    if number_times > 0 then
            o.putstring (str)
            io.new_line
            do_it_recursively (str, number_times - 1) -- recursive call
    end
end -- do_it_recursively
```

The program output is

Eiffel is a wonderful language
Eiffel is a wonderful language
Eiffel is a wonderful language
Eiffel is a wonderful language
Eiffel is a wonderful language

As you might have expected, the input string, "Eiffel is a wonderful language," is output five times. Before we explain the mechanics of this routine, let us add one more simple specification to the problem. Suppose we wish the routine to number the five lines consecutively so that the output becomes:

1. Eiffel is a wonderful language
2. Eiffel is a wonderful language
3. Eiffel is a wonderful language
4. Eiffel is a wonderful language
5. Eiffel is a wonderful language

Listing 8.2 shows our first try at this; it's a modified version of Listing 8.1.

Listing 8.2 Modified version of Listing 8.1

```
do_it_recursively (str : STRING; number_times : INTEGER) is
    do
        if number_times > 0 then
            io.putint (number_times)
            io.putstring (". ")
            io.putstring (str)
            io.new_line
            do_it_recursively (str, number_times - 1) -- recursive call
        end
end -- do_it_recursively
```

In Listing 8.2 two extra lines of code are inserted in front of the output statement for the string, *str*. Unfortunately, the modified *do_it_recursively* routine fails. Its output is

5. Eiffel is a wonderful language
4. Eiffel is a wonderful language
3. Eiffel is a wonderful language
2. Eiffel is a wonderful language
1. Eiffel is a wonderful language

Oh well, at least the third line of output is correct!

Upon entry to the routine the first time, the test, *number_times > 0*, is passed. The value of *number_times*, namely 5, is output followed by a dot and space. Then the routine invokes itself (i.e., recursion) sending the value 4 as input. The same thing happens again, and the routine is recursively invoked with input 3, then later input 2, then later input 1, and finally input 0. When the input is 0, the test, *number_times > 0*, fails and control is passed back to the previous level of recursion (when *value = 1*). The location within the *do_it_recursively* routine at which control is passed back is one line under the call to *do_it_recursively*. But this line is the "end" of the *if then* control structure. Nothing further needs to be done. Control is then passed back to the call to the routine when *value = 2*. Again, nothing further needs to be done. In this same way control is passed back to the recursive call when *value = 3*, then *value = 4*, and finally *value = 5*. In each case no further output or processing occur. The routine terminates.

Suppose we change the first line of code in Listing 8.2 to the following: *io.putint (6 - number_times)*. Now we have it. Now the output will be the desired output given above. Unfortunately, this routine works only if called initially to print exactly five times. This solution therefore is unacceptable.

Suppose we perform one final modification on *do_it_recursively*. This is shown in Listing 8.3 as a complete application.

Listing 8.3 Final version of *do_it_recursively*

```
class APPLICATION

creation
        start

feature
```

```
start is
    do
        do_it_recursively ("Eiffel is a wonderful language", 5)
    end

do_it_recursively (str: STRING; number_times: INTEGER) is
    do
        if number_times > 0 then
            do_it_recursively (str, number_times - 1)
            io.putint (number_times)
            io.putstring (". ")
            io.putstring (str)
            io.new_line
        end
    end

end -- class APPLICATION
```

Let us dissect the recursion of Listing 8.3.

The first recursive call, *do_it_recursively (str, 5)*, is pushed onto the run-time stack (the parameter *number_times* has the value 5). This is followed by five additional calls to *do_it_recursively* that are pushed onto the run-time stack with *number_times* equal to 4, 3, 2, 1, and 0 respectively.

When the last recursive call is invoked, with *number_times* equal to 0, the *if number_times > 0* expression fails causing the run-time stack to be popped. Control is transferred automatically to the *io.putint (number_times)* command with *number_times* equal to 1. This produces the first line of output: **1. Eiffel is a wonderful language**.

The run-time stack is again popped, control again transferred to the *io.putint (number_times)* command, and the parameter *number_times* equal to 2. This produces the second line of output: **2. Eiffel is a wonderful language**.

This pattern is continued until all of the desired output is produced. It is noted that if the user wishes *n* numbered output lines, this final version of the routine allows this by invoking the routine with the appropriate *number_times*.

Let us reinforce our understanding of the mechanics of recursion by considering another relatively simple recursive routine. This is given in Listing 8.4.

Listing 8.4 Another relatively simple recursive routine

```
print_recursively (value : REAL) is
    local
        temporary : REAL
    do
        temporary := 10 * value
        if value > 0.0 then
            io.putreal (value)
            io.new_line
            print_recursively (value - 0.1) -- recursive call
            io.putstring ("%Ntemporary = ")
            io.putreal (temporary)
            io.new_line
    end
end -- print_recursively
```

Suppose the routine is invoked from the creation routine of the application class as *print_recursively (1.0)*. This routine is more challenging to understand because there are three lines of code below the recursive call.

Let us "walk" through the recursion and trace the details to uncover the mechanics.

During the first call of the routine, the value of *temporary* is set to 10.0. The first output to occur is *value*, 1.0. Before any of the last three lines of output occur, the recursive call inputs 0.9 and we return to the beginning of *print_recursively*. The value of temporary is set to 9.0. The next output of 0.9 occurs. The successive recursive calls cause the outputs 0.8, 0.7, 0.6, 0.5, 0.4, 0.3, 0.2, and 0.1 to occur. When the recursive call is made with input 0.0, *temporary* is set to 0.0 but the entire block of code nested in the *if then* structure is bypassed. The last recursive execution of the routine actually reaches its end statement.

Following this event, control is returned to the recursively called routine in the program statement one line below the recursive call statement that has just been completed. The values of all local objects and input parameters are restored to the state that existed just before the recursive call was made. This information is automatically stored on a stack called the run-time stack. When the recursive call (the one just completed) had been made in the first place, the values of all local objects and input parameters had been automatically pushed onto this run-time stack.

Now the last three lines of the routine are executed and "Temporary = 1.0" is output.

When the end of the routine is reached, the recursive stack is again popped and control is returned, as before, to the previous call to *print_recursively* when *temporary* is equal to 2.0. This pattern continues until all recursive calls have been popped from the run-time stack. This leads to the following output for Listing 8.4:

1.0
0.9
0.8
0.7
0.6
0.5
0.4
0.3
0.2
0.1

Temporary = 1.0

Temporary = 2.0

...

Temporary = 10.0

The actual mechanics of recursion are summarized below.

Mechanics of recursion

Each time a recursive call occurs, the values of all local objects and input parameters are pushed onto a run-time stack. Upon hitting the "end" statement of a recursive routine, the previous recursive call, if any, is popped from the run-time stack. All the local variables and input parameters are restored to the values that were in place just before the recursive call was executed. Program control returns to the statement that is one line below the recursive call that was just completed.

One final example is provided to solidify your understanding of the mechanics of recursion. Consider the recursive routine in Listing 8.5. Suppose that it is invoked as *print_recursively (10)*.

Listing 8.5 More recursion to solidify mechanics

```
print_recursively (value : INTEGER) is
do
    if value /= 0 then
        print_recursively (value // 2)
```

```
        io.new_line
        io.putint (value)
        print_recursively (value // 2)
    end
end -- print_recursively
```

Some of the events that occur in Listing 8.5 when the initial value of 10 is passed to *print_recursively* are explained below.

1. Enter the routine with value = 10.

2. The system pushes this input parameter (10) onto the run-time stack before the next recursive call with value = 5 occurs.

3. The system pushes this input parameter (5) onto the run-time stack before the next recursive call with value = 2 occurs.

4. The system pushes this input parameter (2) onto the run-time stack before the next recursive call with value = 1 occurs.

5. The system pushes this input parameter (1) onto the run-time stack before the next recursive call with value = 0 occurs.

6. The routine bypasses the code in the *if then* clause and hits its end statement.

7. The system returns control to the statements *io.new_line* and *io.putint (value)* (output statements) and pops the run-time stack so that value is restored to 1. The value 1 is output.

8. Another recursive call is made with value = 0.

9. The code in the *if then* statement is bypassed and the end statement is reached.

10. The system returns control to the line below this recursive call (the end statement).

11. The system again returns control to one line below the previous recursive call (the first line of output) and restores the input parameter value to 2. This value is output.

12. The routine is called recursively with value = 1.

13. A recursive call is made with value = 0.

14. The code in the *if then* statement is bypassed and the end statement is reached.

15. The system returns control to the line below this recursive call (the end statement).

16. The system again returns control to the output statements and restores the input parameter to 5. This value is output.

17. A recursive call with value = 2 occurs.

It is left as an exercise for you to explain all the remaining events associated with this recursion. The final output is

```
1
2
1
5
1
2
1
10
1
2
1
5
1
2
1
```

8.2   Relationship between recursion and iteration

In section 8.1 the mechanics of recursion were explored. Can a recursive routine be implemented iteratively? The answer is always yes. We demonstrate this by recasting the recursive routine presented in Listing 8.5 iteratively. This revised iterative version of the routine is presented in Listing 8.6.

Listing 8.6 Iterative version of Listing 8.5

```
feature
    a_stack : DYNAMIC_STACK [ INTEGER ]

print_iteratively (number : INTEGER) is
    local
```

```
        value : INTEGER
do
    from value := number
            a_stack.push (value)
    until a_stack.empty
    loop
        if value /= 0 then
            value := value // 2
            if value /= 0 then
                a_stack.push (value)
            end
        else
            a_stack.pop
            value := a_stack.popped_element
            io.new_line
            io.putint (value)
            value := value // 2
            if value /= 0 then
                a_stack.push (value)
            end
        end
    end
end -- print_iteratively
```

When the call *print_iteratively* (10) is made, the output from Listing 8.6 is the same as in Listing 8.5.

In Listing 8.6, the integer stack, *a_stack*, is used directly by the *print_iteratively* routine to accomplish the same sequence of events that occurs automatically in the recursive version given in Listing 8.5. It is extremely instructive to carefully study the details of Listing 8.6 since all of the manual pushes and pops of *a_stack* emulate exactly what the run-time system does automatically in the recursive version.

If the recursive routine had more than one input parameter and possibly one or more local objects, these would all have to be pushed (and later popped) from *a_stack*. An abstract data type, implemented as a class, would have to be created to allow the manually manipulated stack to restore these values when the stack is popped. This is illustrated in Listing 8.7 which re-implements the recursive routine of Listing 8.4 iteratively. This recursive routine has one input parameter and one local object.

Listing 8.7 Listing 8.4 redone as an iterative routine

```
class INFORMATION
-- Built to support routine print_iteratively
    creation
        make
    feature
        value, temporary : REAL

    make (a_value : REAL; a_temporary : REAL) is
        do
            value := a_value
            temporary := a_temporary
        end -- make

end -- INFORMATION

    feature -- Part of class that print_iteratively is contained within
        a_stack : DYNAMIC_STACK [ INFORMATION ]

    print_iteratively (number : REAL) is
        local
            value          : REAL
            temporary      : REAL
            info           : INFORMATION
        do
            from    value := number
                    !info.make (value, 10.0 * value)
                    a_stack.push (info)
            until a_stack.empty
            loop
                if value > 0 then
                    io.putreal (value)
                    io.new_line
                    value := value - 0.1
                    !!info.make (value, 10.0 * value)
                    if value >= 0 then
                        a_stack.push (info)
                    end
                else
                    a_stack.pop
                    info := a_stack.popped_element
                    temporary := info.temporary
```

```
            io.putstring ("%NTemporary = ")
            io.putreal (temporary)
            io.new_line
        end
    end
end -- print_iteratively
```

8.3   Recursion used in design

In the previous sections of this chapter the focus was on mechanics: what actually happens during a recursion. Understanding the mechanics of recursion, although important, provides little clue as to its real importance in program development. Recursion, although supported by many programming languages, is not a language feature. Recursion is a design methodology, thus the title of this chapter.

There are problems or systems that can naturally be modeled recursively. We describe several of these in this section. In CS 2, Data Structures, most if not all of the important algorithms can be described recursively. We provide a glimpse of this world in this section.

8.3.1   Binary search of sorted arrays

Suppose we have built an array containing sorted data in ascending order (we will assume without loss of generality that the index locations of the data range from 1 to *size*). The datum in index 1 is given as smaller than the datum in index 2, which is smaller than the datum in index 3, etc.

We wish to construct an algorithm that efficiently determines whether a particular value is present in this sorted array.

A simple but inefficient method for doing this would be to visit each and every index location of the array and compare its value to the input value. If all of the index values fail to turn up the input value, the function returns FALSE; otherwise it returns TRUE. The asymptotic efficiency of this linear search algorithm would be $O(n)$. Doubling the size of the array would on the average double the search time.

Can we do better? The answer is yes!

Let us consider the following example that searches an array containing ten data items, each an integer:

1   3   5   7   9   11   13   15   17   19

Suppose we wish to search for the value 3.

We start by considering the element in index *(1 + size) // 2*, or the element in index 5, and comparing it to the input value. The input value 3 is less than the value at index 5 (which is 9). We can therefore eliminate from consideration the values from index 5 to index 10 and concentrate our search on the first four index locations. We continue by considering the element at index *(1 + 4) // 2* or the element at index 2. Bingo! We have found a match-up. OK, this was fairly simple.

Let us search for the presence of element 20, which is not present in the array.

We begin again by comparing the input value to the value in index *(1 + 10) // 2* or index 5. Since 9 is less than 20 we can eliminate from further consideration the array indices 1 to 5 and focus our search on indices 6 to 10. We take the midpoint index again in the remaining range, namely index *(6 + 10) // 2*, or index 8. The value 20 is greater than 15. Now we know that if the value 20 is present in the array it must be in either index 9 or 10. We choose the midpoint of the range once again, namely index *(9 + 10) // 2* or index 9. Since 20 is greater than 17, we choose the midpoint of *(10 + 10) // 2* or index 10. The value 20 is greater than 19 so we know for sure now that 20 is not present in the array.

After each comparison, roughly half of the index range being searched can be eliminated. This suggests that the total number of comparison operations, on the average, would be $O(\log_2 n)$, where n is the size of the array. The algorithm that we have informally used is called the *binary search* algorithm.

Listing 8.8 presents a recursive implementation of this algorithm.

Listing 8.8 Recursive implementation of binary search algorithm

```
present (data : ARRAY[ INTEGER ]; first_index : INTEGER;
         second_index : INTEGER; value : INTEGER) : BOOLEAN is
   require
      data_sorted: sorted (data, first_index, second_index)
   local
      index : INTEGER
   do
      if first_index <= second_index then
         index := (first_index + second_index) // 2
         if data.item (index) = value then
            Result := TRUE
         elseif value > data.item (index) then
            Result := present (data, index + 1, second_index, value)
```

```
        else
                Result := present (data, first_index, index - 1, value)
        end
    else
        Result := FALSE
    end
ensure
    --Result = TRUE implies value is present in data
end -- present
```

The precondition with tag *sorted_data* is very important. A function, *sorted*, is invoked to evaluate the precondition. This function is given in Listing 8.9.

Listing 8.9 Precondition function *sorted* for binary search routine

```
sorted (data : ARRAY [ INTEGER ]; first_index : INTEGER;
            second_index : INTEGER) : BOOLEAN is
    -- Returns TRUE if the data is sorted from smallest to largest
    -- otherwise returns FALSE
local
    index : INTEGER
do
    Result := TRUE
    if first_index <= second_index then
        from index := first_index
        until index = second_index or not Result
        loop
            index := index + 1
            if data.item (index) < data.item (index - 1) then
                Result := FALSE
            end
        end
    end
end -- sorted
```

In words, the recursive binary search algorithm of Listing 8.8 does the following: if the *first_index* is equal or less than the *second_index* (if it is not, the algorithm concludes that the input *value* is not present), the local variable *index* is set to the midpoint of the range. The array is tested for the presence of this input *value* at location *index*. If *value* is greater than the information at *index*, the routine is called recursively but with *first_index* set to *index + 1*. Otherwise the routine is called recursively but with *second_index* set to *index - 1*.

To illustrate the workings of this algorithm, we trace the values of *first_index* and *second_index* when we search an array of 10,000 integers loaded with values equal to ten times their index location (i.e., the value at index 1 is 10, the value at index 2 is 20, etc.) for the input value equal to 795 (not present in the array). The trace is the following:

```
first_index = 1 second_index = 10000
first_index = 1 second_index = 4999
first_index = 1 second_index = 2499
first_index = 1 second_index = 1249
first_index = 1 second_index = 624
first_index = 1 second_index = 311
first_index = 1 second_index = 155
first_index = 79 second_index = 155
first_index = 79 second_index = 116
first_index = 79 second_index = 96
first_index = 79 second_index = 86
first_index = 79 second_index = 81
first_index = 79 second_index = 79
first_index = 80 second_index = 79
795 not present in sorted_data
```

We trace the algorithm with the same set of 10,000 integers as before for the value 9000 (which is present):

```
first_index = 1 second_index = 10000
first_index = 1 second_index = 4999
first_index = 1 second_index = 2499
first_index = 1 second_index = 1249
first_index = 626 second_index = 1249
first_index = 626 second_index = 936
first_index = 782 second_index = 936
first_index = 860 second_index = 936
first_index = 899 second_index = 936
first_index = 899 second_index = 916
first_index = 899 second_index = 906
first_index = 899 second_index = 901
9000 present in sorted_data
```

Finally, using the same array of 10,000 integers, we trace for the value 100001 which lies just beyond the range present in the array. The trace is the following:

```
first_index = 1 second_index = 10000
first_index = 5001 second_index = 10000
first_index = 7501 second_index = 10000
first_index = 8751 second_index = 10000
first_index = 9376 second_index = 10000
first_index = 9689 second_index = 10000
first_index = 9845 second_index = 10000
first_index = 9923 second_index = 10000
first_index = 9962 second_index = 10000
first_index = 9982 second_index = 10000
first_index = 9992 second_index = 10000
first_index = 9997 second_index = 10000
first_index = 9999 second_index = 10000
first_index = 10000 second_index = 10000
first_index = 10001 second_index = 10000
100001 not present in sorted_data
```

The efficiency of the binary search algorithm should be evident from these traces.

What would happen if the programmer forgot the test *if first_index <= second_index* ?

What might happen if the precondition were removed from routine *present* in Listing 8.8 and the data were not sorted?

8.3.2 Quicksort—an efficient recursive sorting algorithm

In Chapter 4, several sorting algorithms were presented. These "elementary" sorting algorithms had an asymptotic efficiency of $O(n^2)$. This implies that for large n, if one doubles the size of the data set being sorted, the sort time would quadruple. This is discouraging if one needs to sort very large data sets. It would be most desirable to find more efficient sorting routines.

In this section we present the classic and extremely fast sorting algorithm called *quicksort* (many computer scientists believe that there is no faster sorting algorithm although this is impossible to prove). This algorithm was designed by Tony Hoare, a computer scientist who has contributed greatly to our field.

Before showing the recursive code for the quicksort algorithm, let us discuss the basic idea of the algorithm. We have an array of data to sort (we assume again that the index range is from index 1 to size, without loss of generality).

We invoke a routine, *partition*, on the array of data. This function returns an index location, *pivot*, and manipulates the data in the array so that all of the elements in the array whose index values are less than *pivot* are smaller than the pivot element and all of the elements in the array whose index values are greater than *pivot* are larger than the pivot element. A sample array of 10 values with pivot equal to 4 (element 7) is

1 5 2 7 8 13 9 12 10 11

After the data array has been partitioned into two disjoint ranges (those elements whose index locations and values are equal or less than that of the pivot element and those elements whose index locations and values are greater than those of the pivot element), we recursively sort each of the two smaller ranges of values. Each of these two ranges of values get partitioned. Then four smaller ranges of data are recursively sorted. This approach to problem solving is called *divide and conquer*.

Before we showcase the entire quicksort algorithm, let us focus our attention on the function, *partition*, that returns a pivot index and partitions the data into two disjoint subsets on each side of the pivot index.

The *partition* function is presented in Listing 8.10.

Listing 8.10 Partition function

```
partition (values : ARRAY [ REAL ]; first_index : INTEGER;
                 second_index : INTEGER) : INTEGER is
    require
        first_less_than_second: first_index <= second_index
    local
        pivot              : REAL
        return_index       : INTEGER
        k                  : INTEGER
        temp               : REAL
    do
        pivot := values.item (first_index)
        from k := first_index
        until values.item (k) > pivot or k = second_index
        loop
            k := k + 1
```

```
    end
    from return_index := second_index
    until values.item (return_index) <= pivot
    loop
        return_index := return_index - 1
    end
    from
    until k >= return_index
    loop
        -- Interchange value[ k ] and values[ return_index ]
        temp := values.item (return_index)
        values.put (values.item (k), return_index)
        values.put (temp, k)
        from
        until values.item (k) > pivot or k = second_index
        loop
            k := k + 1
        end
        from
        until values.item (return_index) <= pivot
        loop
            return_index := return_index - 1
        end
    end
    -- Interchange values[ first_index ] and values[ return_index ]
    temp := values.item (return_index)
    values.put (values.item (first_index), return_index)
    values.put (temp, first_index)
    Result := return_index
ensure
    -- all of the elements in index locations less than return_index have
    -- values less than or equal to values.item (return_index) and all the
    -- elements in index locations greater than return_index have
    -- values greater than values.item (return_index)
end -- partition
```

Problem 9 in the Exercises asks you to perform a detailed "walk-through" of this algorithm on a data set of size 10. You may wish to do this problem now in order to enhance your understanding of this algorithm.

The first line of code in Listing 8.10 indicates that this is the pivot element. If this element is near the middle of the range of element values, the pivot index will be near the middle of the index range. If the pivot element is either much smaller than or much larger than most of the other elements in the array, the pivot index will be either near the *first_index* or the *second_index*. The highly efficient and recursive algorithm quicksort is presented in Listing 8.11.

Listing 8.11 Recursive quicksort routine

```
quicksort (values : ARRAY [ REAL ]; first_index : INTEGER;
                    second_index : INTEGER) is
    require
        first_less_than_second: first_index <= second_index
    local
        pivot : INTEGER
    do
        pivot := partition (values, first_index, second_index)
        if first_index < pivot - 1 then
            quicksort (values, first_index, pivot - 1)
        end
        if pivot + 1 < second_index then
            quicksort (values, pivot + 1, second_index)
        end
    ensure
        elements_sorted: sorted (values, first_index, second_index)
    end -- quicksort
```

The postcondition for the quicksort routine given in Listing 8.11 uses the same type of function as the one given in Listing 8.10 except that the array has a base type of REAL rather than INTEGER.

Once the pivot index is computed, if this *index - 1* is greater than *first_index*, quicksort is invoked recursively with the range *first_index, pivot - 1*. If the pivot *index + 1* is less than *second_index*, quicksort is recursively invoked with the range *pivot + 1, second_index*.

It can be shown that the asymptotic efficiency of quicksort is O ($n\log n$) for most data sets. This breaks down when the input data is either already sorted or close to sorted. This is ironic. When the input data is "good" from the standpoint of sorting, the *quicksort* algorithm performs as an O (n^2) algorithm (see problem 12 in the Exercises).

8.3.3 Binary search tree

This is not a book specifically about data structures so this section will not be as detailed as would be the case if this were a book on data structures.

A *binary tree* is a non-linear data structure containing nodes. Each node is the root of a subtree with at most two branches. More specifically, each node of a binary tree can have at most two children. Each child is itself a node that can have at most two children. A typical but small binary tree with integer items is shown in Figure 8.1.

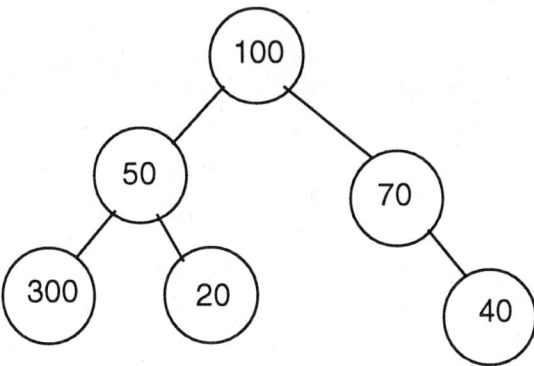

Figure 8.1 Binary Tree

The root node contains the value 100. It has two children. Its left child contains the value 50 whereas its right child contains the value 70. The node with the value 70 has only one child. That right child contains the value 40. The "leaf" nodes are the nodes 300, 20, and 40. They are distinguished by the fact that they each have no children. The nodes with the values 100 and 50 have two children each.

A binary tree is defined recursively and is considered a recursive structure. It is a non-linear structure because one cannot move linearly from a starting node to an ending node as is the case with a linked list. There is one starting node, the root node, but many ending nodes, each leaf node. So how would one traverse a binary tree and output the value of each node?

Listing 8.12 presents a simple recursive algorithm, *pre_order*, that does exactly this.

Listing 8.12 Pre-order traversal algorithm for binary tree

```
pre_order ( n : NODE [ T ]) is
        -- It is assumed here that class NODE has the data fields item of type T,
        -- left of type NODE, and right of type NODE
        do
            if n /= Void then
                print (n.item) -- generic output function from class ANY
                pre_order (n.left)
                pre_order (n.right)
        end
end -- pre_order
```

For the tree of Figure 8.1, the *pre_order* traversal works as follows: The first value for the input node is the root node. Since its value is not Void, the value 100 is output. Then the routine is recursively called with the input node pointing to node 50. This value gets output. Then the routine is recursively called with the input node pointing to node 300. This value gets output. Since 300 is a leaf node, the recursive stack is popped and control resumes at the level of recursion when the input node points to 50. Now a recursive call to node 20 occurs. The value of 20 is output. Since 20 is a leaf node, the recursion backs up so that the input node points to 100. A recursive call to node 70 occurs. The value of this node is output. Then a recursive call to 40 occurs. The value of this node is output. No further output occurs. So the sequence of values that are output is 100, 50, 300, 20, 70, 40.

It is noted that using the pre-order traversal algorithm, each node of the tree is visited exactly once.

Two alternative recursive functions for visiting and outputing each node once are given in Listings 8.13 and 8.14. These functions are in-order and post-order traversals respectively. The only difference among the traversal algorithms is the position of the output statements. For pre-order traversal the output statements (or visit operations) occur before both recursive calls, for in-order traversal they are in between the two recursive calls, and for post-order traversal they are after both recursive calls.

Listing 8.13 In-order traversal algorithm for binary trees

```
in_order (n : NODE [ T ]) is
-- It is assumed here that class NODE has the data fields item of type T,
-- left of type NODE, and right of type NODE
```

```
    do
        if n /= Void then
            in_order (n.left)
            print (n.item)
            io.new_line
            in_order (n.right)
    end
end -- in_order
```

Listing 8.14 Post-order traversal algorithm for binary trees

```
post_order (n : NODE [ T ]) is
-- It is assumed here that class NODE has the data fields item of type T,
-- left of type NODE, and right of type NODE
    do
        if n /= Void then
            post_order (n.left)
            post_order (n.right)
            print (n.item)
            io.new_line
    end
end -- post_order
```

Problem 13 in the Exercises asks you to trace each of the algorithms of Listing 8.13 and 8.14 and show that the output using the in-order traversal is 300, 50, 20, 100, 70, and 40. Using the post-order traversal, the output is 300, 20, 50, 40, 70, and 100.

Now we return to the main subject of this section, binary search trees.

A binary search tree is a binary tree in which each node has a "value" (*item* field of class NODE) that is greater than all its left descendants and smaller than all of its right descendants. This recursive definition leads to efficient algorithms for *insert, present,* and *remove.*

Let us discuss the algorithm for *present*. This function returns TRUE if the element specified through an input parameter is contained within the tree; otherwise it returns FALSE.

Starting at the root node, the input element is compared with the element present in the root node. If the input element is smaller, the entire right subtree of the root can be eliminated because all right descendants of the root node must have values greater than those of the root node (see search tree definition above). The algorithm then calls itself recursively and replaces the root node with its left child. If the input element had been larger than the element present in the root node, the algorithm would call itself recursively replacing the root node with its right child. The maximum depth of the recursion is given by the maximum depth of the tree.

Listing 8.15 shows the class description of NODE. Since this class is for the internal use of class SEARCH_TREE, both its creation routine export scope as well as feature export scope are specified as SEARCH_TREE.

Listing 8.15 Class NODE

```
class NODE [T]

creation {SEARCH_TREE}
    make

feature {SEARCH_TREE}

    item: T

    left: NODE [T]

    right: NODE [T]

    make (element: T; left_child: NODE [T]; right_child: NODE [T]) is
        do
            item := element
            left := left_child
            right := right_child
        end

    set_left (left_child: NODE [T]) is
        do
            left := left_child
        end

    set_right (right_child: NODE [T]) is
        do
            right := right_child
        end

    set_item (value: T) is
        do
            item := value
        end

end -- class NODE
```

A partial class description of SEARCH_TREE that includes routines *insert* and *present* is given in Listing 8.16.

Listing 8.16 Partial class description of SEARCH_TREE (routines *insert* and *present*)

```
class SEARCH_TREE [ T -> COMPARABLE ]
-- Abstract data type for binary search tree
-- The elements that are inserted must be comparable

feature
        number_elements: INTEGER

    insert (element : T) is
        -- Adds element to search tree
        require
            element_not_void: element /= Void
            element_not_present: not present (element)
        do
            number_elements := number_elements + 1
            insert_node (Void, root, element)
        ensure
            number_elements = old number_elements + 1
            present (element)
        end -- insert

    present (element : T) : BOOLEAN is
        require
            element_not_void: element /= Void
        do
            Result := present_node (root, element)
        ensure
            -- Result = TRUE implies element in tree
        end -- present

feature { NONE } -- For internal use only
        root            : NODE [ T ]
        call_left       : BOOLEAN
        -- set to TRUE when replacing curr by curr.left otherwise FALSE

    insert_node (previous : NODE [ T ]; curr : NODE [ T ]; element : T) is
        -- Recursive routine for adding distinct elements to tree. Duplicates not
        -- allowed.
```

```
    local
        tree_node : NODE [ T ]
    do
        if curr = Void then
            !!tree_node.make (element, Void, Void)
            if previous = Void then
                root := tree_node
            elseif call_left then
                previous.set_left (tree_node)
            else
                previous.set_right (tree_node)
            end
        else
            if element < curr.item then
                call_left := TRUE
                insert_node (curr, curr.left, element)
            elseif element > curr.item then
                call_left := FALSE
                insert_node (curr, curr.right, element)
            end
        end
    end -- insert_node

present_node ( p : NODE [ T ]; element : T) : BOOLEAN is
    -- Returns TRUE if element is in the tree, otherwise returns FALSE
    do
        if p = Void then
            Result := FALSE
        elseif element = p.item then
            Result := TRUE
        elseif element < p.item then
            Result := present_node (p.left, element)
        else
            Result := present_node (p.right, element)
        end
    end -- present_node

end -- SEARCH_TREE
```

In examining Listing 8.16, the first important observation is that the public features do not reveal the presence of class NODE. This support class is strictly for internal use only. The interface to routines insert and present involve only an *element* of unspecified comparable type T. The reason for imposing the constraint, COMPARABLE, on the generic parameter is to ensure that the actual type used in creating an instance of a SEARCH_TREE can respond to the operations "<" and "=".

We first examine the query routine, *present*, in Listing 8.16.

The one line of code in this public routine makes a call to the internal recursive routine *present_node* with the 2 parameters *p* of type NODE [T] and *element* of type T. The recursive algorithm descends through the tree, at each step either finding a match-up, or recursively descending to the left or to the right, depending on whether the input element is equal to, less than, or greater than the *item* stored in the tree node *p*.

The routine *insert* invokes the internal routine *insert_node* sending in three parameters. This internal routine keeps track of the previous node, current node, and the input element as it recursively descends down the tree. An internal data feature, *call_left*, keeps track of whether a recursive call has just been made to the left or to the right. When the "bottom" of the tree is finally reached (*curr = Void*), a new *tree_node* is constructed using the creation routine of class NODE. If *previous* equals Void, this implies that the tree was previously empty and *root* is set equal to *new_node*. If the recursive call just before hitting the bottom of the tree was to the left, then node *previous* is linked to the left to *new_node*; otherwise it is linked to the right to *new_node*.

Suppose we wish to output the values stored in a binary search tree in ascending order. The in-order traversal algorithm given in Listing 8.13 can be used to accomplish this. The external interface presented to the user cannot reveal the presence of type NODE. Listing 8.17 shows how this in-order traversal algorithm is hidden in the protected section of the class whereas the interface to routine *display_in_order* has no parameters.

Listing 8.17 Routine *display_in_order*

```
display_in_order is
    -- Outputs the elements of the search tree in ascending order
    do
        in_order (root)
    end -- display_in_order

feature { NONE } -- for internal use only

    in_order (p : NODE [ T ]) is
        -- Performs an in-order traversal of search tree
        do
```

```
        if p /= Void then
            in_order (p.left)
            print (p.item) -- Generic output function from class ANY
            io.new_line
            in_order (p.right)
        end
    end -- in_order
```

It is left as an interesting exercise to explain why the in-order traversal algorithm produces an ordered sequence of output (it is not just because of its name!).

For those readers who wish to stretch themselves and learn more about binary search trees, the recursive code for routine *remove* is given in Listing 8.18. Some readers may wish to skip this listing and continue on to the next subsection. Other readers may wish to solve problem 15.

Listing 8.18 Routines *remove, remove_node,* and *delete* (optional) *reading*

```
    remove (element : T) is
        require
            element_not_void: element /= Void
            element_present: present (element)
        do
            number_elements := number_elements -1
            remove_node (Void, root, element)
        ensure
            number_elements = old number_elements - 1
            not present (element)
        end -- insert

feature { NONE } -- for internal use only

    remove_node (previous : NODE [ T ]; curr : NODE [ T ]; element : T) is
        do
            if element < curr.item then
                call_left := TRUE
                remove_node (curr, curr.left, element)
            elseif element > curr.item then
                call_left := FALSE
                remove_node (curr, curr.right, element)
            else -- element = curr.item
                if previous = Void then -- root node being deleted
```

```
      if curr.right = Void and curr.left = Void then
        root := Void
      elseif curr.right = Void then
        root := curr.left
      elseif curr.left = void then
        root: = curr.right
      else
        delete (curr, curr.left, curr)
      end
    elseif curr.right = Void then -- deleted node has no right child
      if call_left then
        previous.set_left (curr.left)
      else
        previous.set_right (curr.left)
      end
    elseif curr.left = Void then -- deleted node has no left child
      if call_left then
        previous.set_left (curr.right)
      else
        previous.set_right (curr.right)
      end
    else -- deleted node has 2 children
        delete (curr, curr.left, curr)
    end
  end
end -- remove_node

delete (previous : NODE [ T ]; curr : NODE[ T ]; deleted : NODE [ T ]) is
  do
    if curr.right /= Void then
      delete (curr, curr.right, deleted)
    else
      deleted.set_item (curr.item)
      if previous = deleted then
        previous.set_left (curr.left)
      else
        previous.set_right (curr.left)
      end
    end
  end -- delete
```

It should now be evident from the algorithms presented in this section (e.g., *insert_node, present_node, pre-order, in-order, post-order, remove_node, delete*) that recursion appears to fit quite naturally in the context of binary search trees. This is true because, as stated earlier, the tree structure itself is recursive and therefore lends itself to this way of thinking and designing.

Although the primary purpose of exploring binary search trees in this section has been to present a natural application that displays the importance and power of recursion as a design principle, the binary search tree that was produced is an important container class. When the sequence of elements inserted produce a reasonably balanced tree, the search time is proportional to the $\log_2 n$, where n represents the number of elements in the tree. This search-time performance is superior to the linear, $O(n)$, search time of the linked list. For this reason the binary search tree and its variants are the subject of extensive study in a course on Data Structures.

8.4   One final and more advanced but important application of recursion—depth-first search of a graph and airline connection problem

This section of the chapter deals with an interesting but somewhat more advanced application of recursion: a depth-first search of a graph. Some readers may therefore wish to skip this section upon a first reading (or any reading) of this book.

The actual problem that we plan to solve is the following: Suppose an airline maintains flights between a large collection of cities (e.g., New York to Chicago, Chicago to West Palm Beach, Colorado Springs to Denver, etc.). A passenger wishes to fly from city A to city B. What algorithm can be designed to determine whether it is possible for the passenger to fly from city A to B with intermediate stops possible and likely? In other words, is there a path from city A to city B in the graph?

The data structure that will be used to represent the input data is a graph. Each "edge" of the graph represents a connection between two cities for which the airline maintains scheduled flights. Each "node" of the graph represents a particular city.

Consider, Figure 8.2, which contains the route graph for a small commuter airline.

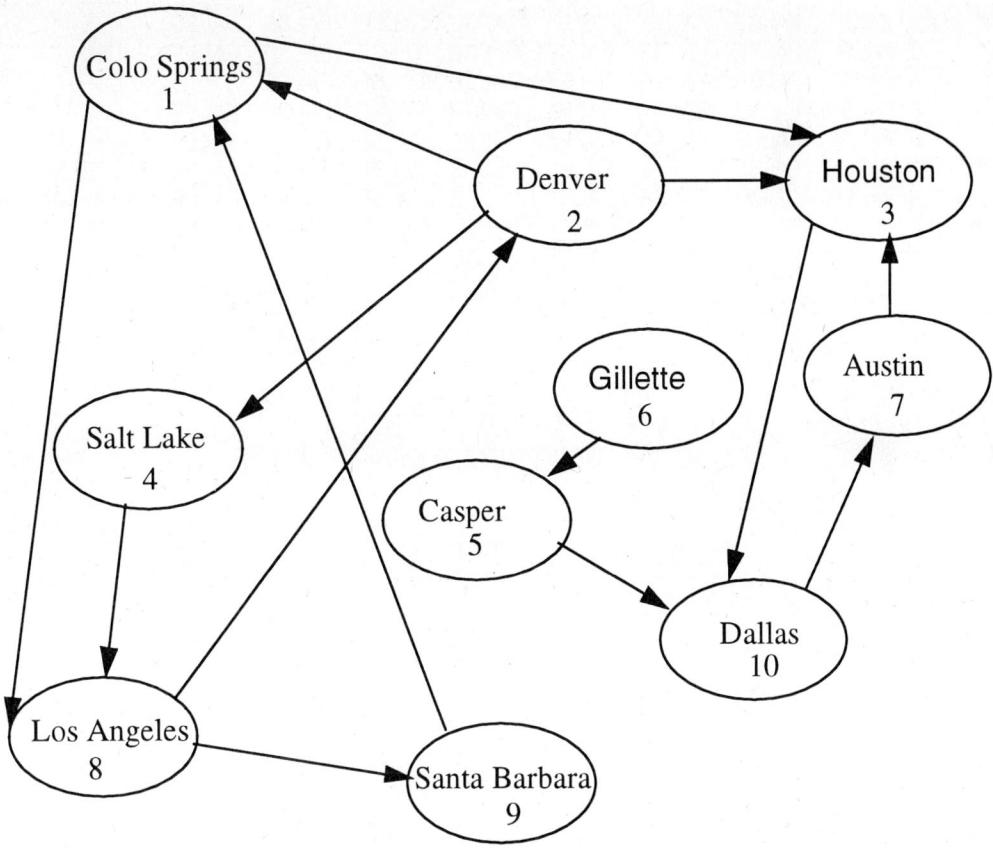

Figure 8.2 Routes for Small Commuter Airline

The graph structure given in Figure 8.2 contains 10 nodes (cities) and 14 edges. The numbers below each city represent an arbitrary numbering of the nodes. It is easier to refer to a node by number than by name. The directed arrows represent the allowable connections (scheduled flights). It is important to note that if a flight is scheduled from city i to j, it does not follow that a flight is scheduled from city j to i.

The graph structure can be represented by a 10 x 10 matrix of base type BOOLEAN. A connection from city i to city j is represented by the presence of the value TRUE in row i and column j. A FALSE value in the same position indicates the absence of a connection between city i and city j.

For the graph given in Figure 8.2, the 10 x 10 connection matrix is the following:

	1	2	3	4	5	6	7	8	9	10
1	FALSE	FALSE	TRUE	FALSE	FALSE	FALSE	FALSE	TRUE	FALSE	FALSE
2	TRUE	FALSE	TRUE	TRUE	FALSE	FALSE	FALSE	FALSE	FALSE	FALSE
3	FALSE	FALSE	FALSE	FALSE	FALSE	FALSE	FALSE	FALSE	FALSE	TRUE
4	FALSE	FALSE	FALSE	FALSE	FALSE	FALSE	FALSE	TRUE	FALSE	FALSE
5	FALSE	FALSE	FALSE	FALSE	FALSE	FALSE	FALSE	FALSE	FALSE	TRUE
6	FALSE	FALSE	FALSE	FALSE	TRUE	FALSE	FALSE	FALSE	FALSE	FALSE
7	FALSE	FALSE	TRUE	FALSE	FALSE	FALSE	FALSE	FALSE	FALSE	FALSE
8	FALSE	TRUE	FALSE	FALSE	FALSE	FALSE	FALSE	FALSE	TRUE	FALSE
9	TRUE	FALSE	FALSE	FALSE	FALSE	FALSE	FALSE	FALSE	FALSE	FALSE
10	FALSE	FALSE	FALSE	FALSE	FALSE	FALSE	TRUE	FALSE	FALSE	FALSE

We wish to design a function, *connection*, with the signature given below that returns TRUE if there exists a set of flights that connect *city1* to *city2*.

connection (city1 : INTEGER; city2 : INTEGER;
graph : ARRAY2[BOOLEAN]) : BOOLEAN

The approach that we will take is called *depth-first* search. Suppose, for example, that we wish to determine whether it is possible to travel from city 1 to city 9 (from Colorado Springs to Santa Barbara).

Using a depth-first approach, from city 1 we attempt to travel to city 2. The entry is FALSE in row 1, column 2 so a direct connection does not exist between these two cities (if a direct connection existed the problem would be quite simple and would be solved—at least in this case!). We then attempt to go from city 1 to city 3. This succeeds because there is an entry TRUE in row 1 and column 3. In general, if failure had occurred, we would continue attempting to go from city 1 to city i, where i increases by 1 at each attempt until a successful link is finally reached (if one exists).

In the present case there is a direct connection from city 1 to city 3 so this becomes the first "leg" of the journey that is tentatively established. Recall that our goal is not to minimize the number of legs between city 1 and city 2 but to merely determine whether a set of legal legs exists that would make such a trip possible.

We now continue what you will shortly see is a recursive process at city 3 (Houston). From this city we determine whether there exists a link from city 3 to city i, as i increases from 1 to 10. It should be evident from the connection matrix given above that the leg from city 3 to city 10 is the only one that exists. We proceed with the second tentative leg of the journey from city 3 to city 10.

From city 10 the same process unfolds. Successive attempts are made to find a link from city 10 to i, as i increases by 1, until the first successful link is found. This link is between city 10 and city 7 and becomes the third leg of the tentative journey. At city 7, the only link that is found using the same consecutive search strategy as before is to city 3. But, city 3 is already part of this journey (i.e., leg 1: city 1 to city 3; leg 2: city 3 to city 10; leg 3: city 10 to city 7). Such a loop is clearly unproductive. To protect against this occurrence, we must mark each city as visited when one of the legs on our tentative journey takes us to a particular city.

With no further links from city 7 (the last city on our tentative journey) possible, the depth-first algorithm backs up to city 10 to determine whether there are other links that can be attempted. There are none in this case. The algorithm backs up again to city 3 where it is again determined that there are no other links that can be tried. So the algorithm backs up to the starting city 1. From this city there is one additional link to be tried, namely the leg from city 1 to city 8. From city 8 the first successful link to be found is to city 2 (the attempts are always made in numerical order). So the connection from city 8 to city 2 becomes the second leg on the new tentative journey.

From city 2, the link to city 1 is rejected because city 1 is marked as previously visited; the link to city 3 is rejected for the same reason (there is no point in going back to a city from a previous journey attempt that failed), so the link to city 4 is the final legal link out of city 2. Now the tentative journey goes from city 1 to city 8 to city 2 to city 4.

From city 4 the only legal link is to city 8, but this city has been marked as visited. The algorithm must back up first to city 2. Since all legal links have been exhausted from this city, the algorithm backs up to city 8. The only remaining link out of city 8 is to city 9. Voila! Since this is the destination city, the tentative journey from city 1 to 8 to 9 becomes solidified as proof that it is possible to travel from Colorado Springs to Santa Barbara on the airline with the connection matrix given above (as you readers might have guessed, this is an important link since the author of this book lives in Colorado Springs and the original vendor and creator of Eiffel lives in Santa Barbara!).

The algorithm just described is called depth-first because an attempt is made to move as far away from the starting node as possible (depth) and then to back up the smallest amount before again attempting to move further and further away from the starting node. The recursive nature of this algorithm should be evident from the fact that at each node the same events unfold (i.e., successively attempt to find the first possible link to another node that has not been previously visited). The process of "backing-up" that has been described above is automated by the recursion. As you recall from section 9, when a recursive call terminates, the run-time system automatically returns control to the previous recursive call and restores all local objects and input parameters to the values that were in place.

In addition to the input matrix of boolean values (the connection matrix), we need to be able to mark cities as having been visited in order to avoid loops and unproductive paths. This can be accomplished using an array of booleans called *visited*. Each time a city is selected on a tentative tour, its index location in visited is changed from FALSE to TRUE. Before allowing a new link to be established, the index location of the proposed new city must be tested in this array to ensure that it has never been visited before.

Listing 8.19 presents a complete application program that includes the recursive function, connection, for determining whether a legal connection exists between two specified cities. The input matrix corresponds to the graph given in Figure 8.2.

Listing 8.19 Implementation of depth-first airline connections function

```
class AIRLINE_CONNECTIONS

creation
    make

feature

    Number_cities: INTEGER is 10

    link: ARRAY2 [BOOLEAN]
            -- entry is TRUE if a link exists
            -- entry is TRUE if city has been visited
            -- holds current "tentative" path

    visited: ARRAY [BOOLEAN]

    path: ARRAY [INTEGER]

    make is
        local
            city1, city2: INTEGER
            index: INTEGER
            quit: CHARACTER
        do
            load_link_matrix
            !! visited.make (1, number_cities)
            !! path.make (1, number_cities)
```

```
from
until
    quit = 'y'
loop
    from
        index := 0
    until
        index = number_cities
    loop
        index := index + 1
        visited.put (false, index)
    end
    io.putstring ("Enter city 1: ")
    io.readint
    io.new_line
    city1 := io.lastint
    io.putstring ("Enter city 2: ")
    io.readint
    io.new_line
    city2 := io.lastint
    visited.put (true, city1)
    if connection (city1, city2, 1) then
        io.putstring ("A legal set of connections exist between city ")
        io.putint (city1)
        io.putstring (" and city ")
        io.putint (city2)
        io.putstring (". That path is: ")
        from
          index := 1
        until
          path.item (index) = city2
        loop
          io.putint (path.item (index))
          io.putstring (" ")
          index := index + 1
        end
        io.putint (city2)
        io.new_line
        io.new_line
    else
        io.putstring ("No legal connections exist between city ")
```

```
                io.putint (city1)
                io.putstring (" and city ")
                io.putint (city2)
                io.putstring (".%N")
            end
            io.putstring ("%NQuit (y/n)? ")
            io.readchar
            quit := io.lastchar
            io.new_line
        end
    end

load_link_matrix is
    do
        !! link.make (number_cities, number_cities)
        link.put (true, 1, 3)
        link.put (true, 1, 8)
        link.put (true, 2, 1)
        link.put (true, 2, 3)
        link.put (true, 2, 4)
        link.put (true, 3, 10)
        link.put (true, 4, 8)
        link.put (true, 5, 10)
        link.put (true, 6, 5)
        link.put (true, 7, 3)
        link.put (true, 8, 2)
        link.put (true, 8, 9)
        link.put (true, 9, 1)
        link.put (true, 10, 7)
    end

connection (city1: INTEGER; city2: INTEGER; next_path_index: INTEGER):
            BOOLEAN is
    local
        destination: INTEGER
    do
        path.put (city1, next_path_index)
        if city1 /= city2 then
            Result := false
            from
                destination := 0
            until
```

```
            destination = number_cities or Result = true
      loop
            destination := destination + 1
            if link.item (city1, destination) and not visited.item (destination) then
                  visited.put (true, destination)
                  Result := connection (destination, city2, next_path_index + 1)
            end
        end
    else
        Result := true
    end
  end
```

end -- class *AIRLINE_CONNECTIONS*

The "global" features of class AIRLINE_CONNECTIONS are *number_cities* (an integer constant), *link* (the two dimensional array of boolean connections), *visited* (a one-dimensional array of cities visited), and *path* (a one-dimensional array that holds the current tentative path).

The details of function *make*, although somewhat lengthy, are straightforward. The two-dimensional *link* array is loaded with the input data. It is noted that the default values for each element is FALSE so only the TRUE values need be set.

Each time around the main loop the first task is to initialize the *visited* array with FALSE in every index location. The user is prompted to enter city 1 and city 2. The function *connection* is invoked. If the function returns TRUE the path from city 1 to city 2 is output; otherwise the user is told that no legal connection exists between the two cities.

Let us examine the function *connection* that employs a depth-first search of the input graph.

The *city1* is added to the *path* array at index location *next_path_index* which is sent in as an input parameter. If *city1* is equal to *city2*, the function exits with the return value TRUE and the problem is solved.

If city1 is not equal to city2 the return value of FALSE is set. In a loop that increments the destination city by 1, it is determined whether a link exists between the current *city1* and *destination* and also whether *destination* has been visited. If the answers are yes and no, then the *destination* city is added to the array of visited cities. The function *connection* is recursively called with *destination* being sent in as *city1* and *next_path_index* being incremented by 1.

When a recursive call to *connection* terminates (e.g., no links or cities not yet visited are found), the value of the loop index, *destination*, is restored at the previous level of recursion. The loop is then able to resume from where it left off. Also, the values of the input parameters *city1*, *city2*, and *next_path_index* are restored. This allows a partial path to be continued.

The entire guts of the depth-first solution to the problem are contained in the 16 lines of code (counting "end" statements) in the body of function *connection*. There is a lot of power in these 16 lines of code. It is fairly typical for recursive solutions to a problem to be relatively compact. There is clearly a lot going on behind the scenes in a recursion as complex as the one given in Listing 8.19. You are urged to test your understanding of this function by "walking" through several examples (different choices of *city1* and *city2* like *city1* = 4 and *city2* = 10).

A weakness in Listing 8.19 is that it is the user's responsibility to ensure that the *visited* array is initialized to FALSE before calling the *connection* routine. This initialization should be performed by the *connection* routine itself. Unfortunately, it is a recursive routine and it would be inappropriate to do this during each recursive call. The remedy is to embed the recursive routine inside of an outer shell that first performs this initialization. This is done in Listing 8.20 in which we consider one final application.

Suppose we consider a larger airline, Random Airlines, Inc., that potentially services 100 cities. There are *100 x 100 = 10,000* possible one-way paths among the 100 cities if one allows paths from a city back to itself (which we in fact do not allow). Random Airlines Inc. takes great pride in doing its schedule assignment randomly. In fact, the algorithm that its executives currently use to determine which pairs of cities the airline serves (in one direction only of course) is the following: A random integer from 1 to 100 is chosen for the first city in the pair. Then another random integer from 1 to 100, but not equal to the first and at a position where a link does not already exist, is chosen. This provides a unique link (entry in the matrix that is set to TRUE). This process is repeated until 200 links (2 percent of the total number of potential links) are established.

We wish to write an application class that counts and lists all the possible legal connection paths among the 100 cities. The code for doing this is presented in Listing 8.20 along with a small change in the *connection* routine that initializes the *visited* array.

Listing 8.20 100-city airline connection application using depth-first search

```
class APPLICATION

creation
    start

feature

    Number_cities: INTEGER is 100

    link: ARRAY2 [BOOLEAN]
        -- entry is TRUE if a link exists
        -- entry is TRUE if city has been visited
        -- holds current "tentative" path

    visited: ARRAY [BOOLEAN]

    path: ARRAY [INTEGER]

    rand: RANDOM_NUMBER

    number_paths: INTEGER

    start is
        local
            city1: INTEGER
            city2: INTEGER
            index: INTEGER
            quit: CHARACTER
        do
            !! visited.make (1, number_cities)
            !! path.make (1, number_cities)
            !! rand.initialize
            load_link_matrix
            from
                city1 := 0
            until
                city1 = number_cities
            loop
                city1 := city1 + 1
                io.putstring ("Finding connections from city ")
                io.putint (city1)
                io.new_line
```

```
        from
            city2 := 0
        until
            city2 = number_cities
        loop
            city2 := city2 + 1
            if city1 /= city2 and connection (city1, city2, 1) then
                number_paths := number_paths + 1
                io.putstring ("A legal set of connections exist between city ")
                io.putint (city1)
                io.putstring (" and city ")
                io.putint (city2)
                io.putstring (". %NThat path is: ")
                from
                    index := 1
                until
                    path.item (index) = city2
                loop
                    io.putint (path.item (index))
                    io.putstring (" ")
                    index := index + 1
                end
                io.putint (city2)
                io.new_line
                io.new_line
            end
        end
    end
    io.putstring ("%NThe total number of legal paths = ")
    io.putint (number_paths)
    io.new_line
end
load_link_matrix is
    local
        row, col: INTEGER
        count: INTEGER
    do
        !! link.make (number_cities, number_cities)
        from
            count := 0
        until
```

```
        count = number_cities * number_cities // 50
    loop
        count := count + 1
        from
            rand.next
            row := rand.value_between (1, number_cities)
            rand.next
            col := rand.value_between (1, number_cities)
        until
            col /= row and not link.item (row, col)
        loop
            rand.next
            row := rand.value_between (1, number_cities)
            rand.next
            col := rand.value_between (1, number_cities)
        end
        link.put (true, row, col)
    end
end

connection (city1: INTEGER; city2: INTEGER; next_path_index: INTEGER):
        BOOLEAN is

local
    index: INTEGER
do
    from
        index := 0
    until
        index = number_cities
    loop
        index := index + 1
        visited.put (false, index)
    end
    Result := connect (city1, city2, next_path_index)
end

connect (city1: INTEGER; city2: INTEGER; next_path_index: INTEGER):
        BOOLEAN is

local
    destination: INTEGER
do
```

```
        path.put (city1, next_path_index)
        if city1 /= city2 then
            Result := false
            from destination := 0
            until
                destination = number_cities or Result = true
            loop
                destination := destination + 1
                if link.item (city1, destination) and not visited.item (destination) then
                    visited.put (true, destination)
                    Result := connect (destination, city2, next_path_index + 1)
                end
            end
        else
            Result := true
        end
    end

    end -- class APPLICATION
```

The output to Listing 8.20 takes awhile to produce but is quite interesting. On two runs of the problem (the actual random link array generated in each case was different), the total number of legal paths that were found were 5878 and 6484. This result is somewhat counterintuitive. With only 200 one-way links between cities, one would certainly not guess that so many legal paths could be produced.

You might wish to experiment with the code and try to predict the number of legal paths if there were 500 cities (25,000 entries in the link matrix) and 500 links were provided (again 2 percent of the total number possible).

This section of the chapter, challenging as it is, has provided you with a glimpse into an important area of computer science, namely algorithm design, and the role that recursion plays in this theory.

8.5 Some parting comments about recursion

```
Recursion
    Recursion is
        Recursion is a
            Recursion is a challenging
                Recursion is a challenging but
                    Recursion is a challenging but important
```

Recursion is a challenging but important technique
Recursion is a challenging but important technique of
Recursion is a challenging but important technique of program
Recursion is a challenging but important technique of program design

Hope you learn to use it well!

8.6 Summary

- An Eiffel routine can invoke itself. This capability, also supported by most modern programming languages, is called **recursion**.

- Recursion is a powerful and sometimes subtle design principle.

- Each time a recursive call occurs, the values of all local objects and input parameters are pushed onto a run-time stack. Upon hitting the "end" statement of a recursive routine, the previous recursive call, if any, is popped from the run-time stack. All the local variables and input parameters are restored to the values that were in place just before the recursive call was executed. Program control returns to the statement one line below the recursive call that was just completed.

8.7 Exercises

1. Explain why the line of code, *io.putint (6 - number_times)*, corrects the routine given in Listing 8.2. Why is this an unsatisfactory solution?

2. What would be the output if the routine given in Listing 8.4 were modified as follows:

```
print_recursively (value : REAL) is
    local
        temporary : REAL
    do
        temporary := 10 * value
        if value >= 0.0 then
            io.putreal (value)
            io.new_line
            io.putstring ("Temporary = ")
            io.putreal (temporary)
            io.new_line
            print_recursively (value - 0.1) -- recursive call
```

```
            io.putstring ("%Ntemporary = ")
            io.putreal (temporary)
            io.new_line
      end
   end -- print_recursively
```

3. How would the routine in Listing 8.1 have to be modified in order to produce the following output (four spaces of additional indentation for each new line):

   Eiffel is a wonderful language.
      Eiffel is a wonderful language.
         Eiffel is a wonderful language.
            Eiffel is a wonderful language.
               Eiffel is a wonderful language.

4. Carefully explain all of the recursive events that lead to the output shown for Listing 8.5.

5. Carefully explain the iterative version of Listing 8.4 given in Listing 8.7.

6. Implement a binary search algorithm iteratively. Please consult the recursive version given in Listing 8.8. Include a test program that loads an array of size 10,000 with integers that are each ten times the index location containing the value (i.e., the value in index 1 is 10, index 2 is 20, ..., the value in index 10,000 is 100,000). Search for the presence of values 795, 9000, 0, and 100001.

7. What would happen if the test *if first_index <= second_index* were removed from the binary search algorithm of Listing 8.8?

8. What might happen if the precondition were removed from routine *present* in Listing 8.8 and the data were not sorted?

9. Perform a detailed "walkthrough" of the algorithm *partition*, given in Listing 8.10, using the following array of 10 values: 7, 9, 2, 4, 6, 5, 2, 15, 3, 17.

10. Perform a detailed "walkthrough" of the quicksort algorithm, given in Listing 8.11, using the same data set as that of problem 9.

11. Do a timing analysis of *quicksort* against the insertion sort algorithm presented in Chapter 4. Load up data sets with random and uniformly distributed numbers of sizes: 100, 200, ..., 1000. For each size, use the same data set for insertion sort as for quicksort. Show a table of sort time versus array size for each algorithm.

12. For what type of input data would quicksort run the slowest? Explain why. Why would the efficiency be $O\ (n^2)$ for this case?

13. Trace the output sequences for the tree given in Figure 8.1 and the in-order and post-order traversal algorithms given in Listings 8.12 and 8.13. Discuss each step of these algorithms.

14. Walk through the binary search tree insert algorithm given in Listing 8.16 and sketch the search tree resulting from the insertion of the following sequence of integers: 45, 13, 12, 17, 19, 21, 17 (recall no duplicates allowed), 34, 64, 22, 9, 11, 8, 9, and 10.

15. (Optional) Explain in detail the workings of the *remove* algorithm given in Listing 8.18. Show how the elements 22, 9, and 11 are removed from the search tree constructed in problem 14.

16. (a) Sketch the binary search tree resulting from the insertion of the following integers: 10, 5, 15, 8, 12, 6, 20, 3, 18, 4, 22, 7, 50, 35, 100, 26, 1, 19, and 60.
    (b) Show the tree resulting after each of the following elements have been removed: 35, 10, 15, 8, 12, and 6.

17. Implement and test an iterative version of *insert* for a binary search tree.

18. Explain why the in-order traversal algorithm given in Listing 8.13 and used in Listing 8.17 produces an ordered sequence of output when applied to a binary search tree.

19. Perform a careful "walk" through the *display_in_order* routine of Listing 8.17 and apply the in-order algorithm to the tree constructed in problem 16 before any elements have been removed.

20. Write and test a recursive function that computes the sum of the integers in an array of integers.

21. Modify Listing 8.19 so that instead of printing out the numbers of the cities visited, the program prints out the sequence of cities visited by name (not number).

22. Implement function *connection*, in Listing 8.19, iteratively rather than recursively.

Chapter 9

Polymorphism as a Design Principle

In the previous chapters you have seen many Eiffel programs or program segments and have hopefully become comfortable with the command/query style of object-oriented programming. An arbitrary object, *an_object*, can receive some command, *an_object.perform_some_action*. Is it conceivable that the programmer might not know what action (i.e., what specific routine) would be invoked by the command *perform_some_action*? The answer is yes! Furthermore, this lack of knowledge on the programmer's part might be an asset rather than a liability! Let us explain.

Suppose that a small hierarchy of specialized classes has been created. Suppose the root class of this small hierarchy is called SOME_ABSTRACT_TYPE and is defined as a deferred class with a deferred routine, *display.* Suppose this root class has three concrete classes as descendants, namely SPECIALIZED1, SPECIALIZED2, and SPECIALIZED3. Each of these concrete classes has defined appropriate implementation details for its *display* routine. Suppose that an array, *collection*, of size 3 is defined with base type SOME_ABSTRACT_TYPE. The user assigns an instance of each of these specialized classes to either index 1, 2, or 3 of the array. These assignments are legal because the objects are of a type that is a descendant of the formal type specified for the array.

Figure 9.1 shows a particular ordering of the specialized objects in the array of size 3.

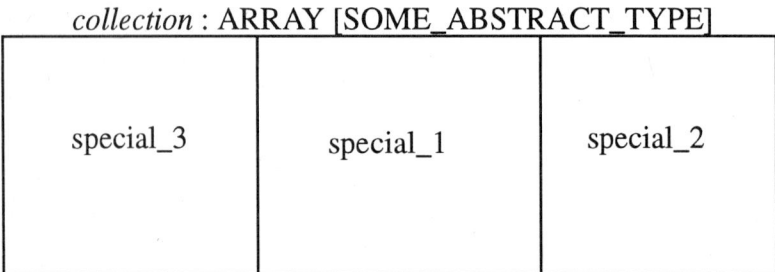

collection : ARRAY [SOME_ABSTRACT_TYPE]

special_3	special_1	special_2

Figure 9.1 Collection of Specialized Objects

Suppose we wish to output the set of specialized objects contained within the array. We iterate through *collection* sending the message *display* to each object. This is accomplished with the following segment of Eiffel code:

```
from index := 0
until index = 3
loop
      index := index + 1
      collection.item (index).display
end
```

Let us examine the last line of code in the loop, *collection.item (index).display*. Which specific *display* method will be invoked (there are three such *display* routines, one in each of the specialized classes)? Neither the programmer nor the compiler knows what type of object is in each index location (this is determined at run time after the user specifies this information as input). The binding (association) between the *display* command and specific *display* routine is made at run time *based on the actual type* of the object receiving the command *display*. This run-time decision by the system is called late-binding or dynamic-binding. This is in contrast to early-binding in which the compiler (and programmer) know the specific routine that is associated with the given command before the program starts executing.

The principle of design that the above example illustrates is called polymorphism. Literally, this word means "to take many forms or shapes" (poly -> many, morph -> shape). Polymorphism in the above example allows the command *display* to be invoked on a set of objects from conforming subclasses. The meaning or semantics of *display* is common to all of the objects. Only the details of *display* are different.

Polymorphism, the ability to establish uniform semantics over a set of disparate objects while allowing each object to respond uniquely to a common message, forms the basis for a powerful approach to design. The command, *an_object.perform_some_action*, allows a particular action to be performed that is based on the actual type of *an_object*, not its formally declared type.

This chapter explores the use and benefit of polymorphism in object-oriented software design.

9.1 Late-binding and polymorphism

The design principle of polymorphism, in which different implementations of a common routine are defined in a set of subclasses that are descendants of some root class, promotes a flexible and decentralized software architecture. The principle can be exploited in actual code if the programming language being used supports late-binding.

Eiffel supports late-binding. In principle, every time a command such as *an_object.perform_some_action* is executed, the system binds the command *perform_some_action* to a specific routine at run time. If only one instance of *perform_some_action* has been defined in the set of conforming subclasses, the Eiffel compiler, during its optimization phase, is able to utilize early-binding which is generally more efficient than late-binding. The programmer need not care about this optimization although it is reassuring to know that efficient code generation is handled by the compiler. The programmer is free to always think "late-binding" in constructing an application.

To clarify the above ideas, a simple and slightly more realistic hierarchy of conforming subclasses is constructed to illustrate the mechanics and concepts of polymorphism.

Consider an abstract class FLOWER with attributes *color*, *number_petals*, and *stem_length*. My apologies to any readers who have studied botany. Two concrete classes are children of class FLOWER: ROSE and COLUMBINE. Class ROSE contains the additional attribute *number_thorn* and COLUMBINE contains the additional attribute *soil_ph*.

Listing 9.1 shows the construction of the tiny hierarchy of flower classes.

Listing 9.1 Tiny hierarchy of flower classes

```
deferred class FLOWER

    feature
        number_petals      : INTEGER
        stem_length        : INTEGER
        color              : STRING

        display is
            deferred
            end

end -- FLOWER

class ROSE

inherit
    FLOWER

creation
    make

feature
    number_thorns : INTEGER

    make (a_color : STRING; petals : INTEGER; stem : INTEGER;
            thorns : INTEGER) is
        do
            color := clone (a_color)
            number_petals := petals
            stem_length := stem
            number_thorns := thorns
        end

    display is
        do
            io.putstring ("%NRose: ")
            io.putstring ("%NColor: ")
            io.putstring (color)
            io.putstring ("%NNumber petals: ")
            io.putint (number_petals)
            io.putstring ("%NNumber thorns: ")
            io.putint (number_thorns)
            io.putstring ("%NStem length: ")
```

```
            io.putint (stem_length)
            io.new_line
        end -- display


        -- Other routines, if any, not shown
end -- ROSE


class COLUMBINE
inherit
    FLOWER
creation
    make
feature
    soil_ph : REAL

    make (a_color : STRING; petals : INTEGER; stems : INTEGER; ph : REAL) is
        do
            color := clone (a_color)
            number_petals := petals
            stem_length := stems
            soil_ph := ph
        end -- make

    display is
        do
            io.putstring ("%NColumbine: ")
            io.putstring ("%NNumber petals: ")
            io.putint (number_petals)
            io.putstring ("%NStem length: ")
            io.putint (stem_length)
            io.putstring ("%NSoil ph required: ")
            io.putreal (soil_ph)
            io.new_line
        end -- display

        -- Other features, if present, not shown

end -- COLUMBINE
```

An application class, FLOWERS, with creation routine, *grow*, is shown in Listing 9.2.

Listing 9.2 Growing flowers application

```
class FLOWERS
    creation
        grow

    feature
        bouquet : ARRAY[ FLOWER ]

        grow is
        local
            a_rose              : ROSE
            a_columbine         : COLUMBINE
            rose_index          : INTEGER
            columbine_index     : INTEGER
            bouquet_index       : INTEGER
        do
            -- Create two flowers
            !!a_rose.make ("Red", 6, 8, 16)
            !!a_columbine.make ("Purple", 4, 4, 1.5)
            -- Prompt user to insert flowers in bouquet
            io.putstring ("Put rose in index (1 or 2): ")
            from io.readint
            until io.lastint = 1 or io.lastint = 2
            loop
                io.readint
            end
            rose_index := io.lastint
            io.putstring ("%NPut columbine in index (1 or 2): ")
            from io.readint
            until io.lastint /= rose_index and (io.lastint = 1 or
                        io.lastint = 2)
            loop
                io.readint
            end
            columbine_index := io.lastint
            -- Create the bouquet
            !!bouquet.make (1, 2)
            bouquet.put (a_rose, rose_index)
            bouquet.put (a_columbine, columbine_index)
            -- Iterate through bouquet and demonstrate late-binding
            from bouquet_index := 0
```

```
        until bouquet_index = 2
        loop
            bouquet_index := bouquet_index + 1
            bouquet.item (bouquet_index).display
        end
    end -- grow

end -- APPLICATION
```

The output of Listing 9.2 is

Put rose in index (1 or 2): 2

Put columbine in index (1 or 2): 1

Columbine:
Number petals: 4
Stem length: 4
Soil ph required: 1.5

Rose:
Color: Red
Number petals: 6
Number thorns: 16
Stem length: 8

The reader is encouraged to carefully study the loop structures in routine *grow* that are used for user input. The first loop terminates when the user has entered an index of either 1 or 2. The second loop terminates when the user has entered an index of either 1 or 2 but not equal to the previously chosen index.

Although the application presented in Listing 9.2 is quite simple and illustrates the concept of late-binding and polymorphism, it is quite sterile. In the next section a complete software application that features polymorphism is presented.

9.2 A case study that features polymorphism

In this section we show an initial object-oriented analysis, design, and Eiffel implementation of a small but typical software application. Late-binding and polymorphism play an important part in the design and implementation.

In section 9.3 we revise the design and present an improved implementation. Some readers may wish to skip the details of the first version presented in section 9.2.3 and read the improved Version 2 in section 9.3. The purpose of presenting both versions is to demonstrate that software development is an iterative process.

The system to be developed is a game. First we state its specifications. This is followed by an initial analysis and design. Finally we present and discuss an initial Eiffel implementation.

9.2.1 Specifications

We wish to build a software system that implements the following game:

- Three players compete against each other.

- Each player starts with a score of 500.

- The first player to acquire a score of 1000 or higher wins the game.

- If a player's score reaches 0 or becomes negative, the player is eliminated from the competition.

- A game may end with no player winning because all may be eliminated.

- Players "play" in sequential order with player 1 going first, followed by player 2, followed by player 3.

- When it is a player's turn, the player generates a random integer index according to a specific set of rules that are different for each player:

For player 1: A random uniformly distributed index between 2 and 12 is generated by simulating the throw of a pair of two ordinary six-sided dice (i.e., an ordinary pair of dice).

For player 2: A random uniformly distributed index between 2 and 6 is generated.

For player 3: A random index uniformly distributed index between 2 and 12 is generated by choosing a uniformly distributed random integer from 2 to 12 (please note that such numbers are distributed differently than for player 1—for player 1 an outcome of 7 is the most likely, followed by outcomes of 6 or 8 followed by outcomes of 5 or 9, etc.).

- A scorekeeper takes the random integer produced by the player and uses it to determine the action to be taken on the player.

- The scorekeeper determines what change of score, if any, is assigned to the given player and to other players, if appropriate.

- As the game progresses, the outcomes may be "rotated" so that a particular dice result is not permanently associated with a given outcome.

- After each player's turn, the output display is updated by the scorekeeper.

- The output display indicates the play number and the score of each player.

- The initial array of outcomes is the following:

Dice value = 2: Increase score by 36.

Dice value = 3: Increase score by 18.

Dice value = 4: Decrease score by 20.

Dice value = 5: Increase score by 15 times the previous dice value for the given player.

Dice value = 6: Decrease score by 8 times the previous dice value for the given player.

Dice value = 7: Shift all the existing outcomes by 1 index in the array (i.e., the new outcome associated with dice value 2 would be the previous outcome associated with 12, the new outcome associated with dice value 3 would be the previous outcome associated with 2, ..., the new outcome associated with dice value 12 would be the previous outcome associated with 11).

Dice value = 8: Decrease score by 5 time the previous dice throw plus 4 times the dice throw before the previous one. At the beginning of the game previous dice throws assume the value 0.

Dice value = 9: Decrease score by 25.

Dice value = 10: Increase score by 10 percent of the sum of the scores of your two opponents, rounded down to the nearest integer, only for opponents with positive scores. Each of the opposing players has their score reduced by 10 percent, rounded down to the nearest integer, if their score is positive.

Dice value = 11: Decrease score by 5 percent of the sum of the scores of your two opponents, rounded down to the nearest integer, only for opponents with positive scores. Each of the opposing players has their score increased by 5 percent, rounded down to the nearest integer, if their score is positive.

Dice value = 12: Shift all the existing outcomes by 1 index in the array, as before.

- Each player must have his or her score updated by a scorekeeper after each roll. In addition to each player knowing their own score, only the scorekeeper knows the score of each player. Players do not have access to each other's score.

- When the scorekeeper detects that a player has a score of 1000 or greater, the scorekeeper announces the winner of the game. The scorekeeper must determine the score of each player after each player has moved.

- When a player has a score of 0 or negative, it can no longer play in the game.

- The interface of each class should be as tight as possible. That is, features should be exported to only the clients that need the information.

- Polymorphism should be exploited wherever it is natural and possible to use it.

9.2.2 The analysis and design

From the description of the game the following five major problem domain classes exist:

GAME - controls the main flow of the game (this is significantly changed in Version 2)

OUTCOME - updates players' scores based on player that has just thrown dice

PLAYER - makes play and then tells the next player to make a play

SCOREKEEPER- updates players' scores based on player that has just thrown dice

DISPLAY - writes the output

An initial class diagram that shows the relationship among these five major domain classes is given in Figure 9.2.

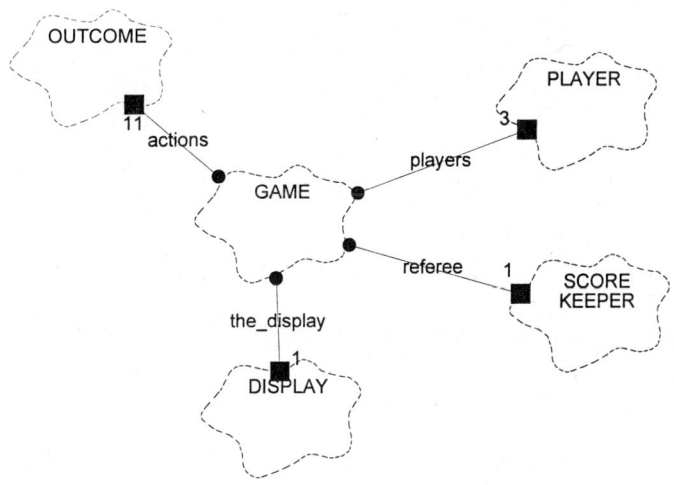

Figure 9.2 First Diagram for Class GAME

Class GAME represents the application class that initiates the simulation. This class is responsible for creating 3 PLAYER objects, a SCOREKEEPER object, a DISPLAY object, and 11 OUTCOME objects. These objects are all "owned" by the GAME class.

The tasks of bringing these objects to life are illustrated in Figure 9.3, an object scenario diagram for creating the game attributes. Three objects are shown, *the_game* (of type GAME), *players* (an array of base type PLAYER) and *referee* (of type SCOREKEEPER). The first five commands that *the_game* object sends to itself bring *the_display, player1, player2, player3*, and the *players* array to life. Steps 6, 7, and 8 insert each player in index locations 1, 2, and 3 respectively in the *players* array. Step 9 creates an actions array (not shown in Figure 9.3) that is not initialized. Step 10 creates a referee object (of type SCOREKEEPER) with the parameters *players, actions*, and *the_display*. These objects are contained by reference in the SCOREKEEPER class. This enables a *referee* object to query each player for its score and dice roll and determine the appropriate outcome (action) with the result sent to *the_display*.

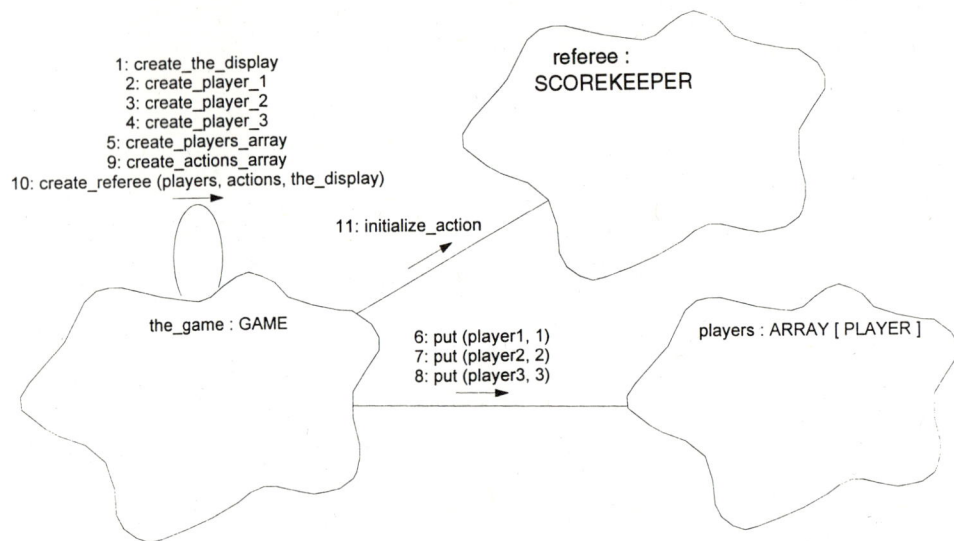

Figure 9.3 Scenario for Creating Game Attributes

Figure 9.4 shows the object scenario diagram that shows the initialization of the *actions* array. This is a key step in the analysis of the software system. Of the 11 possible outcomes that are defined in the game specification, only 5 actions are distinct. These are

- Change a player's score by a fixed amount, making it either higher or lower

- Change a player's score by an amount based on the player's previous dice roll

- Change a player's score by an amount based on the player's two previous dice rolls

- Rotate the outcome objects in the *actions* array by 1 index location

- Change a player's score by a percentage of the opponent's score (if positive) and change each opponent's score by the same percentage (if positive) but in the opposite direction (i.e., if the player's score is increased, the opponent's score is decreased)

Eiffel object creation notation is used to show precisely how each object is created.

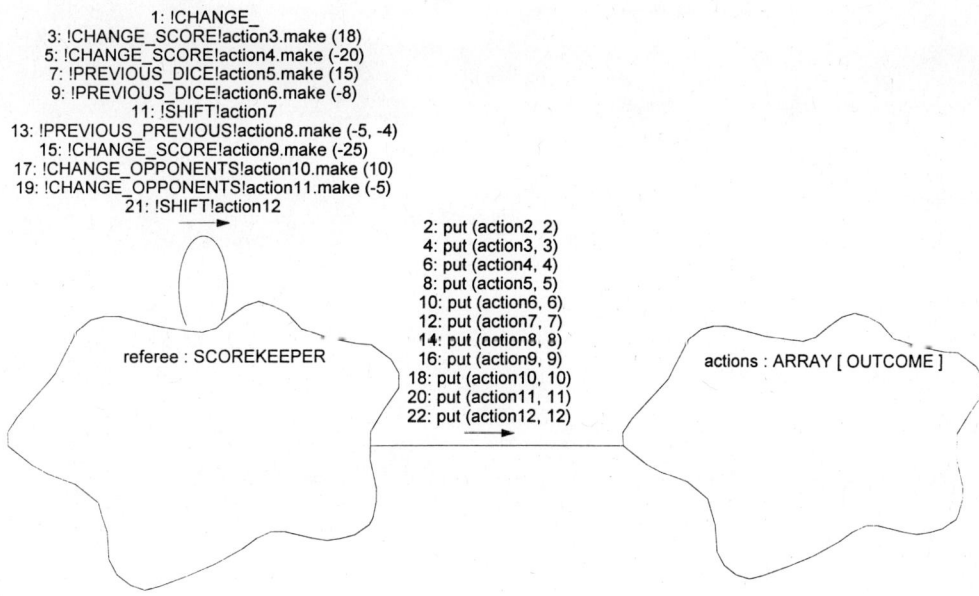

1: !CHANGE_
3: !CHANGE_SCORE!action3.make (18)
5: !CHANGE_SCORE!action4.make (-20)
7: !PREVIOUS_DICE!action5.make (15)
9: !PREVIOUS_DICE!action6.make (-8)
11: !SHIFT!action7
13: !PREVIOUS_PREVIOUS!action8.make (-5, -4)
15: !CHANGE_SCORE!action9.make (-25)
17: !CHANGE_OPPONENTS!action10.make (10)
19: !CHANGE_OPPONENTS!action11.make (-5)
21: !SHIFT!action12

2: put (action2, 2)
4: put (action3, 3)
6: put (action4, 4)
8: put (action5, 5)
10: put (action6, 6)
12: put (action7, 7)
14: put (action8, 8)
16: put (action9, 9)
18: put (action10, 10)
20: put (action11, 11)
22: put (action12, 12)

referee : SCOREKEEPER

actions : ARRAY [OUTCOME]

Figure 9.4 Initialize Action is Class SCOREKEEPER

From the two scenario diagrams (Figures 9.3 and 9.4), a revised class diagram is shown in Figure 9.5. This diagram shows class OUTCOME as an abstract class (the triangle with 'A' in its center). It also shows the five specialized types of actions (classes CHANGE_OPPONENT, CHANGE_SCORE, PREVIOUS_DICE, PREVIOUS_PREVIOUS_DICE, and SHIFT).

The reference relationship between class SCOREKEEPER and classes OUTCOME, PLAYER, and DISPLAY is also shown.

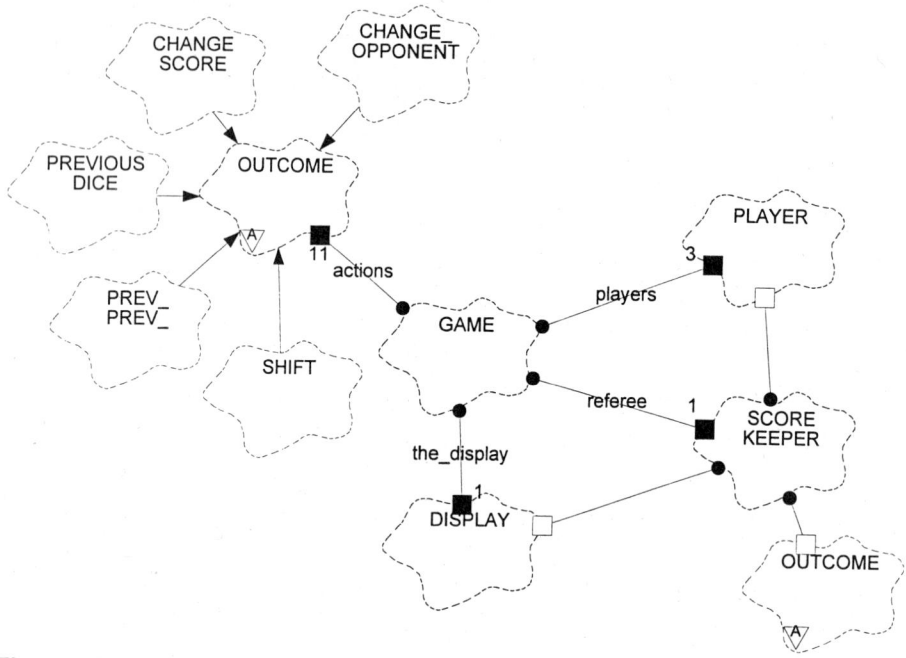

Figure 9.5 Second Class Diagram for GAME

The main event loop is shown in the object scenario diagram of Figure 9.6. The loop continues until the *referee* detects that the conditions for ending the game have been met (any player achieving a score of 1000 or greater or all three players' getting scores of 0 or lower). The first step in the loop is for game object to fetch the next player (this is done cyclically). Next, the player is told to roll his or her dice (the actual mechanism for producing a random index varies of course from player to player). Finally, the *referee* is told to *update_scores_and_display* with *the_player* sent in as a parameter.

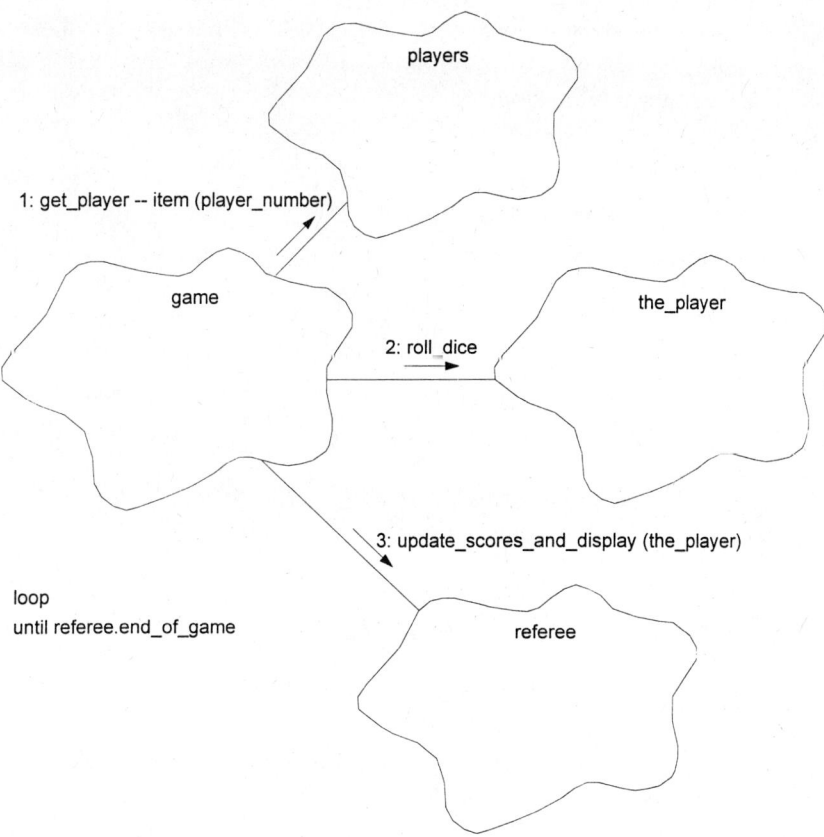

1: get_player -- item (player_number)

game

players

the_player

2: roll_dice

3: update_scores_and_display (the_player)

loop
until referee.end_of_game

referee

Figure 9.6 Main Event Loop

The final analysis class diagram that shows PLAYER as an abstract class with classes PLAYER1_TYPE, PLAYER2_TYPE, and PLAYER3_TYPE as subclasses and also shows the two ARRAY classes is shown in Figure 9.7. Amazingly, this "simple" problem analysis has led to the discovery of 15 classes in Figure 9.7.

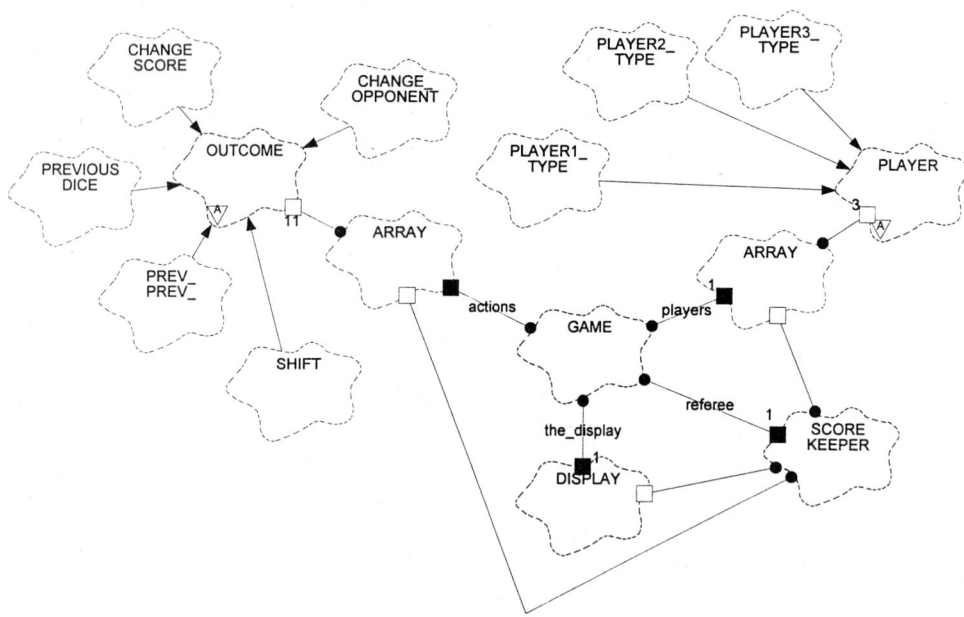

Figure 9.7 Third Class Diagram for GAME

The only remaining classes that need to be added are classes that support the implementation of the *roll_dice* mechanism for each of the three player types. If you recall from the problem description, player 1 rolls a pair of dice to get its random index location. Player 2 rolls a single die accepting only outcomes between 2 and 6. Player 3 chooses a uniformly distributed random number between 2 and 12. Therefore, 3 additional support classes are required in the final design class diagram shown in Figure 9.8. This diagram shows 18 classes.

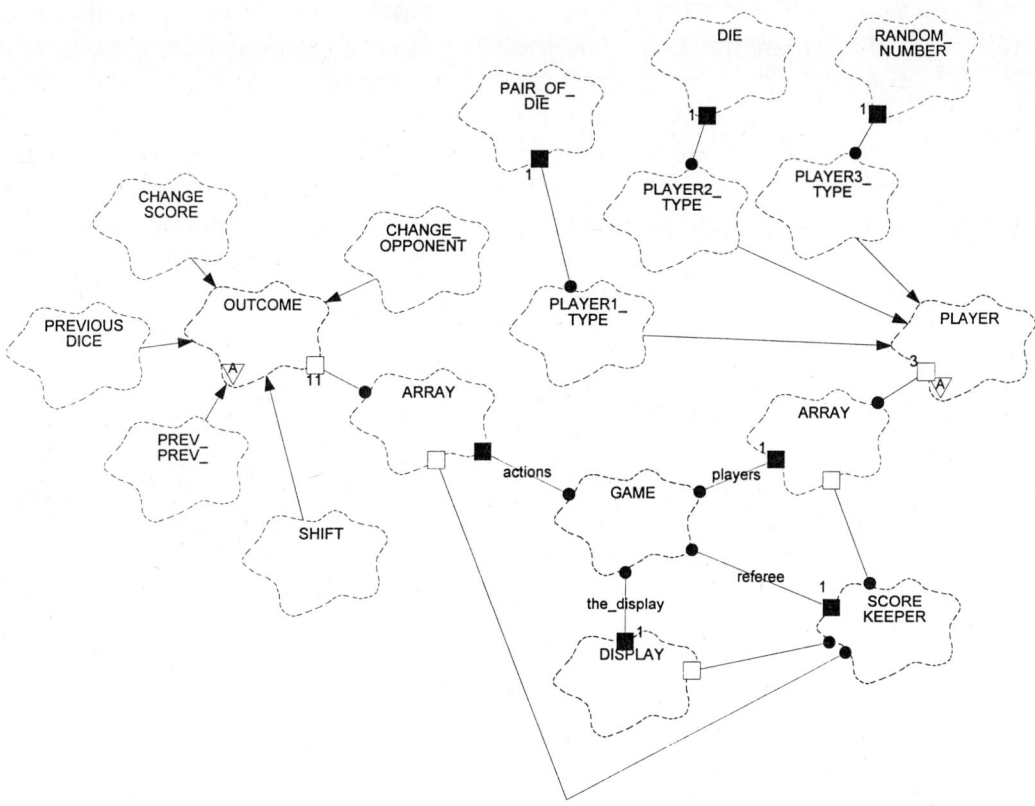

Figure 9.8 Third Class Diagram for GAME

The two areas where late-binding is an essential part of the software design are the methods *roll_dice* and *update_score* for a particular action type. These two polymorphic behavior mechanisms are associated with the two abstract classes (OUTCOME and PLAYER). In a more complex system, many more polymorphic mechanisms might be identified.

We have completed our domain analysis and have entered the stage of late design. All of the key classes have been identified. The nature of their associations have been discovered and modeled. We could continue the process of design with more detailed object scenarios that would allow the discovery of additional methods for each of the key classes. From this design work, detailed class descriptions could be written. For each major class a list of its attributes and methods including a narrative description of each could be constructed. At some point in this process the level of detail would become so low that a form of graphical coding would already have begun. There is a fine and somewhat delicate line that must be established that separates the planning process in which the overall software architecture is defined from the implementation stage in which the final details are discovered and incorporated into the software system. It is rarely obvious when one has hit or crossed this line.

For the current system, further design details are left as an exercise to the reader (see problem 1 in the Exercise section of this chapter). We will now turn our attention to the implementation details of this game.

The reader is asked to provide pre- and postconditions for each of the routines in the many classes that follow (see problem 2).

9.2.3 Implementation details

Listing 9.3 shows the skeletal structure of the software system in class GAME. Even before implementing the supplier classes that it depends on (i.e., class PLAYER, SCOREKEEPER, OUTCOME, and DISPLAY), the overall flow of control is established in this main application class.

The one line of code that implements the first polymorphic mechanism is commented as such. The structure of the code in Listing 9.3 closely follows the object scenario analysis presented in the section 9.2.2.

Listing 9.3

```
class GAME

creation
      start

feature
      player1:    PLAYER

      player2:    PLAYER

      player3:    PLAYER

      players:    ARRAY [PLAYER]

      referee:    SCOREKEEPER

      the_display: DISPLAY

      actions:    ARRAY [OUTCOME]

      start is
          local
            value: INTEGER
```

```
        player_number: INTEGER
        the_player: PLAYER
    do
        !! the_display
        !PLAYER1_TYPE! player1.make (500)
        !PLAYER2_TYPE! player2.make (500)
        !PLAYER3_TYPE! player3.make (500)
        !! players.make (1, 3)
        players.put (player1, 1)
        players.put (player2, 2)
        players.put (player3, 3)
        !! actions.make (1, 12)
        !! referee.make (players, actions, the_display)
        referee.initialize_action
        from
            player_number := 1
        until
            referee.end_of_game
        loop
            the_player := players.item (player_number)
            the_player.roll_dice
            referee.update_scores_and_display (the_player)
            player_number := player_number + 1
            if player_number = 4 then
                player_number := 1
            end
        end
    end

end -- class GAME
```

Listing 9.4 presents the details of deferred class PLAYER, the first of the two abstract classes. Please take note of how features of this class are separated into four distinct export sections (i.e., GAME, SCOREKEEPER and OUTCOME, SCOREKEEPER, and OUTCOME).

The *make* routine is not labeled as a creation routine because it is illegal for a *deferred* class to have any instances and therefore to contain a creation routine. The *make* routine will become a creation routine in the subclasses of PLAYER and as such must be available in class GAME (from our earlier analysis, this class "owns" the player objects). The data features *current_dice_value* and *score* must be accessible to the SCOREKEEPER and to the various OUTCOME classes.

The method *update_previous_dice_values* must be available only in the SCOREKEEPER class since the *referee* issues this command to each player after the appropriate action has been taken. Some of the export scope decisions may be added later in the code development after the various pieces of the system start to emerge. The goal is to keep the "interface bandwidth" (i.e., the regions of visibility for each feature) as small as possible.

The data features *previous_dice_value* and *previous_previous_dice_value* and the method *change_score* must be available only to the various OUTCOME subclasses.

Finally, the polymorphic method *roll_dice* must be available only in class GAME. This method is defined in each of the concrete PLAYER subclasses.

Listing 9.4 Abstract class PLAYER

```
deferred class PLAYER

feature {GAME}

    make (initial_score: INTEGER) is
        do
            score := initial_score
        end

feature {SCOREKEEPER, OUTCOME}

    current_dice_value: INTEGER

    score: INTEGER

feature {SCOREKEEPER}

    update_previous_dice_values is
        do
            previous_previous_dice_value := previous_dice_value
            previous_dice_value := current_dice_value
        end

feature {OUTCOME}

    previous_dice_value: INTEGER

    previous_previous_dice_value: INTEGER

    change_score (amount: INTEGER) is
        do
```

```
        score := score + amount
    end

feature {GAME}

    roll_dice is
        deferred
        end

end -- class PLAYER
```

Listings 9.5, 9.6, and 9.7 present the details of the 3 concrete PLAYER subclasses, PLAYER1_TYPE, PLAYER2_TYPE, and PLAYER3_TYPE.

Listing 9.5 Class PLAYER1_TYPE

```
class PLAYER1_TYPE

inherit
    PLAYER

creation {GAME}
    make

feature {NONE}

    dice: PAIR_OF_DIE

    initialize_dice is
        once
            !! dice.make
        end

feature {GAME}

    roll_dice is
        do
            initialize_dice
            if score > 0 then
                current_dice_value := dice.roll
            end
        end

end -- class PLAYER1_TYPE
```

Before presenting the details of PLAYER2_TYPE and PLAYER3_TYPE, some discussion of Listing 9.5 is in order.

PLAYER1_TYPE is declared as a subclass of PLAYER. It therefore inherits all of the attributes and routines of this parent class. A *creation* clause declares *make* (inherited from class PLAYER) as a creation routine. Furthermore, instances of PLAYER1_TYPE can only be legally produced in class GAME (the export scope next to the *creation* keyword).

In the protected section of the class, the attribute dice (of type PAIR_OF_DIE) is declared. The "once" routine *initialize_dice* uses the keyword *once* instead of *do* in order to guarantee that this routine will be executed one time even though it may be called many times. This is important because the *dice* need to be initialized only once.

The polymorphic *roll_dice* routine sets the value of the attribute *current_dice_value* to the result of *dice.roll*. Only the first time that this routine is invoked from within class GAME will the routine *initialize_dice* be executed.

Similar comments apply to Listings 9.6 and 9.7 which follow.

Listing 9.6 Class PLAYER2_TYPE

```
class PLAYER2_TYPE

inherit
    PLAYER

creation {GAME}
    make

feature {NONE}

    the_die: DIE

    initialize_die is
        once
            !! the_die.initialize
        end

feature {GAME}

    roll_dice is
        do
            initialize_die
            if score > 0 then
                from
                    current_dice_value := the_die.value
                until
```

```
        current_dice_value /= 1
    loop
        current_dice_value := the_die.value
    end
  end
end

end -- class PLAYER2_TYPE
```

Listing 9.7 Class PLAYER3_TYPE

```
class PLAYER3_TYPE

inherit
    PLAYER

creation {GAME}
    make

feature {NONE}

    number: RANDOM_NUMBER

    initialize_random is
        once
            !! number.initialize
        end

feature {GAME}

    roll_dice is
        do
            initialize_random
            if score > 0 then
                number.next
                current_dice_value := number.value_between (2, 12)
            end
        end

end -- class PLAYER3_TYPE
```

We next turn our attention to the second abstract class and its sub-classes, class OUTCOME. This is a class that encapsulates only behavior, not data. The method *update_scores*, which takes *primary_player*, *other_player1*, and *other_player2* as parameters, has five separate concrete implementations as will be seen below. Listing 9.8 presents deferred class

OUTCOME. The deferred routine, *update_scores*, returns TRUE only if the *actions* array is to be rotated by 1 index; otherwise it returns FALSE.

Listing 9.8 Abstract class OUTCOME

```
deferred class OUTCOME

feature {SCOREKEEPER}

      update_scores (primary_player: PLAYER; other_player1: PLAYER;
            other_player2: PLAYER): BOOLEAN is
         deferred
         end

end -- class OUTCOME
```

The five concrete subclasses of class OUTCOME are shown in Listings 9.9, 9.10, 9.11, 9.12, and 9.13.

Listing 9.9 Class CHANGE_SCORE

```
class CHANGE_SCORE

inherit
      OUTCOME

creation {SCOREKEEPER}
      make

feature {NONE}

      change_score_by: INTEGER

      make (value: INTEGER) is
         do
            change_score_by := value
         end

feature {SCOREKEEPER}

      update_scores (primary_player: PLAYER; other_player1: PLAYER;
            other_player2: PLAYER): BOOLEAN is
         do
            primary_player.change_score (change_score_by)
            Result := false
         end

end -- class CHANGE_SCORE
```

Listing 9.10 Class PREVIOUS_DICE

```
class PREVIOUS_DICE

inherit
    OUTCOME

creation {SCOREKEEPER}
    make

feature {NONE}

    multiplicative_factor: INTEGER

    make (factor: INTEGER) is
        do
            multiplicative_factor := factor
        end

feature {SCOREKEEPER}

    update_scores (primary_player: PLAYER; other_player1: PLAYER;
                   other_player2: PLAYER): BOOLEAN is
        do
            primary_player.change_score(multiplicative_factor
                    * primary_player.previous_dice_value)
            Result := false
        end

end -- class PREVIOUS_DICE
```

Listing 9.11 Class PREVIOUS_PREVIOUS

```
class PREVIOUS_PREVIOUS

inherit
    OUTCOME

creation {SCOREKEEPER}
    make

feature {NONE}

    multiplicative_factor1: INTEGER

    multiplicative_factor2: INTEGER
```

```
make (factor1: INTEGER; factor2: INTEGER) is
    do
        multiplicative_factor1 := factor1
        multiplicative_factor2 := factor2
    end

feature {SCOREKEEPER}

update_scores (primary_player: PLAYER; other_player1: PLAYER;
                  other_player2: PLAYER): BOOLEAN is
    do
        primary_player.change_score (multiplicative_factor1 *
            primary_player.previous_dice_value
            + multiplicative_factor2 * primary_player.previous_previous_dice_value)
        Result := false
    end

end -- class PREVIOUS_PREVIOUS
```

Listing 9.12 Class SHIFT

```
class SHIFT

inherit
    OUTCOME

feature {SCOREKEEPER}

update_scores (primary_player: PLAYER; other_player1: PLAYER;
                  other_player2: PLAYER): BOOLEAN is
    do
        Result := true
    end

end -- class SHIFT
```

Listing 9.13 Class CHANGE_OPPONENTS_SCORE

```
class CHANGE_OPPONENTS_SCORE

inherit
    OUTCOME

creation
    make
```

```
feature {NONE}

    increase_percentage: INTEGER

    make (value: INTEGER) is
        do
            increase_percentage := 100 // value
        end

feature {SCOREKEEPER}

    update_scores (primary_player: PLAYER; other_player1: PLAYER;
                other_player2: PLAYER): BOOLEAN is
    local
        score_primary: INTEGER
        score_other1: INTEGER
        score_other2: INTEGER
        increase_by: INTEGER
    do
        score_primary := primary_player.score
        score_other1 := other_player1.score
        score_other2 := other_player2.score
        if score_other1 > 0 then
            other_player1.change_score (- score_other1 // increase_percentage)
            increase_by := increase_by + score_other1 // increase_percentage
        end
        if score_other2 > 0 then
            other_player2.change_score (- score_other2 // increase_percentage)
            increase_by := increase_by + score_other2 // increase_percentage
        end
        primary_player.change_score (increase_by)
        Result := false
    end

end -- class CHANGE_OPPONENTS_SCORE
```

The most complex of the polymorphic *update_scores* routines occurs in class CHANGE_OPPONENTS_SCORE in Listing 9.13. A local variable *increase_by* is incremented only if one of the other players has a score that is greater than 0.

Perhaps the most important class in the system is SCOREKEEPER. This class has the responsibility to evaluate each player's dice throw, update its score, and transmit this information to the display object. It is also responsible for initializing the *actions* array and creating instances of each of the OUTCOME subclasses.

The code for this class is given in Listing 9.14.

Listing 9.14 Class SCOREKEEPER

```
class SCOREKEEPER

creation {GAME}
    make

feature {NONE}

    the_display: DISPLAY

    players: ARRAY [PLAYER]

    actions: ARRAY [OUTCOME]

    iteration: INTEGER

    make (the_players: ARRAY [PLAYER]; the_actions: ARRAY [OUTCOME];
                    a_display: DISPLAY) is
        do
            players := the_players
            actions := the_actions
            the_display := a_display
        end

    shift_actions is
            -- Rotate the action objects within the actions array
        local
            index: INTEGER
            action_12: OUTCOME
        do
            action_12 := actions.item (12)
            from
                index := 13
            until
                index = 3
            loop
                index := index - 1
                actions.put (actions.item (index - 1), index)
            end
```

```
            actions.put (action_12, 2)
        end

    display_scores is
        do
            the_display.display_scores (iteration,
                players.item(1).score,players.item (2).score, players.item (3).score)

        end

feature {GAME}

    initialize_action is
        local
            action2, action3, action4, action5, action6, action7, action8,
                action9, action10, action11, action12: OUTCOME
        do
            !CHANGE_SCORE! action2.make (36)
            actions.put (action2, 2)
            !CHANGE_SCORE! action3.make (18)
            actions.put (action3, 3)
            !CHANGE_SCORE! action4.make (- 20)
            actions.put (action4, 4)
            !PREVIOUS_DICE! action5.make (15)
            actions.put (action5, 5)
            !PREVIOUS_DICE! action6.make (- 8)
            actions.put (action6, 6)
            !SHIFT! action7
            actions.put (action7, 7)
            !PREVIOUS_PREVIOUS! action8.make (- 5, - 4)
            actions.put (action8, 8)
            !CHANGE_SCORE! action9.make (- 25)
            actions.put (action9, 9)
            !CHANGE_OPPONENTS_SCORE! action10.make (10)
            actions.put (action10, 10)
            !CHANGE_OPPONENTS_SCORE! action11.make (- 5)
            actions.put (action11, 11)
            !SHIFT! action12
            actions.put (action12, 12)
        end

    update_scores_and_display (a_player: PLAYER) is
        local
```

```
            player_number: INTEGER
            dice_roll: INTEGER
            the_action: OUTCOME
            perform_shift: BOOLEAN
    do
        if a_player.score > 0 then
            iteration := iteration + 1
            if players.item (1) = a_player then
                player_number := 1
            elseif players.item (2) = a_player then
                player_number := 2
            else
                player_number := 3
            end
            dice_roll := a_player.current_dice_value
            the_action := actions.item (dice_roll)
            if player_number = 1 then
                perform_shift := the_action.update_scores (a_player,
                            players.item (2), players.item (3))
            elseif player_number = 2 then
                perform_shift := the_action.update_scores (a_player,
                            players.item (1), players.item (3))
            else
                perform_shift := the_action.update_scores (a_player,
                            players.item (1), players.item (2))
            end
            a_player.update_previous_dice_values
            if perform_shift then
                shift_actions
            end
            display_scores
        end
    end

end_of_game: BOOLEAN is
        -- Determines whether all players have been eliminated
        -- or one has reached a score of 1000
    do
        if players.item (1).score >= 1000 then
            io.putstring ("%N%NPlayer 1 has won the game%N")
            Result := true
```

```
            elseif players.item (2).score >= 1000 then
                io.putstring ("%N%NPlayer 2 has won the game%N")
                Result := true
            elseif players.item (3).score >= 1000 then
                io.putstring ("%N%NPlayer 3 has won the game%N")
                Result := true
            elseif players.item (1).score <= 0 and players.item (2).score <= 0 and
                    players.item (3).score <= 0 then
                io.putstring ("%N%NNo player has won the game%N")
                Result := true
            else
                Result := false
            end
        end

end -- class SCOREKEEPER
```

Several study questions related to class SCOREKEEPER are given in the Exercise section. The reader is encouraged to solve these problems.

Since output is sent to the screen using ordinary screen output routines, it is not really necessary to have a separate class DISPLAY. This class is included to allow for future maintenance at which time fancier output might be desired. In that case only the routine *display_scores* would have to be modified.

The details of class DISPLAY are shown in Listing 9.15.

Listing 9.15 Class DISPLAY

```
class DISPLAY

feature {SCOREKEEPER}

    display_scores (iteration: INTEGER; score1: INTEGER; score2: INTEGER;
            score3: INTEGER) is
        do
            io.putstring ("%NIteration ")
            io.putint (iteration)
            io.putstring ("%NScore for player 1: ")
            io.putint (score1)
            io.putstring ("%NScore for player 2: ")
            io.putint (score2)
            io.putstring ("%NScore for player 3: ")
            io.putint (score3)
```

```
            io.new_line
        end

end -- class DISPLAY
```

Among the three support classes, DIE, RANDOM_NUMBER, and PAIR_OF_DIE, only the latter class has not been presented before. The code for this class is given in Listing 9.16.

Listing 9.16 Support class PAIR_OF_DIE

```
class PAIR_OF_DIE

creation
    make

feature {NONE}

    die1: DIE

    die2: DIE

feature

    make is
        do
            !! die1.initialize
            !! die2.initialize
        end

    roll: INTEGER is
        do
            Result := die1.value + die2.value
        end

end -- class PAIR_OF_DIE
```

9.2.4 Output

After running the game simulation several times, it is evident that all three players are capable of winning the game and occassionally, all three players are eliminated so the game has no winner. I must confess that it was much more fun to design and implement the game than to play it!

Most typical runs take between 75 and 450 iterations to complete with 200 iterations appearing to be a typical run length. It was not deemed necessary to compute more precise statistics.

The last eight iterations of a typical run are presented below:

Iteration 81
Score for player 1: 392
Score for player 2: 428
Score for player 3: 748

Iteration 82
Score for player 1: 336
Score for player 2: 428
Score for player 3: 748

Iteration 83
Score for player 1: 336
Score for player 2: 518
Score for player 3: 748

Iteration 84
Score for player 1: 303
Score for player 2: 467
Score for player 3: 832

Iteration 85
Score for player 1: 247
Score for player 2: 467
Score for player 3: 832

Iteration 86
Score for player 1: 247
Score for player 2: 447
Score for player 3: 832

Iteration 87
Score for player 1: 247
Score for player 2: 447
Score for player 3: 997

Iteration 88
Score for player 1: 176
Score for player 2: 469
Score for player 3: 1046

9.3   Version 2—improved design and implementation

The major problem with the previous design is that it vests too much control with the GAME class. This class is responsible for creating all of the major objects and then controlling the main game loop. Although "correct" (in the sense that the resulting software system runs properly), the architecture is too centric. An object-oriented system should strive to distribute responsibility and control more equally among its objects.

For example, the game should do little more than create three players and a referee and tell the first player to "play." This first player upon completing the throw of its dice should then tell the next player to move. This player upon completing its move should then pass control to the next player and so on. After each player completes its move, it should query the referee to determine whether the game is over. Only the referee has the information to make this determination. Using this approach, there would no longer be a main event loop. The GAME class would have limited responsibility. Its principal function would be reduced to some simple initialization.

Another problem with the previous design is the use of inheritance among the player classes. What really distinguishes one type of player from another is the unique type of dice that is uses. Instead of creating a hierarchy of player classes, the revised design uses a single PLAYER class. This class contains an attribute *dice* of type DICE_TYPE. A hierarchy of DICE_TYPE classes (three specialized dice classes) are constructed. Each player object receives a unique dice type when it is created.

The revised design further distributes responsibility by creating a new class called ACTION. This class is responsible for determining the particular type of outcome resulting from a player's dice roll. The new class ACTION collaborates with class SCOREKEEPER to update the players' scores after a dice roll. This results in a "cleaner" set of interactions. Players interact only with the referee and the next player. The referee interacts with the ACTION class to update each player's score.

An object scenario diagram that shows the important key mechanism of having the referee update a player's score is shown in Figure 9.9. The class diagram that shows the revised system architecture is given in Figure 9.10.

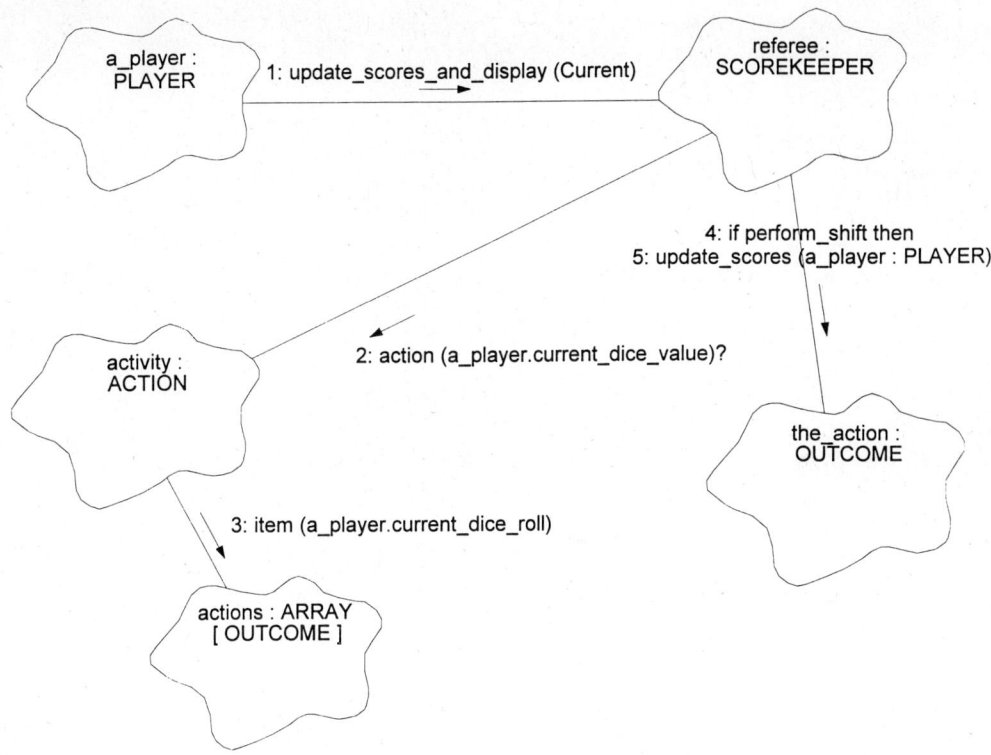

Figure 9.9 Update Scores

9.3.1 Revised implementation
Class GAME is shown in Listing 9.17.

Listing 9.17 Revised class GAME

class GAME

creation
    start

feature
    player1: PLAYER

    player2: PLAYER

    player3: PLAYER

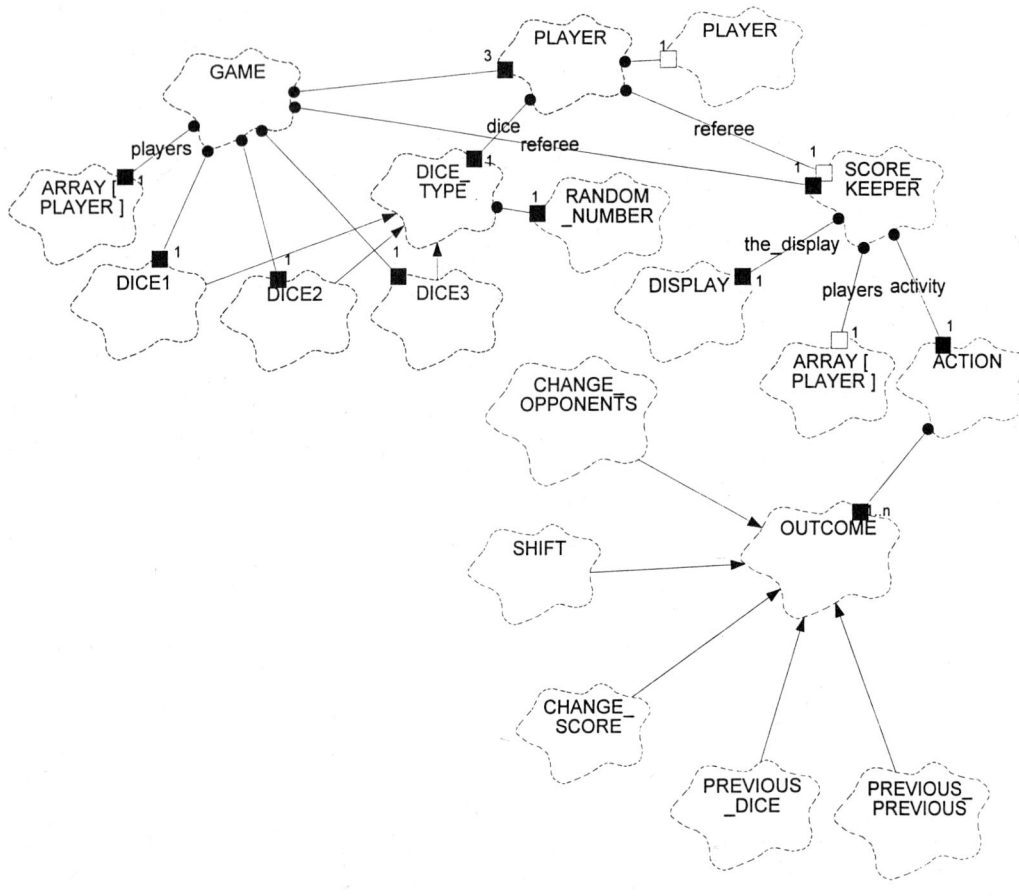

Figure 9.10 Class Diagram for Revised System

players: ARRAY [PLAYER]

referee: SCOREKEEPER

d1: DICE1

d2: DICE2

d3: DICE3

start **is**
    do
        initialize_features
        player1.play
    end

```
    initialize_features is
        do
            !! d1.initialize
            !! d2.initialize
            !! d3.initialize
            !! player1.make (500, d1, 1)
            !! player2.make (500, d2, 2)
            !! player3.make (500, d3, 3)
            player1.set_next_player (player2)
            player2.set_next_player (player3)
            player3.set_next_player (player1)
            !! players.make (1, 3)
            players.put (player1, 1)
            players.put (player2, 2)
            players.put (player3, 3)
            !! referee.make (players)
            player1.set_referee (referee)
            player2.set_referee (referee)
            player3.set_referee (referee)
        end

end -- class GAME
```

The start routine performs 2 steps: *initialize_features* and *player1.play*. Clearly the role of this class is much less centric than the initial design.

Listing 9.18 presents the details of class PLAYER.

Listing 9.18 Class PLAYER

```
class PLAYER

creation {GAME}
    make

feature {NONE}

    next_player: PLAYER    -- owned by GAME

    referee:       SCOREKEEPER  -- owned by GAME

    dice:          DICE_TYPE

    make (initial_score: INTEGER; some_dice: DICE_TYPE; number: INTEGER) is
        do
            score := initial_score
```

```
            dice := some_dice
            player_number := number
        end

    update_previous_dice_values is
        do
            previous_previous_dice_value := previous_dice_value
            previous_dice_value := current_dice_value
        end

feature {GAME}

    set_next_player (nxt_player: PLAYER) is
        do
            next_player := next_player
        end

    set_referee (the_referee: SCOREKEEPER) is
        do
            referee := the_referee
        end

feature {SCOREKEEPER, OUTCOME}

    current_dice_value: INTEGER

    score: INTEGER

    player_number: INTEGER

feature {OUTCOME}

    previous_dice_value:              INTEGER

    previous_previous_dice_value:   INTEGER

    change_score (amount: INTEGER) is
        do
            score := score + amount
        end

feature {PLAYER, GAME}

    play is
        do
            if score > 0 then
                dice.roll
                current_dice_value := dice.value
```

```
            update_previous_dice_values
        end
        referee.update_scores_and_display (Current)
        if not referee.end_of_game then
            next_player.play
        end
    end
```

end -- class *PLAYER*

There are five feature sections, each with its own export scope. The *make* routine has an additional export scope. This "tight bandwidth" ensures that resources are available only where they are needed.

The attributes contained within PLAYER are

- *next_player : PLAYER* - Used to pass control

- *referee : SCOREKEEPER* - Used to update scores and end the game

- *dice : DICE_TYPE* - Used to set *current_dice_value*

- *current_dice_value : INTEGER* - Set by dice

- *score : INTEGER* - Cumulative points

- *player_number : INTEGER* - Used to identify player

Listing 9.19 presents the significantly revised class SCOREKEEPER.

Listing 9.19 Class SCOREKEEPER

```
class SCOREKEEPER

creation {GAME}
    make

feature {NONE}

    the_display: DISPLAY

    players:      ARRAY [PLAYER]  -- Owned by game

    activity:     ACTION

    iteration:    INTEGER

    make (the_players: ARRAY [PLAYER]) is
        do
            !! the_display
```

```
                players := the_players
                !! activity.initialize (players)
            end

    display_scores is
        do

            the_display.display_scores (iteration,
                players.item (1).score, players.item (2).score, players.item (3).score)
        end

feature {PLAYER}

    update_scores_and_display (a_player: PLAYER) is
        local
            the_action: OUTCOME
        do
            iteration := iteration + 1
            if a_player.score > 0 then
                the_action := activity.action (a_player.current_dice_value)
                if the_action.perform_shift then
                    activity.shift_actions
                end
                the_action.update_scores (a_player)
            end
            display_scores
        end

    end_of_game: BOOLEAN is
            -- Determines whether all players have been eliminated
            -- or one has reached a score of 1000
        do
            if players.item (1).score >= 1000 then
                io.putstring ("%N%NPlayer 1 has won the game%N")
                Result := true
            elseif players.item (2).score >= 1000 then
                io.putstring ("%N%NPlayer 2 has won the game%N")
                Result := true
            elseif players.item (3).score >= 1000 then
                io.putstring ("%N%NPlayer 3 has won the game%N")
                Result := true
            elseif players.item (1).score <= 0 and players.item (2).score <= 0 and
                    players.item (3).score <= 0 then
```

```
        io.putstring ("%N%NNo player has won the game%N")
        Result := true
    else
        Result := false
    end
end
```

end -- class *SCOREKEEPER*

In this revised version of SCOREKEEPER the responsibility for updating player scores is shared with the class ACTION. The object scenario diagram of Figure 9.9 sketches the details. Class ACTION is presented in Listing 9.20.

Listing 9.20 Class ACTION

```
class ACTION

creation {SCOREKEEPER}
    initialize

feature {SCOREKEEPER}

    actions: ARRAY [OUTCOME]

    players: ARRAY [PLAYER]   -- Owned by game

    initialize (the_players: ARRAY [PLAYER]) is
        local
            action2, action3, action4, action5, action6, action7, action8,
            action9, action10, action11, action12: OUTCOME
        do
            players := the_players
            !! actions.make (2, 12)
            !CHANGE_SCORE! action2.make (36)
            actions.put (action2, 2)
            !CHANGE_SCORE! action3.make (18)
            actions.put (action3, 3)
            !CHANGE_SCORE! action4.make (- 20)
            actions.put (action4, 4)
            !PREVIOUS_DICE! action5.make (15)
            actions.put (action5, 5)
            !PREVIOUS_DICE! action6.make (- 8)
            actions.put (action6, 6)
```

```
        !SHIFT! action7
        actions.put (action7, 7)
        !PREVIOUS_PREVIOUS! action8.make (- 5, - 4)
        actions.put (action8, 8)
        !CHANGE_SCORE! action9.make (- 25)
        actions.put (action9, 9)
        !CHANGE_OPPONENTS_SCORE! action10.make (10, players)
        actions.put (action10, 10)
        !CHANGE_OPPONENTS_SCORE! action11.make (- 5, players)
        actions.put (action11, 11)
        !SHIFT! action12
        actions.put (action12, 12)
    end


action (dice_roll: INTEGER): OUTCOME is
        -- The action associated with current player dice roll
    do
        Result := actions.item (dice_roll)
    end


shift_actions is
        -- Rotate the actions within the actions array
    local
        index: INTEGER
        action_12: OUTCOME
    do
        action_12 := actions.item (12)
        from
            index := 13
        until
            index = 3
        loop
            index := index - 1
            actions.put (actions.item (index - 1), index)
        end
        actions.put (action_12, 2)
    end

end -- class ACTION
```

Listing 9.21 presents the abstract class OUTCOME.

Listing 9.21 Class OUTCOME

```
deferred class OUTCOME

feature {SCOREKEEPER}

    perform_shift: BOOLEAN

    update_scores (a_player: PLAYER) is
            -- Change the score of the primary player and possibly the
            -- other players. Set perform_shift only if the actions are to
            -- be shifted by 1 in the actions array (in scorekeeper)
        deferred
        end

end -- class OUTCOME
```

Only a single parameter, *a_player*, is passed to the command *update_scores* rather than the three parameters used in the previous version.

Only the subclass CHANGE_OPPONENTS_SCORE is significantly changed from the previous version. Its code is presented in Listing 9.22.

Listing 9.22 Class CHANGE_OPPONENTS_SCORE

```
class CHANGE_OPPONENTS_SCORE

inherit
    OUTCOME

creation {ACTION}
    make

feature {NONE}

    increase_percentage: INTEGER

    players:            ARRAY [PLAYER]  -- Owned by game

    make (value: INTEGER; the_players: ARRAY [PLAYER]) is
        do
            increase_percentage := 100 // value
            players := the_players
        end

feature {SCOREKEEPER}
```

```
update_scores (a_player: PLAYER) is
    local
        score_primary: INTEGER
        score_other1: INTEGER
        score_other2: INTEGER
        increase_by: INTEGER
        other_player1: PLAYER
        other_player2: PLAYER
    do
        if a_player.player_number = 1 then
            other_player1 := players.item (2)
            other_player2 := players.item (3)
        elseif a_player.player_number = 2 then
            other_player1 := players.item (1)
            other_player2 := players.item (3)
        else
            other_player1 := players.item (1)
            other_player2 := players.item (2)
        end
        score_primary := players.item (a_player.player_number).score
        score_other1 := other_player1.score
        score_other2 := other_player2.score
        if score_other1 > 0 then
            other_player1.change_score (- score_other1 // increase_percentage)
            increase_by := increase_by + score_other1 // increase_percentage
        end
        if score_other2 > 0 then
            other_player2.change_score (- score_other2 // increase_percentage)
            increase_by := increase_by + score_other2 // increase_percentage
        end
        a_player.change_score (increase_by)
        perform_shift := false
    end

end -- class CHANGE_OPPONENTS_SCORE
```

The *player_number* attribute plays an important role in Listing 9.22 in determining the *"primary_player"* and the other players. The scoring logic is similar to the first version.

The abstract class DICE_TYPE is presented in Listing 9.23.

Listing 9.23 Class DICE_TYPE

```
deferred class DICE_TYPE
feature {NONE}
    r: RANDOM_NUMBER
feature
    value: INTEGER
    initialize is
        do
            !! r.initialize
        end
    roll is
            -- Sets value
        deferred
        end
end -- class DICE_TYPE
```

The three concrete subclasses of DICE_TYPE are presented in Listings 9.24, 9.25, and 9.26.

Listing 9.24 Class DICE1

```
class DICE1
inherit
    DICE_TYPE
creation
    initialize
feature
    roll is
        local
            die1, die2: INTEGER
        do
            r.next
            die1 := r.value_between (1, 6)
            r.next
            die2 := r.value_between (1, 6)
```

```
            value := die1 + die2
        end

    end -- class DICE1
```

Listing 9.25 Class DICE2

```
    class DICE2

    inherit
        DICE_TYPE

    creation
        initialize

    feature

        roll is
            do
                r.next
                value := r.value_between (2, 6)
            end

    end -- class DICE2
```

Listing 9.26 Class DICE3

```
    class DICE3

    inherit
        DICE_TYPE

    creation
        initialize

    feature

        roll is
            do
                r.next
                value := r.value_between (2, 12)
            end

    end -- class DICE3
```

9.4   Summary

This chapter has presented two versions of the analysis, design, and Eiffel implementation of a game simulation. Both designs feature late-binding and polymorphism. This important design principle permits a common method to enjoy specialized implementations in a set of related subclasses.

Booch class diagrams and object scenario diagrams, discussed in Chapter 2, have been brought to life in this chapter. The process of object modeling has been shown to provide the architectural framework from which the implementation process can be performed.

There is no exact right or wrong way to design a software system. Version 2 improves upon Version 1 because it is less centric and provides a more even distribution of responsibility among the classes. The reader is encouraged to formulate alternative approaches to the analysis, design, and implementation of this game. From such an exercise much can be learned about the process of object-oriented software development.

9.5   Exercises

1. For the game presented in section 9.2, continue the design a little further by showing some additional object scenario diagrams that describe the behavior of the referee.

2. For all of the code in the implementation of the game in section 9.3, add preconditions and postconditions wherever possible and wherever appropriate.

3. In Listing 9.14, routine *shift_actions*, why does the loop index start at 13 and move downward rather than start at index 1 and move upward?

4. In Listing 9.14, routine *update_scores_and_display*, why is it necessary to compute the *player_number*?

5. In Listing 9.14, routine *update_scores_and_display*, where is the polymorphic message?

6. In Listing 9.14, routine *update_scores_and_display*, what is the purpose of sending *a_player* the command *update_previous_dice_values*?

7. Perform a new analysis, design, and implementation of the game specified in section 9.2. Show and explain each class diagram, object scenario diagram, and Eiffel code.

8. Suppose a new player, *player4*, were added to the game. This player when told to *roll_dice* responds by rolling a pair of die (like *player1*) and then subtracting 3 from its total. The subtraction is performed in such a way that if the dice return the value 4, the index chosen is 12; if the dice return the value 3, the index chosen is 11; and if the dice return the value 2, the index chosen is 10.

    Perform the necessary maintenance on the code given in section 9.2 to include the presence of player 4 in the game. Make suitable changes to whatever classes are appropriate.

    When you have finished, write some comments accessing the relative difficulty of performing the maintenance that you have completed. Such an evaluation could serve as the basis for determining the quality of the initial design. If many significant changes have to be made to the original architecture of the system, this would suggest that the original architecture was not robust.

9. Define a small project (like the game in section 9.2) that provides the opportunity to showcase late-binding and polymorphism. Clearly state the specifications of the problem. Then discuss the area(s) where you would employ polymorphism in your analysis and design. Finally, implement a solution in Eiffel.

Special project. The following project might be assigned as a semester project in a lab course. A full implementation and discussion may be found in Chapter 10 of the book *Software Development Using Eiffel: There Can Be Life Other Than C++* (ibid.), Prentice Hall, 1995.

The game consists of four players named A, B, C, and D, and a board with 20 positions on it. There is no required human intervention in this game. Your computer program, through its various objects and mechanisms, will be responsible for playing out a complete game, presenting the user with simple output to be described below and announcing the winner at the end.

There is no entity, such as a centralized game controller, that has any knowledge of the 20 board positions. The four players, A, B, C, and D are all initialized to start at position 1. Each board position knows of the next board position and the twentieth board position knows of the first position.

Each of the players (A, B, C, and D) is randomly assigned one of three investment strategies (1, 2, or 3) at the beginning of the game. Each player starts with an account balance of $50,000. As the game progresses, the original investment strategy may be replaced with another (one of the remaining two). Such swaps may occur from time to time for each player as the game progresses. Each player has no control over these investment strategy swaps.

The referee sequentially tells each of the players in turn (first player A, then B, then C, then D) to move. In response to this, the player rolls a die with an equal probability of outcomes from 1 to 6 and moves that number of board positions forward.

The game ends in one of two ways: (1) The referee has told each player to move 5000 times (each sequence of four "move" commands is defined as a move cycle), (2) one of the players is out of money. If a player is out of money, it must inform the referee who then ends the game and causes the winner to be announced. When the game ends, the player with the most money is declared the winner. Property is not valued in computing the player with the most money. The referee has no other function other than sequentially telling each of the players to move in turn and counting the number of move cycles so the game can be terminated (if in fact the game hasn't already been terminated because of bankruptcy).

There are two kinds of board positions: chance and property.

If a player lands on a chance position, the following possible actions may occur: (1) The player may immediately acquire additional money, (2) the player may immediately lose some money, (3) the player may get a replacement investment strategy, (4) the player may be asked to make another move determined again by a random roll of a die, and (5) the player may be given the option to purchase unowned property.

If a player lands on a property position, the following possible actions may occur: If the property is not owned, the player will be offered the opportunity to purchase the property at a preset price associated with the board position. The player's decision to purchase or not purchase will be based on the investment strategy that it currently has. If the property is owned by another player, the player will pay a fixed rental penalty directly to a banker who will convey this rent to the owner. The rent is based on the number of investment units (the monopoly equivalent of houses) built on the property by the owner. If the property is owned by the player who has landed on the property, the player will be offered the opportunity to purchase from 0 to 5 additional investment units. These investment units on an owned property offer the advantage of increasing the rental fee obtained if another player lands on the property. There is no limit on the number of investment units that can be "built" on an owned property. The decision regarding the number of investment units to purchase (from 0 to 5) will be based on the player's current investment strategy.

The output must be updated at the conclusion of every player's move or when rent is paid to another player. The format for the output is shown below (without the three dots of course) for a typical output (here two players happen to be on the same board position).

Cash A	Cash B	Cash C	Cash D
20799	52114	78043	15398

Move cycle: 12	Owned By	Number Units
1:		
2: A	B	12
3:		
4: C, D		
5:	D	
6:	B	2
7:		
8:		
9:		
10:		
...		
19: B		
20:	A	5

The referee must transmit the updated move cycle number at the beginning of each new move cycle to the display. Each player must transmit its current cash and board position after each move to the display. The display must also be updated each time rent is paid to another player (in order to keep the display of the current cash values current). These data, as indicated in the sample output display given above, are shown on the user's screen.

The specifications for each board position are given below:

For position 1: If a player lands on or passes this board position, the player "earns" $200 (like passing "GO" in Monopoly). That is the only function of position 1.

For position 2: This is a property position. Its cost is $2000. Its rent is $200. Investment units cost $1000 each. For each investment unit, the rent goes up by $100. In general, for all property units the following algorithm holds: Rent is 1/10 the cost of the property. Rent is increased by 1/10 the cost of each additional investment unit. Investment units always cost 1/2 as much as the property. All arithmetic is integer arithmetic with normal truncation. This algorithm allows a property position to be uniquely characterized by its cost. So, as an example, if the property on position 2 has three investment units on it, it will cost another player $500 if it lands on this property (1/10 the worth of the $2000 property and the three investment units).

For position 3: This is a chance position. If a player lands on this position, it receives a new investment strategy randomly chosen from 1 to 3 with equal likelihood. It is possible that it will receive the same investment strategy that it already has (1/3 probability).

For position 4: This is another chance position. A player landing on this position has its cash amount changed by a random integer uniformly distributed from -$300 to $300.

For position 5: This is a property position. The cost to purchase the property is $500. Using the algorithm given above, it would cost the owning player $250 to purchase one additional investment unit and cost a non-owning player landing on this position $50 rent + an extra $25 for each investment sitting on the property. The owning player would be offered the opportunity to purchase between 0 and 5 additional investment units each time it lands on this board position.

For position 6: This is a property position. The cost is $800.

For position 7: This is a chance position. A player landing on this position has its cash amount changed by a random integer uniformly distributed from -$500 to $500.

For position 8: This is a chance position. A player landing on this position must "throw" the die and move again.

For position 9: This is a property position. The cost is $1200.

For position 10: This is a chance position. If a player lands on this position, it receives a new investment strategy randomly chosen from 1 to 3 with equal likelihood. It is possible that it will receive the same investment strategy that it already has (1/3 probability).

For position 11: This is a property position. The cost is $900.

For position 12: This is a chance position. The player immediately receives a bonus of 5 percent of its current cash amount.

For position 13: This is a property position. The cost is $500.

For position 14: This is a chance position. The player immediately receives a penalty of 5 percent of its current cash amount.

For position 15: This is a property position. The cost is $1500.

For position 16: This is a chance position. If a player lands on this position, it receives a new investment strategy randomly chosen from 1 to 3 with equal likelihood. It is possible that it will receive the same investment strategy that it already has (1/3 probability). In addition, a player landing on this position has its cash amount changed by a random integer uniformly distributed from -$200 to $200.

For position 17: This is a property position. The cost is $3000.

For position 18: This is a chance position. A player landing on this position has its cash amount changed by a random integer uniformly distributed from $50 to $250.

For position 19: This is a chance position. A player landing on this position is given the option to purchase the first unowned property (in position 20 or 1 or 2, etc.).

For position 20: This is a property position. The cost is $700.

All monetary transactions (one player paying another rent, player receiving money on a chance board position, player losing money on a chance board position, player receiving $200 dollars every time it completes a circuit, players paying for a property or additional investment units) are handled by a banker. Players do not communicate directly with other players. The banker cannot ever run out of money.

It was stated earlier that when a player is offered the option of purchasing a property (when landing on an unowned property) or offered the option of purchasing from 0 to 5 additional investment units (when later landing on its own property), it makes its decision by "using" its current investment strategy. The algorithms for each of the three investment strategies are given below.

If a player has investment strategy 1: This is a random strategy. When offered the opportunity to purchase an unowned property, it will be decided by a "flip of a fair coin" (i.e., equal chance of accepting or rejecting) provided that it has more cash than the cost of the property. Its decision to purchase between 0 and 5 investment units when later landing on its own property is made by choosing a uniformly distributed random integer from 0 to 5 (providing it has enough cash to make the purchase).

For example, if the random integer chosen is 3 and the player lacks the cash to buy 3 units, it then elects to buy no units.

If a player has investment strategy 2: This is an aggressive strategy. When offered an unowned property, it will always purchase it if it has the cash to cover the purchase price (a player must always have at least one dollar remaining after a purchase—bankruptcy cannot occur as a result of a purchase). When given an opportunity to buy between 0 and 5 additional investment units, it will always purchase the largest number that it has the cash on hand to cover. That is, it will try to purchase 5 units if it has the cash. If not, it will try to purchase 4 units, and so on.

If a player has investment strategy 3: This is a conservative strategy that is based on the player's current cash and rent receipts. When offered the opportunity to purchase an unowned property, it will purchase this property provided that it has at least five times the cost of the property in current cash. When offered the opportunity to purchase between 0 and 5 investment units on its own property, it will purchase as many investment units as it can subject to the following constraints: (1) It has greater than five times as much cash as the total outlay for the additional investment units, (2) the rent already earned from the property exceeds 1/4 the cost of the additional investment units.

When a player runs out of money because it lands on another player's property and must pay rent, or a chance board position imposes a monetary penalty, it cannot sell its property or investment units to acquire additional cash. Property and investment units are not deemed to have any monetary value for avoiding bankruptcy. Their only value is in acquiring wealth during the game. When a player runs out of cash, it must inform the referee. The referee then asks the banker which of the remaining players has the most cash, ends the game, and asks the banker to tell the display to name the winning player.

Each class should limit access to its attributes as much as possible (have the smallest interface bandwidth). That is, each player should know as little about the board position it's on as is feasible, each board position should know as little about the player that has landed on it as is feasible, and the referee knows nothing about any of the players or board positions. In fact, only the banker has direct access to information about the current cash amount of all players and can reveal this information only to the display at the end of the game. Of course each player knows its own cash amount which it must transmit to the display after each move.

Appendix

1

Interface to String Class

class interface *STRING*

creation
    make

feature -- *Access*

    area: SPECIAL [CHARACTER]
        -- Special data zone
        -- (from *TO_SPECIAL*)

    False_constant: STRING **is** *"false"*
        -- Constant string "false"

    fuzzy_index (other: STRING; start: INTEGER; fuzz: INTEGER): INTEGER
        require
            other_exists: other /= void;
            other_not_empty: **not** *other.empty;*
            start_large_enough: start >= 1;
            start_small_enough: start <= count;
            acceptable_fuzzy: fuzz <= other.count

    has (c: CHARACTER): BOOLEAN
        -- Does string include *c*?
        ensure -- from *CONTAINER*
            not_found_in_empty: Result **implies not** *empty*

hash_code: INTEGER
    -- Hash code value
  require -- from *HASHABLE*
    hashable: is_hashable
  ensure -- from *HASHABLE*
    good_hash_value: Result >= 0

index_of (c: CHARACTER; start: INTEGER): INTEGER
    -- Position of first occurrence of *c* at or after *start*;
    -- 0 if none.
  require
    start_large_enough: start >= 1;
    start_small_enough: start <= count
  ensure
    correct_place: Result > 0 **implies** *item (Result) = c*

item (i: INTEGER): CHARACTER
    -- Character at position *i*
  require -- from *TABLE*
    valid_key: valid_index (k)

item_code (i: INTEGER): INTEGER
    -- Numeric code of character at position *i*
  require
    index_small_enough: i <= count;
    index_large_enough: i > 0

*shared_with (other: **like** Current): BOOLEAN*
    -- Does string share the text of *other*?

substring_index (other: STRING; start: INTEGER): INTEGER
    -- Position of first occurrence of *other* at or after *start*;
    -- 0 if none.
  require
    other_nonvoid: other /= void;
    *other_notempty: **not** other.empty;*
    start_large_enough: start >= 1;
    start_small_enough: start <= count
  ensure
    correct_place: Result > 0 **implies** *substring (Result, Result +*
other.count - 1).is_equal (other)

*True_constant: STRING **is** "true"*
    -- Constant string "true"

infix "@" (i: INTEGER): CHARACTER
 -- Character at position *i*
 require -- from *TABLE*
  valid_key: valid_index (k)

feature -- Comparison

 *is_equal (other: **like** Current): BOOLEAN*
  -- Is string made of same character sequence as *other*
  -- (possibly with a different capacity)?
  ensure -- from *COMPARABLE*
   trichotomy: Result = (**not** (Current < other) **and not** (other < makeCurrent))

 *max (other: **like** Current): **like** Current*
  -- The greater of current object and *other*
  -- (from *COMPARABLE*)
  require -- from *COMPARABLE*
   other_exists: other /= void
  ensure -- from *COMPARABLE*
   *current_if_not_smaller: Current >= other **implies** Result = Current;*
   *other_if_smaller: Current < other **implies** Result = other*

 *min (other: **like** Current): **like** Current*
  -- The smaller of current object and *other*
  -- (from *COMPARABLE*)
  require -- from *COMPARABLE*
   other_exists: other /= void
  ensure -- from *COMPARABLE*
   *current_if_not_greater: Current <= other **implies** Result = Current;*
   *other_if_greater: Current > other **implies** Result = other*

 *three_way_comparison (other: **like** Current): INTEGER*
  -- If current object equal to *other*, 0;
  -- if smaller, -1; if greater, 1
  -- (from *COMPARABLE*)
  require -- from *COMPARABLE*
   other_exists: other /= void
  ensure -- from *COMPARABLE*
   equal_zero: (Result = 0) = is_equal (other);
   smaller_negative: (Result = - 1) = (Current < other);
   greater_positive: (Result = 1) = (Current > other)

infix "<" (other: **like Current): BOOLEAN**
  -- Is string lexicographically lower than *other*?

require -- from *PART_COMPARABLE*
other_exists: other /= void
ensure -- from *COMPARABLE*
asymmetric: Result **implies not** *(other < Current)*

infix *">=" (other:* **like** *Current): BOOLEAN*
-- Is current object greater than or equal to *other*?
-- (from *COMPARABLE*)
require -- from *PART_COMPARABLE*
other_exists: other /= void
ensure -- from *COMPARABLE*
definition: Result = (other <= Current)

infix *">" (other:* **like** *Current): BOOLEAN*
-- Is current object greater than *other*?
-- (from *COMPARABLE*)
require -- from *PART_COMPARABLE*
other_exists: other /= void
ensure -- from *COMPARABLE*
definition: Result = (other < Current)

infix *"<=" (other:* **like** *Current): BOOLEAN*
-- Is current object less than or equal to *other*?
-- (from *COMPARABLE*)
require -- from *PART_COMPARABLE*
other_exists: other /= void
ensure -- from *COMPARABLE*
definition: Result = (Current < other) **or** *is_equal (other)*

feature -- Conversion

center_justify
-- Center justify the string using
-- the capacity as the width

character_justify (pivot: CHARACTER; position: INTEGER)
-- Justify a string based on a *pivot*
-- and the *position* it needs to be in
-- the final string.
-- This will grow the string if necessary
-- to get the pivot in the correct place.
require
valid_position: position <= capacity;
positive_position: position >= 1;

pivot_not_space: pivot /= ' ';
*not_empty: **not** empty*

left_justify
　　-- Left justify the string using
　　-- the capacity as the width

linear_representation: LINEAR [CHARACTER]
　　-- Representation as a linear structure

mirror
　　-- Reverse the order of characters.
　　-- "Hello world" -> "dlrow olleH".
　ensure
　　*same_count: count = **old** count*

*mirrored: **like** Current*
　　-- Mirror image of string;
　　-- result for "Hello world" is "dlrow olleH".
　ensure
　　same_count: Result.count = count

right_justify
　　-- Right justify the string using
　　-- the capacity as the width

to_boolean: BOOLEAN
　　-- Boolean value;
　　-- "true" yields *True*, "false" yields *False*
　　-- (case-insensitive)
　require
　　is_boolean: is_boolean

to_c: ANY
　　-- A reference to a C form of current string.
　　-- Useful only for interfacing with C software.

to_double: DOUBLE
　　-- "Double" value;
　　-- for example, when applied to "123.0", will yield 123.0 (double)
　require
　　is_double: is_double

to_integer: INTEGER
　　-- Integer value;

-- for example, when applied to "123", will yield 123
require
   is_integer: is_integer

to_lower
   -- Convert to lower case.

to_real: REAL
   -- Real value;
   -- for example, when applied to "123.0", will yield 123.0
require
   is_real: is_real

to_upper
   -- Convert to upper case.

feature -- Duplication

multiply (n: INTEGER)
   -- Duplicate a string within itself
   -- ("hello").multiply(3) => "hellohellohello"
require
   meaningful_multiplier: n >= 1

substring (n1, n2: INTEGER): like Current
   -- Copy of substring containing all characters at indices
   -- between *n1* and *n2*
require
   meaningful_origin: 1 <= n1;
   meaningful_interval: n1 <= n2;
   meaningful_end: n2 <= count
ensure
   new_result_count: Result.count = n2 - n1 + 1

feature -- Element change

append (s: STRING)
   -- Append a copy of *s* at end.
require
   argument_not_void: s /= void
ensure
   *new_count: count = **old** count + s.count*

append_boolean (b: BOOLEAN)
   -- Append the string representation of *b* at end.

append_character (c: CHARACTER)
    -- Append *c* at end.
   ensure
    item_inserted: item (count) = c

append_double (d: DOUBLE)
    -- Append the string representation of *d* at end.

append_integer (i: INTEGER)
    -- Append the string representation of *i* at end.

append_real (r: REAL)
    -- Append the string representation of *r* at end.

append_string (s: STRING)
    -- Append a copy of *s*, if not void, at end.

*copy (other: **like** Current)*
    -- Reinitialize by copying the characters of *other.*
    -- (This is also used by *clone*.)
   ensure
    new_result_count: count = other.count

extend (c: CHARACTER)
    -- Append *c* at end.
   require -- from *COLLECTION*
    extendible: extendible
   ensure
    item_inserted: item (count) = c
   ensure then -- from *BAG*
    *one_more_occurrence: occurrences (v) = **old** (occurrences (v)) + 1*
   ensure then -- from *COLLECTION*
    item_inserted: has (v)

fill (other: CONTAINER [CHARACTER])
    -- Fill with as many items of *other* as possible.
    -- The representations of *other* and current structure
    -- need not be the same.
    -- (from *COLLECTION*)
   require -- from *COLLECTION*
    other_not_void: other /= void;
    extendible

fill_blank
    -- Fill with blanks.

fill_character (c: CHARACTER)
> -- Fill with *c*.

head (n: INTEGER)
> -- Remove all characters except for the first *n*;
> -- do nothing if *n* >= *count*.
>
> **require**
> non_negative_argument: *n* >= 0
> **ensure**
> new_count: *count* = *n.min* (**old** *count*)

*insert (s: **like** Current; i: INTEGER)*
> -- Add *s* to the left of position *i* in current string.
>
> **require**
> string_exists: *s* /= void;
> index_small_enough: *i* <= count;
> index_large_enough: *i* > 0
> **ensure**
> new_count: *count* = **old** *count* + *s.count*

left_adjust
> -- Remove leading whitespace.
>
> **ensure**
> new_count: (*count* /= 0) **implies** ((*item* (1) /= ' ') **and**
> (*item* (1) /= '%T') **and** (*item* (1) /= '%R') **and** (*item* (1) /= '%N'))

precede (c: CHARACTER)
> -- Add *c* at front.
>
> **ensure**
> new_count: *count* = **old** *count* + 1

prepend (s: STRING)
> -- Prepend a copy of *s* at front.
>
> **require**
> argument_not_void: *s* /= void
> **ensure**
> new_count: *count* = **old** *count* + *s.count*

prepend_boolean (b: BOOLEAN)
> -- Prepend the string representation of *b* at front.

prepend_character (c: CHARACTER)
> -- Prepend the string representation of *c* at front.

prepend_double (d: DOUBLE)
    -- Prepend the string representation of *d* at front.

prepend_integer (i: INTEGER)
    -- Prepend the string representation of *i* at front.

prepend_real (r: REAL)
    -- Prepend the string representation of *r* at front.

prepend_string (s: STRING)
    -- Prepend a copy of *s*, if not void, at front.

put (c: CHARACTER; i: INTEGER)
    -- Replace character at position *i* by *c*.
    require -- from *TABLE*
    valid_key: valid_index (k)
    ensure -- from *INDEXABLE*
    insertion_done: item (k) = v

*replace_substring (s: **like** Current; start_pos, end_pos: INTEGER)*
    -- Copy the characters of *s* to positions
    -- *start_pos .. end_pos.*
    require
    string_exists: s /= void;
    index_small_enough: end_pos <= count;
    order_respected: start_pos <= end_pos;
    index_large_enough: start_pos > 0
    ensure
    *new_count: count = **old** count + s.count - end_pos + start_pos - 1*

*replace_substring_all (original, new: **like** Current)*
    -- Replace every occurence of *original* with *new.*
    require
    original_exists: original /= void;
    new_exists: new /= void;
    *original_not_empty: **not** original.empty;*
    *not_empty: **not** empty*

right_adjust
    -- Remove trailing whitespace.
    ensure
    *new_count: (count /= 0) **implies** ((item (count) /= ' ') **and***
        *(item (count) /= '%T') **and** (item (count) /= '%R') **and** (item (count) /= '%N'))*

*set (t: **like** Current; n1, n2: INTEGER)*
>   -- Set current string to substring of *t* from indices *n1*
>   -- to *n2*, or to empty string if no such substring.
>   **require**
>   *argument_not_void: t /= void*
>   **ensure**
>   *is_substring: is_equal (t.substring (n1, n2))*

*share (other: **like** Current)*
>   -- Make current string share the text of *other*.
>   -- Subsequent changes to the characters of current string
>   -- will also affect *other*, and conversely.
>   **require**
>   *argument_not_void: other /= void*
>   **ensure**
>   *shared_count: other.count = count*

tail (n: INTEGER)
>   -- Remove all characters except for the last *n*;
>   -- do nothing if *n >= count*.
>   **require**
>   *non_negative_argument: n >= 0*
>   **ensure**
>   *new_count: count = n.min (**old** count)*

feature -- Initialization

*adapt (s: STRING): **like** Current*
>   -- Object of a type conforming to the type of *s*,
>   -- initialized with attributes from *s*

from_c (c_string: POINTER)
>   -- Reset contents of string from contents of *c_string*,
>   -- a string created by some external C function.
>   **require**
>   *c_string_exists: c_string /= void*

make_from_string (s: STRING)
>   -- Initialize from the characters of *s*.
>   -- (Useful in proper descendants of class STRING,
>   -- to initialize a string-like object from a manifest string.)
>   **require**
>   *string_exists: s /= void*

ensure
  shared_implementation: shared_with (s)

remake (n: INTEGER)
    -- Allocate space for at least *n* characters.
  require
    non_negative_size: n >= 0
  ensure
    empty_string: count = 0;
    area_allocated: capacity >= n

setup (other: **like** Current)
    -- Perform actions on a freshly created object so that
    -- the contents of *other* can be safely copied onto it.

feature -- Measurement

additional_space: INTEGER
    -- Proposed number of additional items
    -- (from *RESIZABLE*)
  ensure -- from *RESIZABLE*
    at_least_one: Result >= 1

capacity: INTEGER
    -- Allocated space

count: INTEGER
    -- Actual number of characters making up the string

Growth_percentage: INTEGER **is** 50
    -- Percentage by which structure will grow automatically
    -- (from *RESIZABLE*)

Minimal_increase: INTEGER **is** 5
    -- Minimal number of additional items
    -- (from *RESIZABLE*)

occurrences (c: CHARACTER): INTEGER
    -- Number of times *c* appears in the string
  ensure -- from *BAG*
    non_negative_occurrences: Result >= 0

feature -- Output

out: **like** Current
    -- Printable representation

feature -- Removal

> *prune (c: CHARACTER)*
> > -- Remove first occurrence of *c*, if any.
> > **require**
> > > **true**
> >
> > **require else** -- from *COLLECTION*
> > > *prunable: prunable*

> *prune_all (c: CHARACTER)*
> > -- Remove all occurrences of *c*.
> > **require**
> > > **true**
> >
> > **require else** -- from *COLLECTION*
> > > *prunable*
> >
> > **ensure**
> > > *changed_count: count = (old count) - (old occurrences (c))*
> >
> > **ensure then** -- from *COLLECTION*
> > > *no_more_occurrences:* **not** *has (v)*

> *prune_all_leading (c: CHARACTER)*
> > -- Remove all leading occurrences of *c*.

> *prune_all_trailing (c: CHARACTER)*
> > -- Remove all trailing occurrences of *c*.

> *remove (i: INTEGER)*
> > -- Remove *i*-th character.
> > **require**
> > > *index_small_enough: i <= count;*
> > > *index_large_enough: i > 0*
> >
> > **ensure**
> > > *new_count: count =* **old** *count - 1*

> *wipe_out*
> > -- Remove all characters.
> > **require** -- from *COLLECTION*
> > > *prunable*
> >
> > **ensure**
> > > *empty_string: count = 0;*
> > > *empty_area: capacity = 0*
> >
> > **ensure then** -- from *COLLECTION*
> > > *wiped_out: empty*

feature -- Resizing

> *adapt_size*
> > -- Adapt the size to accommodate *count* characters.
>
> *automatic_grow*
> > -- Change the capacity to accommodate at least
> > -- *Growth_percentage* more items.
> > -- (from *RESIZABLE*)
> > **ensure** *-- from RESIZABLE*
> > increased_capacity: capacity >= **old** capacity +
> > > **old** capacity * growth_percentage // 100
>
> *grow (newsize: INTEGER)*
> > -- Ensure that the capacity is at least *newsize*.
> > **require**
> > new_size_non_negative: newsize >= 0
> > **require else** *-- RESIZABLE*
> > precursor: True
> > **ensure** *-- from RESIZABLE*
> > new_capacity: capacity >= i
>
> *resize (newsize: INTEGER)*
> > -- Rearrange string so that it can accommodate
> > -- at least *newsize* characters.
> > -- Do not lose any previously entered character.
> > **require**
> > new_size_non_negative: newsize >= 0

feature -- Status report

> *Changeable_comparison_criterion: BOOLEAN* **is false**
>
> *consistent (other: **like** Current): BOOLEAN*
> > -- Is object in a consistent state so that *other*
> > -- may be copied onto it? (Default answer: yes).
>
> *empty: BOOLEAN*
> > -- Is structure empty?
> > -- (from *FINITE*)
>
> *Extendible: BOOLEAN* **is true**
> > -- May new items be added? (Answer: yes.)

full: BOOLEAN
> -- Is structure full?
> -- (from *BOUNDED*)

is_boolean: BOOLEAN
> -- Is the string representing a boolean?

is_double: BOOLEAN
> -- Is the string representing a double?

is_hashable: BOOLEAN
> -- May current object be hashed?
> -- (True if it is not its type's default.)
> -- (from *HASHABLE*)
> **ensure** -- from *HASHABLE*
> *ok_if_not_default: Result* **implies** *(Current /= default)*

is_integer: BOOLEAN
> -- Is the string representing an integer?

is_real: BOOLEAN
> -- Is the string representing a real?

object_comparison: BOOLEAN
> -- Must search operations use *equal* rather than =
> -- for comparing references? (Default: no, use =.)
> -- (from *CONTAINER*)

prunable: BOOLEAN
> -- May items be removed? (Answer: yes.)

resizable: BOOLEAN
> -- May *capacity* be changed? (Answer: yes.)
> -- (from *RESIZABLE*)

valid_index (i: INTEGER): BOOLEAN
> -- Is *i* within the bounds of the string?

feature -- Status setting

compare_objects
> -- Ensure that future search operations will use *equal*
> -- rather than = for comparing references.
> -- (from *CONTAINER*)
> **require** -- from *CONTAINER*
> *changeable_comparison_criterion*

ensure -- from *CONTAINER*
   object_comparison

compare_references
   -- Ensure that future search operations will use =
   -- rather than *equal* for comparing references.
   -- (from *CONTAINER*)
   require -- from *CONTAINER*
   changeable_comparison_criterion
   ensure -- from *CONTAINER*
   reference_comparison: **not** *object_comparison*

invariant
   extendible: extendible;
   compare_character: object_comparison = **false;**
   -- from *RESIZABLE*
   increase_by_at_least_one: minimal_increase >= 1;
   -- from *BOUNDED*
   valid_count: count <= capacity;
   full_definition: full = (count = capacity);
   -- from *FINITE*
   empty_definition: empty = (count = 0);
   non_negative_count: count >= 0;
   -- from *COMPARABLE*
   irreflexive_comparison: **not** *(Current < Current);*

end -- class *STRING*

Interface to Class PLAIN_TEXT_FILE

class interface PLAIN_TEXT_FILE

creation
> *make,*
> *make_open_read,*
> *make_open_write,*
> *make_open_append,*
> *make_open_read_write,*
> *make_create_read_write,*
> *make_open_read_append*

feature -- Access

> *access_date: INTEGER*
>> -- Time stamp of last access made to the inode.
>> -- (from *FILE*)
>> **require** -- from *FILE*
>> *file_exists: exists*

> *date: INTEGER*
>> -- Time stamp (time of last modification)
>> -- (from *FILE*)
>> **require** -- from *FILE*
>> *file_exists: exists*

descriptor: INTEGER
    -- File descriptor as used by the operating system.
    -- (from *FILE*)
  require -- from *FILE*
    file_opened: **not** *is_closed*
  require else -- from *IO_MEDIUM*
    valid_handle: descriptor_available

descriptor_available: BOOLEAN
    -- (from *FILE*)

file_info: UNIX_FILE_INFO
    -- Collected information about the file.
    -- (from *FILE*)

file_pointer: POINTER
    -- File pointer as required in C
    -- (from *FILE*)

group_id: INTEGER
    -- Group identification of owner
    -- (from *FILE*)
  require -- from *FILE*
    file_exists: exists

has (v: **like** *item): BOOLEAN*
    -- Does structure include an occurrence of *v*?
    -- (Reference or object equality,
    -- based on *object_comparison.*)
    -- (from *LINEAR*)
  ensure -- from *CONTAINER*
    not_found_in_empty: Result **implies not** *empty*

index_of (v: **like** *item; i: INTEGER): INTEGER*
    -- Index of *i*-th occurrence of *v.*
    -- 0 if none.
    -- (Reference or object equality,
    -- based on *object_comparison.*)
    -- (from *LINEAR*)
  require -- from *LINEAR*
    positive_occurrences: i > 0
  ensure -- from *LINEAR*
    non_negative_result: Result >= 0

inode: INTEGER
> -- I-node number
> -- (from *FILE*)
> **require** -- from *FILE*
> file_exists: exists

item: CHARACTER
> -- Current item
> -- (from *FILE*)
> **require** -- from *ACTIVE*
> readable: readable
> **require else** -- from *TRAVERSABLE*
> not_off: **not** off

links: INTEGER
> -- Number of links on file
> -- (from *FILE*)
> **require** -- from *FILE*
> file_exists: exists

name: STRING
> -- File name
> -- (from *FILE*)

occurrences (v: CHARACTER): INTEGER
> -- Number of times *v* appears.
> -- (Reference or object equality,
> -- based on *object_comparison*.)
> -- (from *LINEAR*)
> **ensure** -- from *BAG*
> non_negative_occurrences: Result >= 0

owner_name: STRING
> -- Name of owner
> -- (from *FILE*)
> **require** -- from *FILE*
> file_exists: exists

position: INTEGER
> -- Current cursor position.
> -- (from *FILE*)

protection: INTEGER
> -- Protection mode, in decimal value

-- (from *FILE*)
require -- from *FILE*
file_exists: exists

separator: CHARACTER
-- ASCII code of character following last word read
-- (from *FILE*)

user_id: INTEGER
-- User identification of owner
-- (from *FILE*)
require -- from *FILE*
file_exists: exists

feature -- Conversion

linear_representation: LINEAR [CHARACTER]
-- Representation as a linear structure
-- (from *LINEAR*)

feature -- Cursor movement

back
-- Go back one position.
-- (from *FILE*)
require -- from *BILINEAR*
not_before: **not** before
ensure -- from *BILINEAR*
moved_back: position = **old** position - 1

finish
-- Go to last position.
-- (from *FILE*)
require -- from *FILE*
file_opened: **not** is_closed

forth
-- Go to next position.
-- (from *FILE*)
require -- from *FILE*
file_opened: **not** is_closed
require else -- from *LINEAR*
not_after: **not** after

go (abs_position: INTEGER)
>>>> -- Go to the absolute *position*.
>>>> -- (New position may be beyond physical length.)
>>>> -- (from *FILE*)
>>> **require** -- from *FILE*
>>>> *file_opened:* **not** *is_closed;*
>>>> *non_negative_argument: abs_position >= 0*

move (offset: INTEGER)
>>>> -- Advance by *offset* from current location.
>>>> -- (from *FILE*)
>>> **require** -- from *FILE*
>>>> *file_opened:* **not** *is_closed*

next_line
>>>> -- Move to next input line.
>>>> -- (from *FILE*)
>>> **require** -- from *FILE*
>>>> *is_readable: file_readable*

recede (abs_position: INTEGER)
>>>> -- Go to the absolute *position* backwards,
>>>> -- starting from end of file.
>>>> -- (from *FILE*)
>>> **require** -- from *FILE*
>>>> *file_opened:* **not** *is_closed;*
>>>> *non_negative_argument: abs_position >= 0*

search (v: **like** *item)*
>>>> -- Move to first position (at or after current
>>>> -- position) where *item* and *v* are equal.
>>>> -- If structure does not include *v* ensure that
>>>> -- *exhausted* will be true.
>>>> -- (Reference or object equality,
>>>> -- based on *object_comparison*.)
>>>> -- (from *BILINEAR*)
>>> **ensure** -- from *LINEAR*
>>>> *object_found:* **(not** *exhausted* **and then** *object_comparison* **and then** *v /= void*
and then *item /= void)* **implies** *v.is_equal (item);*
>>>> *item_found:* **(not** *exhausted* **and not** *object_comparison)* **implies** *v = item*

>> *start*
>>>> -- Go to first position.

-- (from *FILE*)
require -- from *FILE*
    file_opened: **not** *is_closed*

feature -- Element change

    add_permission (who, what: STRING)
        -- Add read, write, execute or setuid permission
        -- for *who* ('u', 'g' or 'o') to *what.*
        -- (from *FILE*)
    require -- from *FILE*
        who_is_not_void: who /= void;
        what_is_not_void: what /= void;
        file_descriptor_exists: exists

    append (f: **like** *Current)*
        -- Append a copy of the contents of *f.*
        -- (from *FILE*)
    require -- from *FILE*
        target_is_closed: is_closed;
        source_is_closed: f.is_closed
    require else -- from *SEQUENCE*
        argument_not_void: s /= void
    ensure -- from *FILE*
        new_count: count = **old** *count + f.count;*
        files_closed: f.is_closed **and** *is_closed*
    ensure then -- from *SEQUENCE*
        new_count: count >= **old** *count*

    change_date: INTEGER
        -- Time stamp of last change.
        -- (from *FILE*)
    require -- from *FILE*
        file_exists: exists

    change_group (new_group_id: INTEGER)
        -- Change group of file to *new_group_id* found in
        -- system password file.
        -- (from *FILE*)
    require -- from *FILE*
        file_exists: exists

    change_mode (mask: INTEGER)
        -- Replace mode by *mask.*

```
                -- (from FILE)
        require -- from FILE
            file_exists: exists

change_name (new_name: STRING)
            -- Change file name to new_name
            -- (from FILE)
        require -- from FILE
            not_new_name_void: new_name /= void;
            file_exists: exists
        ensure -- from FILE
            name_changed: name.is_equal (new_name)

change_owner (new_owner_id: INTEGER)
            -- Change owner of file to new_owner_id found in
            -- system password file. On some systems this
            -- requires super-user privileges.
            -- (from FILE)
        require -- from FILE
            file_exists: exists

extend (v: CHARACTER)
            -- Include v at end.
            -- (from FILE)
        require -- from COLLECTION
            extendible: extendible
        ensure -- from BAG
            one_more_occurrence: occurrences (v) = old (occurrences (v)) + 1
        ensure then -- from COLLECTION
            item_inserted: has (v)

fill (other: CONTAINER [CHARACTER])
            -- Fill with as many items of other as possible.
            -- The representations of other and current structure
            -- need not be the same.
            -- (from COLLECTION)
        require -- from COLLECTION
            other_not_void: other /= void;
            extendible

flush
            -- Flush buffered data to disk.
            -- Note that there is no guarantee that the operating
```

-- system will physically write the data to the disk.
-- At least it will end up in the buffer cache,
-- making the data visible to other processes.
-- (from *FILE*)
require -- from *FILE*
is_open: **not** is_closed

force (v: **like** item)
-- Add *v* to end.
-- (from *SEQUENCE*)
require -- from *SEQUENCE*
extendible: extendible
ensure -- from *SEQUENCE*
new_count: count = **old** count + 1;
item_inserted: has (v)

link (fn: STRING)
-- Link current file to *fn*.
-- *fn* must not already exist.
-- (from *FILE*)
require -- from *FILE*
file_exists: exists

new_line
-- Write a new line character at current position.
-- (from *FILE*)
require -- from *IO_MEDIUM*
extendible: extendible

put (v: **like** item)
-- Add *v* to end.
-- (from *SEQUENCE*)
require -- from *COLLECTION*
extendible: extendible
ensure -- from *SEQUENCE*
new_count: count = **old** count + 1
ensure then -- from *COLLECTION*
item_inserted: has (v)

put_character (c: CHARACTER)
-- Write *c* at current position.
-- (from *FILE*)

require -- from *IO_MEDIUM*
extendible: extendible

put_string (s: STRING)
    -- Write *s* at current position.
    -- (from *FILE*)
require -- from *IO_MEDIUM*
extendible: extendible;
non_void: s /= void

putchar (c: CHARACTER)
    -- Write *c* at current position.
    -- (from *FILE*)
require -- from *IO_MEDIUM*
extendible: extendible

putstring (s: STRING)
    -- Write *s* at current position.
    -- (from *FILE*)
require -- from *IO_MEDIUM*
extendible: extendible;
non_void: s /= void

remove_permission (who, what: STRING)
    -- Remove read, write, execute or setuid permission
    -- for *who* ('u', 'g' or 'o') to *what*.
    -- (from *FILE*)
require -- from *FILE*
who_is_not_void: who /= void;
what_is_not_void: what /= void;
file_descriptor_exists: exists

set_access (time: INTEGER)
    -- Stamp with *time* (access only).
    -- (from *FILE*)
require -- from *FILE*
file_exists: exists
ensure -- from *FILE*
access_date_updated: access_date = time;
*date_unchanged: date = **old** date*

set_date (time: INTEGER)
    -- Stamp with *time* (modification time only).
    -- (from *FILE*)

> **require** -- from *FILE*
> *file_exists: exists*
> **ensure** -- from *FILE*
> *access_date_unchanged: access_date = **old** access_date;*
> *date_updated: date = time*

stamp (time: INTEGER)
> -- Stamp with *time* (for both access and modification).
> -- (from *FILE*)
> **require** -- from *FILE*
> *file_exists: exists*
> **ensure** -- from *FILE*
> *date_updated: date = time*

touch
> -- Update time stamp (for both access and modification).
> -- (from *FILE*)
> **require** -- from *FILE*
> *file_exists: exists*
> **ensure** -- from *FILE*
> *date_changed: date /= **old** date*

feature -- Initialization

make (fn: STRING)
> -- Create file object with *fn* as file name.
> -- (from *FILE*)
> **require** -- from *FILE*
> *string_exists: fn /= void;*
> *string_not_empty: **not** fn.empty*
> **ensure** -- from *FILE*
> *file_named: name.is_equal (fn);*
> *file_closed: is_closed*

make_create_read_write (fn: STRING)
> -- Create file object with *fn* as file name
> -- and open file for both reading and writing;
> -- create it if it does not exist.
> -- (from *FILE*)
> **require** -- from *FILE*
> *string_exists: fn /= void;*
> *string_not_empty: **not** fn.empty*
> **ensure** -- from *FILE*

exists: exists;
open_read: is_open_read;
open_write: is_open_write

make_open_append (fn: STRING)
    -- Create file object with *fn* as file name
    -- and open file in append-only mode.
    -- (from *FILE*)
  require -- from *FILE*
    string_exists: fn /= void;
    string_not_empty: **not** *fn.empty*
  ensure -- from *FILE*
    exists: exists;
    open_append: is_open_append

make_open_read (fn: STRING)
    -- Create file object with *fn* as file name
    -- and open file in read mode.
    -- (from *FILE*)
  require -- from *FILE*
    string_exists: fn /= void;
    string_not_empty: **not** *fn.empty*
  ensure -- from *FILE*
    exists: exists;
    open_read: is_open_read

make_open_read_append (fn: STRING)
    -- Create file object with *fn* as file name
    -- and open file for reading anywhere
    -- but writing at the end only.
    -- Create file if it does not exist.
    -- (from *FILE*)
  require -- from *FILE*
    string_exists: fn /= void;
    string_not_empty: **not** *fn.empty*
  ensure -- from *FILE*
    exists: exists;
    open_read: is_open_read;
    open_append: is_open_append

make_open_read_write (fn: STRING)
    -- Create file object with *fn* as file name
    -- and open file for both reading and writing.

```
            -- (from FILE)
      require -- from FILE
          string_exists: fn /= void;
          string_not_empty: not fn.empty
      ensure -- from FILE
          exists: exists;
          open_read: is_open_read;
          open_write: is_open_write

  make_open_write (fn: STRING)
          -- Create file object with fn as file name
          -- and open file for writing;
          -- create it if it does not exist.
          -- (from FILE)
      require -- from FILE
          string_exists: fn /= void;
          string_not_empty: not fn.empty
      ensure -- from FILE
          exists: exists;
          open_write: is_open_write

feature -- Input

  read_character
          -- Read a new character.
          -- Make result available in last_character.
          -- (from FILE)
      require -- from FILE
          is_readable: file_readable
      require else -- from IO_MEDIUM
          is_readable: readable

  read_double
          -- Read the ASCII representation of a new double
          -- from file. Make result available in last_double.
      require -- from FILE
          is_readable: file_readable
      require else -- from IO_MEDIUM
          is_readable: readable

  read_integer
          -- Read the ASCII representation of a new integer
          -- from file. Make result available in last_integer.
```

require -- from *FILE*
    is_readable: file_readable
require else -- from *IO_MEDIUM*
    is_readable: readable

read_line
    -- Read a string until new line or end of file.
    -- Make result available in *last_string*.
    -- New line will be consumed but not part of *last_string*.
    -- (from *FILE*)
require -- from *FILE*
    is_readable: file_readable
require else -- from *IO_MEDIUM*
    is_readable: readable

read_real
    -- Read the ASCII representation of a new real
    -- from file. Make result available in *last_real*.
require -- from *FILE*
    is_readable: file_readable
require else -- from *IO_MEDIUM*
    is_readable: readable

read_stream (nb_char: INTEGER)
    -- Read a string of at most *nb_char* bound characters
    -- or until end of file.
    -- Make result available in *last_string*.
    -- (from *FILE*)
require -- from *FILE*
    is_readable: file_readable
require else -- from *IO_MEDIUM*
    is_readable: readable

read_word
    -- Read a string, excluding whitespace and stripping
    -- leading whitespace.
    -- Make result available in *last_string*.
    -- Whitespace characters are: blank, new_line, tab,
    -- vertical tab, formfeed, end of file.
    -- (from *FILE*)
require -- from *FILE*
    is_readable: file_readable

readchar

    -- Read a new character.

    -- Make result available in *last_character*.

    -- (from *FILE*)

  require -- from *FILE*

    is_readable: file_readable

  require else -- from *IO_MEDIUM*

    is_readable: readable

readdouble

    -- Read the ASCII representation of a new double

    -- from file. Make result available in *last_double*.

  require -- from *FILE*

    is_readable: file_readable

  require else -- from *IO_MEDIUM*

    is_readable: readable

readint

    -- Read the ASCII representation of a new integer

    -- from file. Make result available in *last_integer*.

  require -- from *FILE*

    is_readable: file_readable

  require else -- from *IO_MEDIUM*

    is_readable: readable

readline

    -- Read a string until new line or end of file.

    -- Make result available in *last_string*.

    -- New line will be consumed but not part of *last_string*.

    -- (from *FILE*)

  require -- from *FILE*

    is_readable: file_readable

  require else -- from *IO_MEDIUM*

    is_readable: readable

readreal

    -- Read the ASCII representation of a new real

    -- from file. Make result available in *last_real*.

  require -- from *FILE*

    is_readable: file_readable

  require else -- from *IO_MEDIUM*

    is_readable: readable

readstream (nb_char: INTEGER)
>   -- Read a string of at most *nb_char* bound characters
>   -- or until end of file.
>   -- Make result available in *last_string*.
>   -- (from *FILE*)
>   **require** -- from *FILE*
>   *is_readable: file_readable*
>   **require else** -- from *IO_MEDIUM*
>   *is_readable: readable*

readword
>   -- Read a string, excluding whitespace and stripping
>   -- leading whitespace.
>   -- Make result available in *last_string*.
>   -- Whitespace characters are: blank, new_line, tab,
>   -- vertical tab, formfeed, end of file.
>   -- (from *FILE*)
>   **require** -- from *FILE*
>   *is_readable: file_readable*

feature -- Measurement

count: INTEGER
>   -- Size in bytes (0 if no associated physical file)
>   -- (from *FILE*)

feature -- Obsolete

lastchar: CHARACTER
>   -- Last character read by *read_character*
>   -- (from *IO_MEDIUM*)

lastdouble: DOUBLE
>   -- Last double read by *read_double*
>   -- (from *IO_MEDIUM*)

lastint: INTEGER
>   -- Last integer read by *read_integer*
>   -- (from *IO_MEDIUM*)

lastreal: REAL
>   -- Last real read by *read_real*
>   -- (from *IO_MEDIUM*)

laststring: STRING
-- Last string read
-- (from *IO_MEDIUM*)

feature -- Output

put_boolean (b: BOOLEAN)
-- Write ASCII value of *b* at current position.
require -- from *IO_MEDIUM*
extendible: extendible

put_double (d: DOUBLE)
-- Write ASCII value *d* at current position.
require -- from *IO_MEDIUM*
extendible: extendible

put_integer (i: INTEGER)
-- Write ASCII value of *i* at current position.
require -- from *IO_MEDIUM*
extendible: extendible

put_real (r: REAL)
-- Write ASCII value of *r* at current position.
require -- from *IO_MEDIUM*
extendible: extendible

putbool (b: BOOLEAN)
-- Write ASCII value of *b* at current position.
require -- from *IO_MEDIUM*
extendible: extendible

putdouble (d: DOUBLE)
-- Write ASCII value *d* at current position.
require -- from *IO_MEDIUM*
extendible: extendible

putint (i: INTEGER)
-- Write ASCII value of *i* at current position.
require -- from *IO_MEDIUM*
extendible: extendible

putreal (r: REAL)
-- Write ASCII value of *r* at current position.
require -- from *IO_MEDIUM*
extendible: extendible

feature -- Removal

delete
> -- Remove link with physical file.
> -- File does not physically disappear from the disk
> -- until no more processes reference it.
> -- I/O operations on it are still possible.
> -- A directory must be empty to be deleted.
> -- (from *FILE*)
>
> *require* -- from *FILE*
> *exists: exists*

dispose
> -- Ensure this medium is closed when garbage collected.
> -- (from *IO_MEDIUM*)

*prune_all (v: **like** item)*
> -- Remove all occurrences of *v*; go *off*.
> -- (from *SEQUENCE*)
>
> *ensure* -- from *COLLECTION*
> *no_more_occurrences: **not** has (v)*

reset (fn: STRING)
> -- Change file name to *fn* and reset
> -- file descriptor and all information.
> -- (from *FILE*)
>
> *require* -- from *FILE*
> *valid_file_name: fn /= void*
>
> *ensure* -- from *FILE*
> *file_renamed: name = fn;*
> *file_closed: is_closed*

wipe_out
> -- Remove all items.
> -- (from *FILE*)
>
> *require* -- from *FILE*
> *is_closed: is_closed*
>
> *ensure* -- from *COLLECTION*
> *wiped_out: empty*

feature -- Status report

access_exists: BOOLEAN
> -- Does physical file exist?

-- (Uses real UID.)
-- (from *FILE*)

after: BOOLEAN
    -- Is there no valid cursor position to the right of cursor position?
    -- (from *FILE*)

before: BOOLEAN
    -- Is there no valid cursor position to the left of cursor position?
    -- (from *FILE*)

changeable_comparison_criterion: BOOLEAN
    -- May *object_comparison* be changed?
    -- (Answer: yes by default.)
    -- (from *CONTAINER*)

empty: BOOLEAN
    -- Is structure empty?
    -- (from *FINITE*)

end_of_file: BOOLEAN
    -- Has an EOF been detected?
    -- (from *FILE*)
   require -- from *FILE*
   opened: **not** *is_closed*

exhausted: BOOLEAN
    -- Has structure been completely explored?
    -- (from *LINEAR*)
   ensure -- from *LINEAR*
   exhausted_when_off: off **implies** *Result*

exists: BOOLEAN
    -- Does physical file exist?
    -- (Uses effective UID.)
    -- (from *FILE*)

extendible: BOOLEAN
    -- May new items be added?
    -- (from *FILE*)

file_prunable: BOOLEAN
    -- May items be removed?
    -- (from *FILE*)

file_readable: BOOLEAN
>   -- Is there a current item that may be read?
>   -- (from *FILE*)

file_writable: BOOLEAN
>   -- Is there a current item that may be modified?
>   -- (from *FILE*)

Full: BOOLEAN **is false**
>   -- Is structure filled to capacity?
>   -- (from *FILE*)

is_access_executable: BOOLEAN
>   -- Is file executable by real UID?
>   -- (from *FILE*)
> **require** -- from *FILE*
> *file_exists: exists*

is_access_owner: BOOLEAN
>   -- Is file owned by real UID?
>   -- (from *FILE*)
> **require** -- from *FILE*
> *file_exists: exists*

is_access_readable: BOOLEAN
>   -- Is file readable by real UID?
>   -- (from *FILE*)
> **require** -- from *FILE*
> *file_exists: exists*

is_access_writable: BOOLEAN
>   -- Is file writable by real UID?
>   -- (from *FILE*)
> **require** -- from *FILE*
> *file_exists: exists*

is_block: BOOLEAN
>   -- Is file a block special file?
>   -- (from *FILE*)
> **require** -- from *FILE*
> *file_exists: exists*

is_character: BOOLEAN
>   -- Is file a character special file?
>   -- (from *FILE*)

> ***require*** *-- from FILE*
> *file_exists: exists*

is_closed: BOOLEAN
>   -- Is file closed?
>   -- (from *FILE*)

is_creatable: BOOLEAN
>   -- Is file creatable in parent directory?
>   -- (Uses effective UID to check that parent is writable
>   -- and file does not exist.)
>   -- (from *FILE*)

is_device: BOOLEAN
>   -- Is file a device?
>   -- (from *FILE*)
> ***require*** *-- from FILE*
> *file_exists: exists*

is_directory: BOOLEAN
>   -- Is file a directory?
>   -- (from *FILE*)
> ***require*** *-- from FILE*
> *file_exists: exists*

is_executable: BOOLEAN
>   -- Is file executable?
>   -- (Checks execute permission for effective UID.)
>   -- (from *FILE*)
> ***require*** *-- from IO_MEDIUM*
> *handle_exists: exists*

is_fifo: BOOLEAN
>   -- Is file a named pipe?
>   -- (from *FILE*)
> ***require*** *-- from FILE*
> *file_exists: exists*

is_open_append: BOOLEAN
>   -- Is file open for appending?
>   -- (from *FILE*)

is_open_read: BOOLEAN
>   -- Is file open for reading?
>   -- (from *FILE*)

is_open_write: BOOLEAN
  -- Is file open for writing?
  -- (from *FILE*)

is_owner: BOOLEAN
  -- Is file owned by effective UID?
  -- (from *FILE*)
 require -- from *FILE*
 file_exists: exists

is_plain: BOOLEAN
  -- Is file a plain file?
  -- (from *FILE*)
 require -- from *FILE*
 file_exists: exists

is_plain_text: BOOLEAN
  -- Is file reserved for text (character sequences)? (Yes)

is_readable: BOOLEAN
  -- Is file readable?
  -- (Checks permission for effective UID.)
  -- (from *FILE*)
 require -- from *IO_MEDIUM*
 handle_exists: exists

is_setgid: BOOLEAN
  -- Is file setgid?
  -- (from *FILE*)
 require -- from *FILE*
 file_exists: exists

is_setuid: BOOLEAN
  -- Is file setuid?
  -- (from *FILE*)
 require -- from *FILE*
 file_exists: exists

is_socket: BOOLEAN
  -- Is file a named socket?
  -- (from *FILE*)
 require -- from *FILE*
 file_exists: exists

is_sticky: BOOLEAN
      -- Is file sticky (for memory swaps)?
      -- (from *FILE*)
    require -- from *FILE*
     file_exists: exists

is_symlink: BOOLEAN
      -- Is file a symbolic link?
      -- (from *FILE*)
    require -- from *FILE*
     file_exists: exists

is_writable: BOOLEAN
      -- Is file writable?
      -- (Checks write permission for effective UID.)
      -- (from *FILE*)
    require -- from *IO_MEDIUM*
     handle_exists: exists

last_character: CHARACTER
      -- Last character read by *read_character*
      -- (from *IO_MEDIUM*)

last_double: DOUBLE
      -- Last double read by *read_double*
      -- (from *IO_MEDIUM*)

last_integer: INTEGER
      -- Last integer read by *read_integer*
      -- (from *IO_MEDIUM*)

last_real: REAL
      -- Last real read by *read_real*
      -- (from *IO_MEDIUM*)

last_string: STRING
      -- Last string read
      -- (from *IO_MEDIUM*)

object_comparison: BOOLEAN
      -- Must search operations use *equal* rather than =
      -- for comparing references? (Default: no, use =.)
      -- (from *CONTAINER*)

off: *BOOLEAN*
> -- Is there no item?
> -- (from *FILE*)

readable: *BOOLEAN*
> -- Is there a current item that may be read?
> -- (from *SEQUENCE*)
> **require** -- from *IO_MEDIUM*
> handle_exists: exists

writable: *BOOLEAN*
> -- Is there a current item that may be modified?
> -- (from *SEQUENCE*)

feature -- Status setting

close
> -- Close file.
> -- (from *FILE*)
> **require** -- from *IO_MEDIUM*
> medium_is_open: **not** is_closed
> **ensure** -- from *FILE*
> is_closed: is_closed

compare_objects
> -- Ensure that future search operations will use *equal*
> -- rather than = for comparing references.
> -- (from *CONTAINER*)
> **require** -- from *CONTAINER*
> changeable_comparison_criterion
> **ensure** -- from *CONTAINER*
> object_comparison

compare_references
> -- Ensure that future search operations will use =
> -- rather than *equal* for comparing references.
> -- (from *CONTAINER*)
> **require** -- from *CONTAINER*
> changeable_comparison_criterion
> **ensure** -- from *CONTAINER*
> reference_comparison: **not** object_comparison

create_read_write
> -- Open file in read and write mode;

      -- create it if it does not exist.
      -- (from *FILE*)
    require -- from *FILE*
      is_closed: is_closed
    ensure -- from *FILE*
      exists: exists;
      open_read: is_open_read;
      open_write: is_open_write

fd_open_append (fd: INTEGER)
      -- Open file of descriptor *fd* in append mode.
      -- (from *FILE*)
    ensure -- from *FILE*
      exists: exists;
      open_append: is_open_append

fd_open_read (fd: INTEGER)
      -- Open file of descriptor *fd* in read-only mode.
      -- (from *FILE*)
    ensure -- from *FILE*
      exists: exists;
      open_read: is_open_read

fd_open_read_append (fd: INTEGER)
      -- Open file of descriptor *fd*
      -- in read and write-at-end mode.
      -- (from *FILE*)
    ensure -- from *FILE*
      exists: exists;
      open_read: is_open_read;
      open_append: is_open_append

fd_open_read_write (fd: INTEGER)
      -- Open file of descriptor *fd* in read-write mode.
      -- (from *FILE*)
    ensure -- from *FILE*
      exists: exists;
      open_read: is_open_read;
      open_write: is_open_write

fd_open_write (fd: INTEGER)
      -- Open file of descriptor *fd* in write mode.
      -- (from *FILE*)

      ensure -- from *FILE*
        exists: exists;
        open_write: is_open_write

open_append
      -- Open file in append-only mode;
      -- create it if it does not exist.
      -- (from *FILE*)
    require -- from *FILE*
      is_closed: is_closed
    ensure -- from *FILE*
      exists: exists;
      open_append: is_open_append

open_read
      -- Open file in read-only mode.
      -- (from *FILE*)
    require -- from *FILE*
      is_closed: is_closed
    ensure -- from *FILE*
      exists: exists;
      open_read: is_open_read

open_read_append
      -- Open file in read and write-at-end mode;
      -- create it if it does not exist.
      -- (from *FILE*)
    require -- from *FILE*
      is_closed: is_closed
    ensure -- from *FILE*
      exists: exists;
      open_read: is_open_read;
      open_append: is_open_append

open_read_write
      -- Open file in read and write mode.
      -- (from *FILE*)
    require -- from *FILE*
      is_closed: is_closed
    ensure -- from *FILE*
      exists: exists;
      open_read: is_open_read;
      open_write: is_open_write

open_write
>> -- Open file in write-only mode;
>> -- create it if it does not exist.
>> -- (from *FILE*)
> **ensure** -- from *FILE*
>> *exists: exists;*
>> *open_write: is_open_write*

recreate_read_write (fname: STRING)
>> -- Reopen in read-write mode with file of name *fname*;
>> -- create file if it does not exist.
>> -- (from *FILE*)
> **require** -- from *FILE*
>> *is_open:* **not** *is_closed;*
>> *valid_name: fname /= void*
> **ensure** -- from *FILE*
>> *exists: exists;*
>> *open_read: is_open_read;*
>> *open_write: is_open_write*

reopen_append (fname: STRING)
>> -- Reopen in append mode with file of name *fname*;
>> -- create file if it does not exist.
>> -- (from *FILE*)
> **require** -- from *FILE*
>> *is_open:* **not** *is_closed;*
>> *valid_name: fname /= void*
> **ensure** -- from *FILE*
>> *exists: exists;*
>> *open_append: is_open_append*

reopen_read (fname: STRING)
>> -- Reopen in read-only mode with file of name *fname*;
>> -- create file if it does not exist.
>> -- (from *FILE*)
> **require** -- from *FILE*
>> *is_open:* **not** *is_closed;*
>> *valid_name: fname /= void*
> **ensure** -- from *FILE*
>> *exists: exists;*
>> *open_read: is_open_read*

reopen_read_append (fname: STRING)
    -- Reopen in read and write-at-end mode with file
    -- of name *fname*; create file if it does not exist.
    -- (from *FILE*)
  require -- from *FILE*
    is_open: **not** is_closed;
    valid_name: fname /= void
  ensure -- from *FILE*
    exists: exists;
    open_read: is_open_read;
    open_append: is_open_append

reopen_read_write (fname: STRING)
    -- Reopen in read-write mode with file of name *fname*.
    -- (from *FILE*)
  require -- from *FILE*
    is_open: **not** is_closed;
    valid_name: fname /= void
  ensure -- from *FILE*
    exists: exists;
    open_read: is_open_read;
    open_write: is_open_write

reopen_write (fname: STRING)
    -- Reopen in write-only mode with file of name *fname*;
    -- create file if it does not exist.
    -- (from *FILE*)
  require -- from *FILE*
    is_open: **not** is_closed;
    valid_name: fname /= void
  ensure -- from *FILE*
    exists: exists;
    open_write: is_open_write

invariant
    plain_text: is_plain_text;
    -- from *FILE*
    name_exists: name /= void;
    name_not_empty: **not** name.empty;
    -- from *FINITE*
    empty_definition: empty = (count = 0);
    non_negative_count: count >= 0;

-- from *ACTIVE*
writable_constraint: writable **implies** *readable;*
empty_constraint: empty **implies** **(not** *readable)* **and** **(not** *writable);*
-- from *BILINEAR*
not_both: **not** *(after* **and** *before);*
empty_property: empty **implies** *(after* **or** *before);*
before_constraint: before **implies** *off;*
-- from *LINEAR*
after_constraint: after **implies** *off;*
-- from *TRAVERSABLE*
empty_constraint: empty **implies** *off;*

end -- class *PLAIN_TEXT_FILE*

Appendix

3

Class RANDOM_NUMBER

```
class RANDOM_NUMBER

creation
    initialize

feature {NONE} -- For internal use only

    c_init is
            -- C function seeds random number generator using current clock time
        external
            "C"
        alias
            "initial"
        end

    c_uniform: REAL is
        external
            "C"
        alias
            "rrandom"
        end

    initialize_and_warm_up_generator is
        local
            index: INTEGER
```

```
          value: INTEGER
      once
        c_init
        from
          index := 0
        until
          index = 500
        loop
          index := index + 1
          next
        end
      end

  uniform: REAL is
      -- Returns a uniform random real number between 0.0 and 1.0
    do
      Result := c_uniform
    end

feature -- public

  next_value: REAL
      -- Set by next

  initialize is
    do
      initialize_and_warm_up_generator
    end

  next is
    do
      next_value := uniform
    end

  value_between (low: INTEGER; high: INTEGER): INTEGER is
    local
      t: REAL
    do
      t := (high - low + 1) * next_value
      Result := low + t.truncated_to_integer
    end

end -- class RANDOM_NUMBER
```

```
#include <time.h>
#include <stdlib.h>

double drand48();

void initial()
{
      long seed;
      time_t t;
      time( &t );
      seed = ( long ) t;
      seed *= seed;
      seed = abs( seed );
      srand48( seed );
}

float rrandom()
{
      return drand48();
}
```

Index

A

Abstract, 11
Abstract classes
    in Eiffel programs, 164
    preconditions and postconditions, 175–176
Abstract data type, 26, 35
Abstraction, 13–14, 34
Ace file, 41–42, 92
Ada, 4, 8
ADT, *See* Abstract data type
Aggregation, 11, 24–25, 29
Algol, 4
Algorithms, *See also* Routines
    binary search, 236–237
    computational efficiency of, 97,
        104–105, 121
    defined, 97, 121
    depth-first, 254–255
    design of, 97–98, 121
    examples of
        array values, 99–101

sorting, *See* Sorting algorithms
hard problems
    defined, 119
    examples of, 119–121
problems *versus* instances in, 98
recursive sorting, 239–242
speed increases in, illustrative
    example, 105–110
"and then" operators, 52–53
Applications programs, 3
Arrays, *See also* String
    algorithms for, 99–101
    creation process, 61–66
    recursion use for, 235–239
    sorting process, 66–69
    subvector problem for, 105–110
Assembly language, 3–4, 7
Assertion handling mechanism, 167,
    174–176
Assignment operator, 4
Asymptotic complexity, 104, 122
Attributes
    classification using, 23, 35